Kenneth Burke's Rhetoric of Identification

Photograph of Kenneth Burke, 1989, by Robert Taylor Brewer. © David Blakesley. Used by permission.

KENNETH BURKE'S RHETORIC OF IDENTIFICATION

Lessons in Reading, Writing, and Living

Tilly Warnock

Parlor Press
Anderson, South Carolina
www.parlorpress.com

Parlor Press LLC, Anderson, South Carolina, USA
© 2024 by Parlor Press.
All rights reserved.
Printed in the United States of America on acid-free paper.

S A N: 2 5 4 - 8 8 7 9

Library of Congress Cataloging-in-Publication Data on File

1 2 3 4 5

978-1-64317-3448-8 (paperback)
978-1-64317-449-5 (PDF)
978-1-64317-450-1 (EPUB)

Cover and interior design by David Blakesley.
Cover photo by Filip Kominik on Unsplash. Used by permission.

Parlor Press, LLC is an independent publisher of scholarly and trade titles in print and multimedia formats. This book is available in print and ebook formats from Parlor Press on the World Wide Web at www.parlorpress.com or through online and brick-and-mortar bookstores. For submission information or to find out about Parlor Press publications, write to Parlor Press, 3015 Brackenberry Drive, Anderson, South Carolina, 29621, or email editor@parlorpress.com.

Contents

Abbreviations *vi*

Part I: A Lesson in Reading: Ways In, Ways Out, Ways Roundabout *1*

1 Another Partial Overview: What's Missing in Rhetoric? *3*

Part II: A Lesson in Writing: Attitudes and Actions for Writing and Rewriting *41*

2 Reading as Revision to Identify: Burke's Rewriting of Aristotle's Enthymeme into Identification *43*

3 A Burkean Reading of Fish's Tale of Freud's Analysis of the Wolf-Man's Account: The Long-Lasting Effects of Sisterly Persuasion *98*

Part III: A Lesson in Writing: Attitudes and Actions for Writing and Rewriting *147*

4 Burke's Writing Theories and Practices: "Human Life as a Project in 'Composition'" *149*

5 Burke's Lesson in Writing to Identify Compared to Berlin's Call for Writing as Ideological Action *182*

Part IV: A Lesson in Living as Rebirth Ritual: Getting Along by Going Along Until the Negative Sets In *229*

6 Burke's Epilogue on Earth: A "Return to Inconclusiveness" as Equipment for Living Today *231*

Works Cited *263*

Index *271*

About the Author *279*

Abbreviations

ATH: *Attitudes Toward History*
CS: *Counter-Statement*
LASA: *Language as Symbolic Action*
GM: *A Grammar of Motives*
PC: *Permanence and Change*
RM: *A Rhetoric of Motives*
RR: *Rhetoric of Religion*

PART I
A LESSON IN READING: WAYS IN, WAYS OUT, WAYS ROUNDABOUT

67 - 3987 Gordon Head Road
Victoria, B.C. V8N 3X5, CANADA
March 18, 1986

Tilly Dawlink,

~~Garsh~~, on my map Victoria is less than an inch from Wyoming, so I've felt
~~f t~~ close despite the sluggish mail service twixt here and USA. While I was trying to make up my mind about your first heart-warming invitation to return thither
this June, and also delaying because I have been wanting to write you and John in
connection with developments from my ~~fmmmmm~~ last-year's sojourn among youenz (and it
                                                                                    w a)
~~sas~~ an expeeeerience the very thought of which makes me glow), there came the announce-
ment about my fellow-thinker, Frank Lentricchia, being engaged forh this year. So,
being in a jam, I delayed writing you because I thought you had made up my mind for
me, and I could write youenz later when things quieted down.

But/they haven't quieted down yet - and there came your later missives (one
          a
with ~~a~~ document attesting to your generous attitude, for inclusion in the Texas
Pre-Text Project, for which know of my humble thanks indeed). But my entanglements
(both professional and psychologic) are such that I still caint make up my mindifany
However, the need to begin clearing things up here for a Next Phase elsewhere has
required me to trying decently by my mail, and thy name is the Abou Ben Adam that
leads all the rest.

I Excaped N.J.'S TEN DAMNEDEST WEEKS this year by staying m here at Butchie's
place, in this section of Canada that is so paradoxically different from the East
frontiers of Canada, which ships its wintryn blasts right down from the Arctic to
my kitchen in And/Or. But I am scheduled to be at Iowan U. from April 7 to 24, whe
20 graduate students will have been reading boikwoiks and arrangements have been
for the video-taping of my conferences with them. It should be a ~~gmnin~~ great oppor
tunityhn to get my position on record. And a priceless honor. At least, damnea:
          since
priceless, ~~fmm~~ I am getting but One Grand sans my fare for mm at least six two-

Letter from Kenneth Burke to Tilly Warnock, 18 March 1986.

1 Another Partial Overview: What's Missing in Rhetoric?

It operates on the miso-philanthropic assumption that getting along with people is one devil of a difficult task, but that, in the last analysis, we should all want to get along with people (and do want to) (Burke, *ATH* "Introduction" n.p.).

For rhetoric as such is not rooted in any past condition of human society. It is rooted in an essential function of language itself, a function that is wholly realistic, and is continually born anew; the use of language as a symbolic means of inducing cooperation in beings that by nature respond to symbols. Though rhetorical considerations may carry us far afield, leading us to violate the principle of autonomy separating the various disciplines, there is an intrinsically rhetorical motive, situated in the persuasive use of language (Burke, *RM* 43).

The universe would appear to be something like a cheese; it can be sliced in an infinite number of ways—and when one has chosen his own pattern of slicing, he finds that other men's cuts fall at the wrong places (Burke, *PC* 103).

Any Selection Is a Deflection, Including My Own

What's missing in Burke's rhetoric is what's missing in all rhetoric: that which readers do to create meaning together with writers. Burke builds his theory of identification as action by writer and reader together, not necessarily at the same time or place, motivated by his overall desire to replace physical war with verbal sparring and by his more specific desire to teach us how to use and yet not misuse the tendencies in *animal symbolicum* and in language toward hierarchy, the negative, alienation, and perfection. These are Burke's choices, his "cuts" in the cheese that is the universe, which he understands as rhetoric, "not right but necessary"

(*RM* 47), and our best chance for learning to survive by cooperating with each other.

Burke's theory operates at a high level of generalization that tends to be inclusive rather than exclusive: "wherever there is 'meaning,' there is 'persuasion'" (*RM* 172). This is the strength and limitation of his rhetoric and of rhetoric traditionally. He defines all of us as *animal symbolicum* and yet as divided in individual bodies, with language as the means he explores to connect us and to divide us further. We are all, by his definition, "symbol-using (symbol-making, symbol-misusing)"; we are inventors of the negative "(or moralized by the negative)"; "separated from [our] natural condition by instruments of [our] own making"; "goaded by the spirit of hierarchy (or moved by the sense of order)"; and "rotten with perfection" (*LASA* 16). Moreover, the "principal of perfection is central to the nature of language as motive" (*LASA* 16).

Given the world according to Burke, we can choose, within limitations in us, in language, and in situations, to use the divisions and differences that separate us as the motives and grounds for identification. Burke selects *rhetoric* as his key term and explores and develops the resources of rhetoric throughout his life to teach us how to identify with each other and avoid violence. By defining reading, writing, and living as acts of identification, he teaches us how to come to terms, not to war. This is his choice: this is our choice.

What's missing in language, then, is paradoxically the "*symbolic means of inducing cooperation*" (Burke, *RM* 43). We must discount language, according to Burke, because "the *word* 'tree' is *not* a tree" (*RR* 18, 283), because motives are mixed if not contradictory, and because language, people, and situations change. We must remind ourselves and others that it is "naïve verbal realism" to assume that what we and others write and speak is true, complete, or final (*RR* 18). Burke's is a rhetorical world of doubt and uncertainty, a world after the fall: Here on earth, language is partial, changing, and hierarchical; people are incomplete and imperfect.

To stress the emphasis on choice in Burke's rhetoric, I want to begin again by offering another "way in" to his rhetoric. By juxtaposing the personal and indirect introduction to this more direct and argumentative one, I am trying to convince readers that we need to use all available means of persuasion today and not limit ourselves and others by claiming that one method of proof or one interpretation is right for all occasions. I am also drawing lines and making cuts that I argue Burke makes as he selects *rhetoric* as his key term and thereby subordinates other terms, including *philosophy, literature, economics, politics, religion,* and *ideology,* to the status of means of persuading people to identify. Over time, the term *rhetoric* has been subordinated to all the terms above, as Burke explores and attempts to revise throughout his works. Today, *rhetoric* is most often equated with *ideology*, made synonymous or analogous or collapsed into or subsumed under *ideology* as the dominant and privileged term.

While Burke himself advocates and practices such conversions of terms, he seems to maintain *rhetoric* as a key term, along with *terministic screen*, gambling that he can best exploit the resources of rhetoric and revise the term and the attitudes, other terms, and actions he associates with rhetoric, trying everything he can to identify with readers and to have readers identify with him. Identification on his part and on the part of readers is possible only if writer and reader accept the limitations in themselves and in language and, for mutual good, learn to curb their tendencies and *not* rush to judgment and *not* define action only as assertive, self-protective, and violent. In other words, identification requires writer and reader alike *not* to believe that they are right and *not* to fight for their ideological beliefs but, instead, to fight together verbally for something better for both that neither already knows nor does. This is how we *animal symbolicum* can be "moralized by the negative," which we invented.

In Burke's conception of life on earth, *ideology* as a key term does not provide for consideration of alternative actions or allow for the flexibility in using language that is necessary for getting along. Ideology is integral to his understanding of how and why people communicate, but it does not promote the use of language to transcend "social estrangement" (Burke, *RM* 208), because ideological critics are asking others to identify with them and with what is right; the ideological critic is inviting others to change. It is not, however, as simple as that, and we can understand Burke's rhetoric of identification only by examining how he applies it, by his actions.

RHETORIC AND IDEOLOGY: PROSPECTS FOR IDENTIFICATION AND PERSUASION

To examine the motives and consequences of equating rhetoric and ideology and to assess the gains and losses of Burke's choice of rhetoric as identification, I enter uninvited into a conversation about Burke by three literary, cultural, and ideological critics. I begin with Fredric R. Jameson's 1978 article, "The Symbolic Inference; or, Kenneth Burke and Ideological Interpretation," because this essay marks the shift in Burke studies from formalist interpretations of what Burke's texts mean to readings that use Burke primarily for the critic's purposes, in Jameson's case, to evaluate Burke as an ideological critic. I then examine more briefly Frank Lentricchia's use of

Burke in his 1983 *Criticism and Social Change*, Terry Eagleton's discussion on the subject, and Stephen Bygrave's interpretation in his 1993 *Kenneth Burke: Rhetoric and Ideology*. In brief, Jameson claims that Burke is deficient as an ideological critic; Lentricchia writes an implicit counterstatement to Jameson, arguing that Burke is a model literary, ideological intellectual; and Eagleton and Bygrave reconcile the two by explaining that Burke is a rhetorician and an ideological critic because language and ideology are inextricably related.

I agree with Jameson's conclusion that Burke is deficient as an ideological critic by his standards, and I disagree with Lentricchia's and Bygrave's interpretations of him as an ideological critic who understands ideologies as language and therefore as rhetoric. But I understand each of their readings as partial and therefore as invitations for other interpretations that inevitably "fall at the wrong places" (Burke, *PC* 103). What's missing for me in Jameson's analysis is rhetoric understood and practiced as identification or enthymeme-making. What's missing from Lentricchia's reading is also rhetoric, as I argue Burke defines it.[1] Lentricchia collapses rhetoric and ide-

---

1. Lentricchia begins part 5 with Burke's statement about Nietzsche's later style as "a sequence of *darts*," which he first explained to himself as a "simple conversion of his fighting, hunting attitude into its behavioristic equivalents" (145). He does so to argue for "the writer as political force" (145), but Lentricchia ignores Burke's use of the word "first" and how his understanding of Nietzsche's style changed as he began to understand the style as related to his "cult of perspective," which became "perspective by incongruity" for Burke. Instead, Lentricchia turns immediately to the "scary, ironic discourse of Mafia dons," in which "the rhetorician is one who persuades us by making us an offer we believe we can't refuse" (146). Although he distinguishes between apparently "friendly persuasion" and "otherwise," he states that "[r]hetoric is a form of powerful action: darting, killing, drug dispensing, (doctor, pusher, hit-man, poisoner, healer)" (146). He explains: "But Burke's metaphor for Nietzsche's stylistic effect of 'darting' foregrounds rhetoric's intention to control and dominate, to pin us to the wall" (147). Lentricchia fails to recognize Burke's association of Nietzsche's dartlike style not only with his pages as "a battlefield of thought" but also with perspective: "reasons for relating his cult of perspectives to his dartlike style" (145). He also fails to link this style and perspective with Burke's notion of perspective by incongruity. In chapter 2, I associate Burke's "cult of perspective" with his reading of symbolist methods, particularly the juxtaposition of incongruous parts, with how writers engage readers in qualitatively connecting the disparate angles and parts. For Lentricchia's purposes, Burke remains the man "forever striking out at this or that, exactly like a man in the midst of game, or enemies (qtd. by Lentricchia 145). His conclusion is that "[t]o write is to know is to dominate" (147), and his reading of Burke continues to dominate. For an insightful analysis of Burke's symbolic action, see Greig E. Henderson's *Kenneth Burke: Literature and Language as Symbolic Action*, particularly chapters 1 and 3.

ology and defines both as "radical work of transformation" (*Social Change* 6), without distinguishing among transformations that identification and other forms of persuasion generate, and without distinguishing between transformations upward and downward.

What's missing for me in Bygrave's study are the distinctions between rhetoric and ideology discussed above. He recognizes knowledge and disciplines as rhetorical, in that they are motivated, constructed by language, and consequential in the world, but he finally reads Burke's "rhetoric" as offering a "means of connecting all sorts of 'symbolic action' to ideology" (Bygrave 17). At times he equates rhetoric and ideology; more often he privileges ideology over rhetoric.

JAMESON'S CRITIQUE OF
BURKE: CARDS-FACE-UP-ON-THE-TABLE

In "The Symbolic Inference; or, Kenneth Burke and Ideological Analysis," published first in 1978 in *Critical Inquiry* and reprinted in 1982 in *Representing Kenneth Burke*, Jameson declares his purpose: "I want to determine whether his work can be reread or rewritten as a model for contemporary ideological analysis, or what in my own terminology I prefer to call the study of the ideology of form: the analysis, in other words, of the linguistic, narrative, or purely formal ways in which ideology expresses itself through and inscribes itself in the literary text" (509). He expresses this purpose differently mid-way in his essay: "This is therefore the moment to evaluate Kenneth Burke's theory of verbal praxis and to reach some judgment as to his contribution to a theory of ideological analysis proper" (513).

Right away, yet indirectly, Jameson expresses his doubts about Burke as an ideological critic, for why else would he assess him? As he assumes the role of evaluator, he also implicitly presents himself a model ideological critic. We identify with Jameson as an authority who knows from the start where he's taking us. Even if we question his assumptions, such as the idea that ideology is something real that somehow "expresses itself through and inscribes itself in the literary text," we want to see how Jameson does what he sets out to do—to rewrite Burke's rhetoric as ideological analysis. Even if he fails at this, which seems doubtful, he will surely succeed on other accounts through surprising twists and turns.

In establishing his authority, Jameson efficiently encourages readers to align with him, to identify with him and "our world." He draws a line between the old and the new, between "our world" and "those who speak an historical language," and between literary theory and "older 'philosophical' criticism" with "its emphasis on the primacy of language" (Jameson, "Symbolic Inference" 507). He explains that "it has come to be widely, if loosely, felt that it is the discovery of the Symbolic in the most general sense which marks the great divide between thinkers and writers who belong to our world and those who speak an historical language we have first to learn" (507). We want to be included with the "thinkers and writers who belong to our world" (507).

Like Burke, Jameson defines terms and draws lines to set up his argument and to position his readers alongside him. In doing so, he involves readers from the beginning in accepting his logical distinctions and consequently his conclusions as true. He constructs his readers as like-minded or as critics who want to be so, not as collaborators. In only a few sentences Jameson locates himself with the new and his readers beside him as analysts of the ideology of form. This act of inclusion is also an act of exclusion: the suspense is not *where* he will locate Burke outside his circle but *how*. Today, over twenty years later, even that suspense is gone as Jameson's essay can be read only in the contexts of Burke's reply to him in "Methodological Repression and/or Strategies of Containment" and of his reply to Burke in the same winter 1978 issue of *Critical Inquiry*, "Ideology and Symbolic Action." Even without the suspense, the article still invites us to experience *his* rhetorical moves.

> Setting up "Symbolic Inference," Jameson writes, "In what follows I will have much to say, at least implicitly, about this proposition," andthen proceeds to directly address the issue stating, "it is certain that the older philosophical criticism was content simply to 'apply' various philosophical systems to literature in an occasional way, so that we had the curiosities of an existential or a phenomenological criticism, or a Hegelian or a gestalt, or indeed a Freudian criticism available on specialized shelves for the philosophically venturesome. (507)

His claim and attitude here mark a significant difference, for me, between an ideological and a rhetorical approach. Even though he is a master of persuasion by authority, his key term is *ideology* and his primary means of persuasion is the logical argument of the academy, not the enthymeme, the body of proof in rhetoric.

I am asking readers of this study to distinguish themselves for the time being from "our world," as Jameson constructs it, and am inviting readers to assume a rhetorical rather than an ideological, literary, or even cultural interpretive screen. Indeed, I want readers to accept Jameson's definition of the older critics' task, but with two significant revisions: to identify the older critics as rhetoricians, not only as philosophers, philologists, historians, and formalists, and to extend the application of rhetoric beyond literature to other cultural texts and contexts. The aim of rhetoricians (as I am defining Burke's motives and rhetoric) is to make various terms, theories, attitudes, and practices "available on specialized shelves" for the rhetorically venturesome to choose among and to apply in specific contexts where they are judged to be most likely persuasive.

In Burke's words: "The main ideal of criticism, as I conceive it, is to use all that is there to use" (*PLF* 23), no matter how "far afield" it takes him. He aims to accomplish his purposes, not to be consistent, correct, or totally systematic within a particular school of criticism or theory. In fact, Burke combines biographical, ideological, philological, impressionistic, formalist, New Critical, historical, New Historicist, psychoanalytic, reader response, and deconstructionist criticism.[2] Words such as "autonomy" and "intact" are useful at times in his rhetoric, but they are not accurate representations of states of being or of texts. The rhetorical critic tries to figure out which among the various options on the shelf will probably work best for a specific occasion.

Jameson makes another set of cuts in his second paragraph and uses epideictic rhetoric of praise and blame to suggest again that he is ambivalent about Burke and that his readers should be also, but he's willing to give him

---

2. Lentricchia, in *After the New Criticism*, refers to Burke once in a note, perhaps because he cannot be placed into one of the categories of "critical thematics" or ranked as one of "Four exemplary Careers," along with Murray Krieger, E. D. Hirsch, Paul de Man, and Harold Bloom. The note appears in chapter 4, "Uncovering History and the Reader: Structuralism," following a discussion of Levi-Strauss's "distinction between *bricoleur* and engineer" and how Levi-Strauss and Frye "both present themselves as transparencies, innocents who somehow elude the clutches of perspective" (128–29):

> The most candid statement of this idea in contemporary theory is made by Hayden White, whose structuralism is worked up explicitly through Kenneth Burke and Northrop Frye. White contends that, though discourse is inevitably shaped by a writer's commitments to a pre-critical linguistic protocol (a dominant trope), *his* readings of such discourse are given from a value-neutral point of view—a self-consciously ironic perspective which, by virtue of its self-consciousness, moved beyond irony and all other constitutive tropes. (See *Metahistory: The Historical Imagination in Nineteenth–Century Europe* [Baltimore: Johns Hopkins University Press, 1973], pp. ix-xii, 426-34). Self-conscious irony, however, is probably on the essence of irony, the irony of irony, not its transcendence. See chapter 2, above, for a critique of this very issue (Lentricchia, *New Criticism* 129).

a chance. He acknowledges Burke as "precursor of literary theory in this new, linguistics-oriented sense" and in his "pioneering work on the tropes" (Jameson, "Symbolic Inference" 507). In this sense, Burke is not one of the "older 'philosophical' critics" but a more recent linguistic-oriented critic. On the other hand, Burke has succumbed to "a wider latitude for the exercise of personal themes and the free play of private idiosyncrasies" (508).

He rightly belongs, Jameson asserts, among "the greatest of contemporary critics and virtuoso readers" ("Symbolic Inference" 508). Apparent praise is in fact blame. Jameson's disguised scapegoats throughout the article are those critics whose "practice of peculiar and sometimes eccentric textual interpretations is at one with the projection of a powerful, non-systematized theoretical resonance" (508). By Jameson's standards, and by most traditional academic standards, words such as *latitude, free play, virtuoso, personal themes*, and *non-systematized*, are loaded against Burke. Consequently, he cannot be included as a practicing member of the contemporary group who studies the ideology of forms.

Jameson stops short again, as if reluctant to classify Burke among those with "peculiar and sometimes eccentric textual interpretations" now that he has already done so. Instead of following through on his naming, he praises Burke, but he does so as preparation for symbolically slaying him with just two sentences, albeit very long ones:Yet it is not enough to say that Burke's notion of the symbolic act is an anticipation, indeed a privileged expression, of current notions of the primacy of language; seen from a different angle, it allows us to probe the insufficiencies of the latter, which is in so much of today's critical practice little more than a received or unexamined presupposition. Indeed, Burke's conception of the symbolic as act or *praxis* may equally well be said to constitute a critique of the more mindless forms of the fetishism of language, and this to the point where one of the most interesting historical issues raised by his work finds its implicit resolution, *I mean the question as to why this immense critical corpus, to which lip service is customarily extended in passing, has—read by virtually everybody—been utterly without influence in its fundamental lessons*, has had no following, save perhaps among social scientists, and is customarily saluted as a monument of personal inventiveness and ingenuity (in the sense in which I've just spoken of the idiosyncrasies of the great critics) rather than as an interpretive model to be studied and a method to emulated (508–09; my emphasis).Jameson is accurate, I believe, in saying that lip service has been given *in passing* to Burke's "immense critical corpus," though less accurate in his casual insertion—"read by virtually everybody." He would have stretched his credibility to the breaking point if he'd written, "read completely by everybody." But any of these is less surprising, particularly in retrospect, than his statement that Burke's "fundamental lessons" have been "utterly without influence."

All of Jameson's judgments, the lessons he teaches us about Burke, and the lessons he attributes to Burke are critical to our current understanding of possible relationships between rhetoric and ideology and of Burke's relationships to both. Jameson does not distinguish between rhetoric and ideology and does not identify Burke as a rhetorician; he evaluates Burke as an inadequate ideological critic and uses rhetoric for his ideological ends. Nevertheless, Jameson's analysis marks the beginning of interpretations of Burke as an ideological critic and allows me to focus by contrast on the rhetorical lessons that Burke teaches. Having reached his conclusion about Burke early in his essay, Jameson historicizes, perhaps to soften his blow, explaining that in Burke's day his work was not out-of-date:

> A very different Burke emerges, indeed, when we have understood that, in the period in which his most important work was being elaborated, Burke's stress on language, far from reinforcing as it does today the ideologies of the intrinsic and of the anti-referential text, had on the contrary the function of restoring to the literary text its value as activity and its meaning as a gesture and a response to a determinate situation ("Symbolic Inference" 509).

It is likewise necessary to remember that Jameson first presented his essay as a paper at the 1977 English Institute panel on "The Achievement of Kenneth Burke." He published it the next year in *Critical Inquiry* and then reprinted it in the 1982 collection, *Representing Kenneth Burke*. It is equally important to remember that Jameson writes in this essay as a literary theorist and ideological critic to other literary and ideological theorists and critics. Over the two decades since the publication of his article on Burke, a different Jameson and different understandings of ideological criticism, rhetoric, and Burke have emerged. Still, many continue to follow Jameson in reading Burke *as* an ideological critic, and many challenge his evaluation of Burke as inadequate, out-of-date, and on the shelf.

Jameson and Burke: Replying Without Tears in Their Eyes

Jameson gives his final assessment of Burke in his reply, "Ideology and Symbolic Action," to Burke's reply, "Methodological Repression" both in the Winter 1978 issue of *Critical Inquiry*. This is the evaluation I agree with and argue for in this book, except that I emphasize identification as the subject and body of proof in Burke's symbolic action:

> This might then be the most appropriate way of sharpening the differences between us: for Burke, *the concept of ideology is essentially an instrumental one whose usefulness lies in its effectiveness in dramatizing the key concept of symbolic action. My own priorities are the reverse of these*, since I have found the concept of symbolic action a most effective way of demonstrating the ideological function of culture. (Jameson, "Ideology and Symbolic Action" 421; my emphasis)

Burke states a similar understanding of the differences between his motives, terms, and actions and Jameson's in the opening paragraph of his reply to Jameson:

> For any expression of something implies a repression of something else, and any statement that goes only so far is analyzable as serving to forestall a statement that goes farther. And I can't go as far as I think I should if I share with Jameson what I take to be his over investment in the term "ideology" ("Methodological Repression" 401).

While Jameson emphasizes ideology at the expense of rhetoric, Burke weights rhetoric over ideology. From Burke's rhetorical perspective, one is not right and the other wrong, but the motives and probable consequences of these readings are significantly different and must be assessed for "social reasons," summarized for him as *ad bellum purificandum*.

Burke states his two major complaints about Jameson's essay. First, near the end of his essay, "Jameson speaks of 'Burke's strange reluctance to pronounce the word ideology itself'" ("Methodological Repression" 401), but Burke says he builds on this term in two books published twenty years apart, and "[i]t's quite possible that Jameson never read my discussion of 'form and ideology' in *Counter-Statement*" ("Methodological Repression" 403). For most of the reply, Burke charts his uses of the term. Burke responds to Jameson's judgment that he fails to go far enough with the term "ideology" and that this "failure" is Burke's "strategy of containment," by proposing "methodological repression" to describe Jameson's "emphasis upon [his] relation to the term" as a "strategy of containment" ("Methodological Repression" 401).

This leads to Burke's second and related complaint: Jameson does not follow "the proper expository procedure" which "would require that he explicitly 'report' my statement of my position (preferably at least *somewhat* in my own terms) and then proceed to demolish it as he sees fit" ("Methodological Repression" 403). His point is not a formal matter of correctness or convention but of rhetoric: Jameson doesn't first try to identify with Burke by understanding and presenting his arguments before he promotes his own. Burke asks or rather exclaims: "Surely Jameson is not asking his readers to take the sheer Quietus as a 'model' for his way of 'rereading' or 'rewriting' a text" (403).

For Burke, forms are actions, and writers and readers must identify with each other, through formal or stylistic identification or through identification based on other "margins of overlap," *before* writers try to persuade readers to other actions. Identification is both an end and means of persuasion. Persuasion by authority, coercion, or violence does not develop writer's and reader's experiential knowledge and praxis in constructing meaning collectively; it does not lead to further *collaborative* actions of getting along and staying alive. Identification is a method of educating people to act, in Burke's terms, whereas ideological persuasion is a method of training people to move. Both methods of persuasion may be useful for different purposes and situations. The task is figuring out what to do when, where, how, why, and for or with whom.

Burke is not reluctant to pronounce the word ideology, but Jameson's point is well-taken: Burke is reluctant to make ideology his key term, for reasons that Jameson articulates, as we shall see shortly, in his criticism of the "provisional hesitancy" that characterizes Burke's work. In the rhetorical world of doubt and uncertainty, a rush to judgment and end-of-the-line thinking and acting are acts of inflexibility, certainty, and hierarchy, in which writers and readers are unwilling to accept the limitations in ourselves and in language and the necessity of changing our identities and situations in order to get along and stay alive. Rhetoric cultivates flexibility, ambiguity, change, and "provisional hesitancy" as "equipment for living" in a world in which ideologies propel, conflicts among ideologies prevail, and wars are underway and always imminent. In *Counter-Statement*, Burke explicitly defines ideology in terms of its rhetorical effects that artists (writers and readers) can exploit to encourage identification:

> By an ideology is meant the nodus of beliefs and judgments which the artist can exploit for his effects. It varies from one person to another, and from one age to another—but in so far as its general acceptance and its stability are more stressed than its particular variations from person to person and from age to age, an ideology is a "culture." [. . .] But there are cultures within cultures, since a society can be subdivided into groups with divergent standards and interests. Each of

these subdivisions of a culture may possess its own characteristic ideology. . . . Generally, the ideology of an individual is a slight variant of the ideology distinguishing the class among which he arose" (*CS* 161–62).

He reinforces his point that ideologies are multiple and contradictory, changeable, and cultural: "An ideology is not a harmonious structure of beliefs or assumptions; some of its beliefs militate against others, and some of its standards militate against our nature." He expands this definition further to emphasize action: "An ideology is an aggregate of beliefs sufficiently at odds with one another to justify opposite kinds of conduct" (*CS* 163). In general, throughout his rhetoric, ideology is a means of persuading people to identify with each other in order to take further action, and the conflicts of ideologies can help define the grounds for rhetoric and the motives for identification, or they can make communication impossible.

In his reply to Jameson, Burke turns from his discussions of ideology in *Counter-Statement* to *A Rhetoric of Motives*, the "other book in which I deal specifically with the term 'ideology'" ("Methodological Repression" 403). He explains:

> My dealings with the term [ideology] here form an integral part of my thesis that, although Aristotle's *Rhetoric* remains as enviable a text as it ever was, and I still view it as our central text, the term "persuasion" did not cover the ground that I felt should be part of a modern rhetoric. To this end I proposed the term "identification," not as a substitute for the traditional approach but as "an accessory to the standard lore." ("Methodological Repression" 403).

Again, Burke repeats his claim that "identification" does not replace "persuasion"; it just "does not cover the ground" needed for a modern rhetoric.

Burke continues to explain: "Metaphysically, a thing is identified by its *properties*. In the realm of Rhetoric, such identification is frequently by property in the most materialistic sense of the term, economic property" (Burke, "Methodological Repression" 403). People are ethical in "surrounding" themselves "with properties that name [their] number or establish [their] identity" (Burke, "Methodological Repression" 403). Property is "*par excellence* a topic to be considered in a rhetoric having 'identification' as its key term" and therefore "we see why one should expect to get much insight from Marxism as a study of capitalist rhetoric" (Burke, "Methodological Repression" 403). People "buy refrigerators, not merely to keep their butter hard, but to show that they 'belong'" (Burke, *ATH* 124). Our identities and lives are threatened when people want the properties that are "ours"; likewise, we identify with others with whom we share aspects of our identities and properties.

Despite the differences in their terministic screens, both Burke and Jameson acknowledge that they weight language and ideology differently. For my purposes, Jameson clearly and convincingly articulates the problems that result from reading Burke as an ideological critic, problems that become his strengths from a rhetorical perspective. Ideological action is the end of Jameson's ideological analysis; identification is the end of Burke's rhetoric, with ideologies as possible means. I am indebted to Jameson for reading Burke as an educator and for understanding his criticism as lessons for readers. At the same time, I disagree with him about the lessons Burke teaches and about the lessons he says Burke should have taught.

JAMESON'S ASSESSMENT OF BURKE'S LESSON IN HISTORY

What Jameson finds absent in Burke is what I find or rather make present. He states near the end of his article a point he has been making implicitly from the beginning: "I will therefore regret that Burke finally did not want to teach us history, even though he wanted to teach us how to grapple with it" ("Symbolic Inference" 523). He adds that he will argue for the "*bon usage* of his work, that it be used to learn history, even against his [Burke's] own inclination" (523). He contrasts Burke with Yvor Winters, who in his "Experimental School in American Poetry" rewrites "Burke's already classic 'Lexicon Rhetoricae,'" and he offers Winters as "a model of how productively to historicize a powerful but nonhistorical set of aesthetic observations, and of the transformation of the purely formal Burkean interpretive scheme into a powerful historical statement" ("Symbolic Inference" 523).

Without turning to Winters's lessons and influence, I suggest that Burke teaches history *as* rhetoric, as motivated constructions that are often accepted as true. Oral or written histories may be interpreted variously for different purposes and contexts, as true, accurate, biased, economic, psychological, religious, ideological, or other. In all cases, they must stand pragmatic tests. Burke explains this position directly in his reply to Jameson: "we can have but *attitudes* toward whatever of history is either past or not yet here" ("Methodological Repression" 410). As Jameson says, Burke teaches not history but how to grapple with history or, more accurately, how and why to grapple with and interpret the language of history. We *can* deal with and do something about the rhetoric of the past. We don't deny "history itself" as we recognize histories as motivated, situated, and consequential rhetorics. Burke admits, however, "the distinction is far from being as clean-cut as a yes-or-no answer to a question whether a sum in simple arithmetic is correctly added" (410).[3]

In his reply, Jameson restates his ambivalences in 1978 toward Burke and others who promote "notions of the primacy of language," and he does so in a way that usefully dissociates Burke from poststructuralist critics with whom he has been aligned.[4,5] He moves from his point that Burke distinguishes himself from those who fetishize language by his "conception of the symbolic as act or *praxis*" (Jameson, "Symbolic Inference" 508), to make his most damning claim, which I referred to briefly above and want to repeat and examine now:

> Yet it is not enough to say that Burke's notion of symbolic action is an anticipation, indeed a privileged expression, of current notions of the primacy of language; seen from a different angle, it allows us to probe the insufficiencies of the latter, which is in so much of today's critical practice little more than a received idea or unexamined presupposition. Indeed, Burke's conception of the symbolic as act or *praxis* may equally well be said to constitute a critique of the more mindless forms of the fetishism of language, and this to the point where *one of the most interesting historical issues*

---

3. Victor J. Vitanza in *Negation, Subjectivity, and The History of Rhetoric* says initially that Burke "privileges the negative over the affirmative" in rejecting "Nietzsche's cult of Yea-saying" in *Language as Symbolic Action* on page 433" (58). Later he explains that for Burke and Lacan "when we leave the imaginary for the symbolic, we take on the moral-political negative and become subjects 'rotten with perfection' (Burke) or subjects given to the 'fantasy to seize reality' (Lacan; Lyotard; Zizek)" (249). He declares later: "Burke is completely committed to the negative, though he attempts to ameliorate it by multiplying it" (275). He then acknowledges that "Burke tells us that we ('inventors of the negative') cannot say what a thing is, but we can say what it is not (1966, 9)" and "thereby, paradoxically, say what it 'is'" (315). Vitanza calls this action "a modernist questioning and inventing by way of negation" (315). Finally, he acknowledges the dialectical dimension of Burke's negative: "*In Sum, KB writes*: 'The aesthetic would seek to discourage the most stimulating values of the practical, would seek—by wit, by fancy, by anathema, by versatility—to throw into confusion the code which underlies commercial enterprise, industrial competition, the 'heroism' of economic warfare; would seek to endanger the basic props of industry (115)" (334).

4. Robert Wess also discusses terms for order, such as yes/no, no/no, and others; see particularly 217–39 in chapter 8, "*The Rhetoric of Religion*: History in Eclipse, in *Kenneth Burke: Rhetoric, Subjectivity, Postmodernism*.

5. See, for example, Cary Nelson's "Writing as the Accomplice of Language: Kenneth Burke and Poststructuralism.".

raised by his work finds its implicit resolution, I mean the question as to why this immense critical corpus, to which lip service is customarily extended in passing, has—read by virtually everybody—been utterly without influence in its fundamental lessons, has had no following, save perhaps among the social scientists, and is customarily saluted as a monument of personal inventiveness and ingenuity (in the sense in which I've just spoken of the idiosyncrasies of the great critics) rather than as an interpretive model to be studied and a method to be emulated (508–09; my emphasis).

Having made this strong statement not only about Burke's "notions of the primacy of language" but also about his influence or, rather, lack of influence, Jameson concludes this part of his essay by explaining ideological analysis of a literary text *as* action, as "rewriting or restructuration" that occurs "after the fact, for the purposes of the analysis":

> This is why it has seemed more satisfactory to me to describe ideological analysis as the rewriting of the literary text in such a way that it may itself be grasped as the rewriting or restructuration of a prior ideological or historical subtext, provided it is understood that the latter—what we used to call the "context"—must always be (re)constructed after the fact, for the purposes of the analysis ("Symbolic Inference" 511).

Here Jameson blurs his earlier line between grappling with history and history itself, as he distinguishes between "prior ideological or historical subtext," with "the latter—what we used to call 'context'"—understood as reconstruction. Jameson revises his earlier claims about history and language: "But this does not mean that history is itself a text, only that it is inaccessible to us except in textual form or, in other words, that we approach it only by way of its prior textualization" ("Symbolic Inference" 511). For Burke, everything is not language, but the everything he deals with is language. Language, however, affects the world and is affected by the world; language and reality are dialectically related.

Burke's and Jameson's Uses of Symbolic Action: Identification and Ideology

For Jameson, ideological analysis describes "the rewriting of a particular narrative trait or seme as a function of its social, historical, or political context" ("Symbolic Inference" 511). For Burke, symbols are abstractions from situations—they are motives and contexts—that we use to interact with each other. Figures and tropes are actions that draw on similar thought processes and on shared values, assumptions, ideologies, and more, to engage people in collaborative meaning-making. He understands forms of the world, mind, and text as dialectically interrelated by people. In his reply to Jameson, Burke says his "theory of literary form is largely concerned with the role of an 'ideology' in the arousing and fulfilling of an audience's expectation" ("Methodological Repression" 402) and with identification as "property in the most materialistic sense of the term" that names a man's "number and establish[es] his identity" (403).

In his conclusion, Jameson refers back to his proposed "checklist of the great contemporary critics, the great readers of an age that has discovered the symbolic," to explain further what as readers we gathered then and have had confirmed throughout: "what I then neglected to add was that the art and practice of virtuoso reading does not seem to me to be the noblest function, the most urgent mission, of the literary and cultural critic of our time" (523). Jameson is still concerned with literary and cultural critics who practice ideological analysis and with distinguishing them from the "virtuoso readers." Virtuosity is not a virtue in its relationship to the rhetorical choices writers and readers make when they select among the possible means of persuasion in a given context. Flexibility, pliancy, and liquidity in language are valued in that they can encourage identification and a coming to terms not war.

Jameson locates "history itself" above reading. He recognizes Burke as a teacher of reading but not as a teacher of history, although he links the teaching of history and the "telling of the tale of the tribe." His own mode, however, is logical argument rather than narration:

> In a society like ours . . . there is a higher priority than reading and that is History itself: so the very greatest critics of our time—Lukacs, for example, or, to a lesser degree, a Leavis—are those who have construed their role as the teaching of history, as the telling of the tale of the tribe, the most important story any of us will ever have to listen to, the narrative of that implacable yet also emancipatory logic whereby the human community has evolved into its present form and developed the sign systems by which we live and explain our lives to ourselves. So urgently do we need these history lessons, indeed, that they outweigh the palpable fact that neither critic just mentioned is good, let alone a virtuoso, reader, that each could justly be reproached for his tin ear and his puritanical impatience with the various *jouissances* of the literary text. (Jameson, "Symbolic Inference" 523)

Differences between Jameson's ideological analysis and Burke's rhetorical analysis are obvious. In his previous discussion about the relationship between history and texts, Jameson says that ideology, like history, is known through textualization, but he seems reluctant to pronounce the term rhetoric. This should not be surprising, given his terministic screen. What is surprising is that Jameson would expect a rhetorical critic to be primarily concerned with ideology, because he sees clearly around the corners of his own terministic screen when he explains in his reply that ideology is for Burke a means not the end of persuasion:

> [F]or Burke, the concept of ideology is essentially an instrumental one whose usefulness lies in its effectiveness in dramatizing the key concept of symbolic action. My own priorities are the reverse of these, since I have found the concept of symbolic action a most effective way of demonstrating the ideological function of culture. ("Ideology and Symbolic Action" 421)

Jameson's Related Lessons on Agency: "Strategy," "Purpose," and "Self"

Jameson refers to two specific lessons he "want[s] us to learn and then to unlearn from Burke" ("Symbolic Inference" 513). The first, he says, "is associated with that word which more than anyone else he added to our critical vocabulary, namely the notion of a literary 'strategy'; while the second inevitably enough centers on his fundamental theory of dramatism and of the organization of all symbolic action according to the five basic coordinates of Act, Scene, Agent, Agency, and Purpose" ("Symbolic Inference" 513–14). As we shall see, his two lessons are one, in that they both teach us his lesson on the subject, which he doesn't name until his conclusion, and in that they are both extensions of his ongoing lesson about ideological forces and the limitations of human agency.

I want to examine this concluding lesson about the concept of self or subject, before turning to his earlier lessons about "strategy" and dramatism, to demonstrate how Jameson persuades his readers to accept the conclusions we have already accepted earlier, in part by reading along with him and participating in the symbolic action he generates. More specifically, I want to focus on the qualitative progressions he includes in his overall syllogistic argument and raise questions about the rhetoric of the writer as self, subject, and agent who makes choices.

Jameson builds "The Symbolic Inference" toward an ideological analysis of, and challenge to, American notions of individuality, self, and identity and the relationships between these terms and notions of "bourgeoise individualism" and the "market system." In the following long passage, he sets up an opposition between the self and "new collective structures," without Burke's stress on how terms define each other, how the collective and individual may be read as different in degree or in kind, and how "post-individual" is a rhetorical action, motivated, consequential, yet revisable, as are all terms:

> Nowhere do the continental and the Anglo-American critical traditions diverge more dramatically than on this whole issue of the subject, or the ego, or the self, and the value and reality to be accorded to it. We do not have to go all the way with the current French repudiation of ego psychology and what they call the "philosophies of the subject" to recognize in the American myths of the self and of its identity crises and ultimate reintegration some final trace and survival of that old ideology of bourgeois individualism whose basic features—juridical equality, autonomy, freedom to sell your own labor power—had crucial functions to fulfill in the establishment and organization of the market system. To repudiate that ideological tradition, to valorize the decentering of the subject with its optical illusion of centrality, does not, I would argue, have to lead to anarchism or to that glorification of the schizophrenic hero and the schizophrenic text which has become of the latest French fashions and exports; on the contrary, it should signal a transcendence of the older individualism and the appearance of new collective structures and of ways of mapping our own decentered place with respect to them.
>
> However this may be, it is clear that the rhetoric of the self in American criticism will no longer do, any more than its accompanying interpretive codes of identity crisis and mythic reintegration, and that a post-individualistic age needs new and post-individualistic categories for grasping both the production and the evolution of literary form as well as the semantic content of the literary text and the latter's relationship to collective experience and to ideological contradiction. ("Symbolic Inference" 520–21)

While his claim that "the rhetoric of the self in American criticism will no longer do" may be accepted by some as true, a rhetorical critic understands the claim as rhetorically motivated, analyzes the possible consequences of it, and contrasts it with other claims to assess the gains and losses for use in specific contexts—without denying either the history or the current consequences of American myths of individualism or the physiological distinctions and connections between individual bodies that use language to connect.⁶ The rhetorician asks: No longer do for whom? When? Where? How? Why? Why and how is the association between individualism and the market system constructed as a causal relationship? Can the two be dissociated? What are the probable consequences of such symbolic actions? Is the current rhetoric of the self dead, no longer persuasive, or under reconstruction? When psychologies and ideologies of the self no longer do, what does do, how, and why? What are the possible gains and losses of Jameson's claim?

Jameson supports his claim about the death of myths of the self by first drawing on Burke and then by distinguishing himself from Burke:

> What is paradoxical about Burke's own critical practice in this respect is that he has anticipated many of the fundamental objections to such a rhetoric of self and identity at the same time that he may be counted among its founding fathers: this last and most important of what we have called his "strategies of containment" provides insights which testify against his own official practice ("Symbolic Inference" 521).

What is paradoxical or contradictory from Jameson's perspective is only rhetoric from Burke's. He understands the limitations of a rhetoric of self and identity; he also understands that, despite and because of these limitations, a rhetoric of self and identity might be useful in some situations. In addition, terms such as *self* and *other* and *individual* and *collective* define each other and can be read as polar opposites or terms along a continuum. He uses terms rhetorically not referentially, and one is not inherently or always better or worse than another. He chooses rhetoric because it addresses communication and miscommunication between and among people. Collapsing the two terms rhetoric and ideology may be perilous for both rhetoric and ideology in limiting the resources of both, though doing so might serve other purposes at times.

As Jameson says, Burke does use language temporarily as "strategies for containment," for encompassing situations, and as "strategies for coping,"

---

6. See Robert Wess's "rhetoric of the self," developed throughout *Kenneth Burke: Rhetoric, Subjectivity, Postmodernism*, particularly in chapter 6 "*A Grammar of Motives*: The Rhetorical Constitution of the Subject." Also see Barbara A. Biesecker's *Addressing Postmodernity: Kenneth Burke, Rhetoric, and a Theory of Social Change* for discussions of individual agency and collective identification, particularly in chapter 3, "A Rhetoric of Motives, or, Toward an Ontology of the Social.".

but all uses of language are partial, temporary, and situated. Identification for Burke is a "terministic choice" (*RM* 20) from which actions and consequences follow, but he recognizes that one choice does not necessarily replace another as right forever. It's not as simple as that: we must figure out when it will probably be more useful to use notions of "self" and the "individual" rather than "collective." Burke's choice of "identification" includes both individuals and groups and both as motivated and situated. Identification is always partial and temporary, not whole and permanent.[7] And within his rhetoric, people are divided but can choose and be moved to act collectively through identification.

In his reply to Jameson, Burke explains his conception of the individual and its place in rhetoric as he demonstrates that he is not reluctant to use the term ideology. He points to the second paragraph of *The German Ideology* for support: "'The first premise of all human history is of course the existence of living human individuals. The first fact to be established is therefore the physical organization of these individuals and their consequent relation to the rest of nature'" ("Methodological Repression" 404). He then distinguishes between the "physiological organism as a principle of individuation" and the "*individual* (as distinct from the kind of 'ideological' identity that is intended in a social term, such as 'individualism') in the human body, the 'original economic plant,' distinct from all others owing to the divisive centrality of each body's particular nervous system" (404).

Burke's drawing and redrawing distinctions and definitions are familiar practices in his rhetoric. They are also critical to his rhetoric that assumes agency and choice *and* limitations to both that must be assessed and nevertheless acted upon. He recognizes the uncertainty of his claims and probable conclusions: they are the flexible rather than firm grounds for action, and consequently they are revisable.

Jameson constructs an argument that from beginning to end leads his readers to accept his conclusion that the "rhetoric of the self is dead in American criticism." He challenges what he calls Burke's lessons on "literary 'strategy,'" on the "fundamental theory of dramatism," and on "the organization of all symbolic action according to the five basic coordinates" (Jameson, "Symbolic Inference" 513–14), because all imply individual agency. But for Burke, as we have seen, there is the individual, but the individual must act collaboratively to survive. Jameson provides "perspective by incongruity":

---

7. Bender and Wellbery conclude their article "Rhetoricality: On the Modernist Return of Rhetoric" with the point they repeat throughout but which does not seem to inform their own practices, as it does Burke's: "Rhetoricality, then, also designates the partial and provisional character of every attempt to know it" (39).

> In one sense, of course, the term "strategy" is itself merely shorthand for that complex of symbolic determinants: it is the term which governs their respective relations to each other, which names the *provisional hierarchy established between them on the occasion of a given act—that dominance of Agency over Scene, or alternatively of Scene over Agent and Act*. (514; my emphasis)

The problem for Jameson with the term *strategy* is that it assumes individuals who create, select, and use them; the problem with dramatism is that it posits agents, purposes, and agencies as possibly useful individually and dialectically. For Burke, these terms may be useful distinctions for analytical purposes *and* useful as terms that define each other and can be interrelated, as indicated by ratios among them.

In general, Burke conceives of terms as dialectically related to each other; to the motives, psychologies, biologies, and bodies of *animal symbolicum*; and to situations which we name and from which we abstract our terms. We may select among these possible ways of naming relationships, wisely but not freely, because our choices are constrained by situations and must stand the test of the pragmatic. Neither Jameson nor Burke is right: it's not as simple as that. In rhetoric, agents choose what they figure will work. Burke includes all that is there to use, including rhetorical analysis and ideological analysis, for the purposes of *ad bellum purificandum*.

While Burke understands language as symbolic action and the advantage of such action is the fact it *is* symbolic, Jameson interprets Burke's motive and those of other virtuoso readers as a "rage for patterns and symmetries and the mirage of the metasystem" ("Symbolic Inference" 508). The more agonizing problem for Jameson is that "strategy precedes accomplishment and indeed action or realization itself" (514). What follows from this is even worse for the ideological critic, but essential for the rhetorician:

> There is a sense in which none of the symbolic acts in question can be said to have come to its execution, in which all will have remained forever at the stage of project or sheer intention—*a kind of permanently provisional hesitation* on the threshold of being which the term "strategy" strategically perpetuates (514; my emphasis).

From a rhetorical perspective, "provisional hesitation" about how, when, where, why, and for whom to act is the power of symbolic action by individuals and by groups. It distinguishes rhetorical action that considers alternative means of reaching its ends from ideological action that is certain about its aims. Provisional hesitation or decision-making is by definition and practice "permanent" though always changing in Burke's rhetoric. It does not necessarily prevent or force action; it can delay action and equip us for action. Hesitation, decision-making, consideration of alternatives, and judgment all characterize rhetoric because rhetoric deals in matters of doubt and uncertainty that must be made convincing to others. This "provisional hesitation," this moment of uncertainty, is critical in a rhetoric for reading and writing and for daily life—if the goal is to stay alive through cooperation rather than killing.

Jameson is correct in his ideological analysis of the "fundamental ambiguities of the concept of symbolic action" and his interpretation of these as limiting if not preventing ideological actions:

> One of the fundamental ambiguities of the concept of symbolic action is indeed precisely this shifting distance from non-symbolic or practical or instrumental action itself, which sometimes it seems to want to absorb into itself on the grounds that in that sense all action is symbolic, all production is really communication, and from which, at other times or on other occasions, it seems to ebb and retreat, leaving behind it some inhospitably arid and stony ledge to which all mere practical activity in the world is summarily assigned. ("Symbolic Inference" 514)

From a rhetorical perspective, the ambiguities, the "shifting distance," the "ebb and retreat," and the "ledge" are sites of uncertainty and of rhetoric.

What for Jameson is a "fundamental ambiguity" to resolve or correct is for Burke the human condition: in the rhetorical world it is a practical and wise decision to accept ambiguities and to learn to act in uncertainty. Jameson is right in suggesting that Burke's terministic screen makes him see almost everything as rhetorical and that this is a limitation. Burke acknowledges the partiality of all attitudes, terms, and frames, and he consequently adopts an attitude of uncertainty and inconclusiveness about his own.

Jameson's Critique of Burke's Lesson on Dramatism and the "Shrunken Function" of Purpose

A little more than halfway through "Symbolic Inference," Jameson asks permission of his readers to move from his critique of Burke's lesson on strategy to his lesson on dramatism: "Let me now quickly generalize this critique and apply it to the larger dimensions of the overall theory of dramatism itself" (515). Having completed his case about the word *strategy*, "which more than anyone else [Burke] added to our critical vocabulary" (513), he begins his second lesson:

I believe that the Achilles heel of this system is to be located in the shrunken function left over for Purpose in its grandiose mapping scheme (Purpose being, in the *Grammar of Motives*, amalgamated with Agency, and rather summarily dispatched as a kind of providential survival, a mystical or metaphysical "telos") ("Symbolic Inference" 515).

He explains that the "category of Purpose turns out to designate two very different things at once": "it names the inner logic of the symbolic act itself, its immediate aims and official objectives or, in other words, the terms in which it explains its own activity to itself"; and it "would designate the strategic organization of the gesture, the immediate end toward which this particular muscular effort is mobilized" (Jameson, "Symbolic Inference" 516).

For Jameson, the "restricted concept of Purpose thus stands to this generalized one as an immanent interpretation to a transcendent one or, to use another opposition which has been central in recent debates on hermeneutics, as the study of the *Sinn* or 'sense' of a given text, its inner structure and syntax, as opposed to that of its *Bedeutung* or 'meaning,' its 'historically operative' significance or function" ("Symblic Inference" 516). He adds, "Only the first operation can be carried out without attention to the situation of the work" and "the second, interpretation proper, is impossible without some preliminary (re-)construction of what I have called its subtext" (516).

Burke presents scene as a discrete element of the Pentad and combines it with others through ratios, but throughout his rhetoric, purposes and motives arise from scenes and in turn influence how we understand situations. In addition, Burke as rhetorician understands that we create "scenes" and frame situations in language, without denying that reality exists. His theory of language as symbolic action addresses forms as actions in the world and texts as dialectically related to contexts. People can still choose a more formal rather than contextual weighting for certain circumstances.

Jameson illustrates his point through Burke's rewriting of Keat's *Ode*, specifically Burke's uses of substitution and of the subtext created by Burke's revision of "truth" and "beauty" as Science and Poetry ("Symbolic Inference" 516). For Jameson, the "operation by which this subtext has been constructed remains essentially incomplete" and needs more than a "scene or background, not an inert context alone, but rather a structured and determinate situation, such that the text can be grasped as an active response to it (of whatever type)" (517).

Burke begins *The Philosophy of Literary Form* by explaining that "[c]ritical and imaginative works are answers to questions posed by the situation in which they arose" and that we adopt strategies for the "encompassing of situations" and sizing up situations (*PLF* 1). He does not, as Jameson claims, pinpoint that to which a text is "precisely a response" ("Symbolic Inference" 517). It's not as simple or precise as that for Burke. According to Jameson, Burke uses "a strategy of containment, a substitution," instead of constructing "a subtext in the form of a situation," and this substitution, he says, is "designed to arrest the movement of ideological analysis before it can begin to draw in the social, historical, and political parameters which are the ultimate horizon of every cultural artifact" ("Symbolic Inference" 517). Burke's "specification of the ideological context" here "only allows us to admire the more intelligently the prestidigitation, the intellectual acrobatics, by which he manages to square this particular circle" (517).

In general, the "'dialectical opposition' Burke posits between poetry and science is not yet a situation of that kind," in which the "text's meaning then, in the larger sense of *Bedeutung*, will be the meaningfulness of a gesture that we read back from the situation to which it is precisely a response" (Jameson, "Symbolic Inference" 517). As Burke deals with language to develop pliancy and flexibility, it is not surprising that "this opposition might take on the form of a contradiction or an antinomy, a dilemma or a double-bind, a crisis that required some immediate resolution" (517). Given Jameson's reading, which he admits is "from the point of view of ideological analysis" (518), he claims "[w]e must therefore take the passage just quoted as evidence for a discouraging reversal in Burke's critical strategy":

> His conception of literature as a symbolic act, which began as a powerful incitement to the study of a text's mode of activity in the general cultural and social world beyond it, now proves to have slipped back over the line and, passing from the generalized sense of the word Purpose to its immanent and strategic, restricted sense, now to furnish aid and comfort to those who want to limit our work to texts whose autonomy has been carefully secured in advance, all the blackout curtains drawn before the lights are turned back on (518).

Given Burke's rhetorical perspective, his analysis of Keats's symbolic action is action "in the general cultural and social world beyond it." In his reply, Burke says that "Jameson pictures me trying to solve problems that I had no notion of" ("Methodological Repression" 411). He then states what he was trying to do:

> But here's all I thought I was doing: in my works generally (even when discussing such an "ideological" exhibit as Hitler's *Mein*

Kampf) I have laid great stress upon the study of symbolic constructs that lend themselves readily to analysis as embodying secular traces of religious patterns. And when writing of Keats's "Ode on a Grecian Urn," all that I thought I was doing was analyzing an exceptionally well-put-together art-heaven, as per my references to such matters in my "Motion/Action" essay (pp. 830–32). (411).

In his reading and rewriting of Keats, Burke teaches us to act rather than move and to exercise agency by using language to maintain or transgress distinctions in order to revise our current understandings and to figure out what might help us get along with each other and stay alive. Instead of having to draw the blackout curtains to defend ourselves against bombs, Burke advocates that we use the resources of rhetoric to revise ourselves, others, and the world.

In sum, Burke accurately distinguishes his position from Jameson's in his *Critical Inquiry* reply when he statistically documents his own uses of ideology and criticizes Jameson for his "overinvestment" in the term and his "thumbs-down sense" of ideology ("Methodological Repression" 415). Burke invests in the term rhetoric, and he teaches lessons in rhetoric; Jameson's capital is ideology, and he teaches lessons in ideology. or all the reasons Jameson gives, Burke is deficient as an ideological critic. Nevertheless, Jameson's article positioned Burke as an ideological critic for many, and his negative evaluation of Burke has continued to provoke counterstatements. I refer to Jameson's essay published in *Critical Inquiry*, volume 4, in the Spring of 1978 (507–24).

Lentricchia's Academic Literary Intellectual and Traditional Academic Appeal

Frank Lentricchia uses Burke to justify the ways of the academic literary intellectual as ideologically effective in the world. He interprets Burke not as a rhetorician but as the model "literary intellectual," the "sort of intellectual who works mainly on texts and produces texts," the "university humanist," and the "*specific intellectual* described by Foucault—one whose radical work of transformation, whose fight against repression is carried on at the specific institutional site where he finds himself and on the terms of his own expertise, on the terms inherent to his own functioning as an intellectual" (*Criticism and Social Change* 6–7).

He begins his "pursuit of the issue of criticism as social force with a look at an event in the life of Kenneth Burke"—the first American Writers' Congress in 1935, the purpose of which, he says, was "to extend the reach of the

John Reed Clubs by providing the basis for a much broader organization of American writers." Lentricchia explains that "[i]f writers could effectively band together, then maybe they could accelerate what had to happen anyway—the destruction of capitalism and the creation of a workers' government" (*Criticism and Social Change* 21). Within this context, Burke gave a brief paper that Lentricchia says was "cunningly titled," "Revolutionary Symbolism in America." The paper had "the discomforting feel of ideological deviance," first because Burke discusses symbolism "in those years of Marxist history (Gramsci was Mussolini's dying prisoner in 1935)" and, second, because he discusses America, which is "to put on the blinders of nationalism which will prevent us from seeing the real world-historical dimension of revolution" (22).

Lentricchia says that what Burke "does in the essay as a whole is to rewrite and elaborate Marx's immensely suggestive first thesis on Feuerbach, which was itself a dialectical rewriting of materialism as it had been hitherto understood: the thing, reality, sensuousness, must not be conceived, Marx argued, as an object exterior (and opposed) to practice, to intellection, to subjectivity, but as '*sensuous human activity, practice*,' with 'practice' now understood as an integrated and indivisible whole of physical, intellectual, and emotional coordinates" (*Criticism and Social Change* 22–23). What Burke does specifically, Lentricchia says, is recover the textual, the symbolic, as ideological action:

> One of his most significant contributions to Marxist theory (beyond his lonely American performance of "Western Marxism") is his pressing of the difficult, sliding notion of ideology, bequeathed to us by *The German Ideology*, out of the areas of intellectual trickery and false consciousness and into the politically productive textual realms of practical consciousness—rhetoric, the literary, and the media of what he tellingly called "adult education in America." The political work of the hegemonic, as well as that of a would-be counter-hegemonic culture, Burke saw (as Marx did not) as most effectively carried thorough at the level of a culture's various verbal and nonverbal languages. (23–24)

He explains that "Burke was saying to America's radical left" revolution must be "culturally as well as economically rooted" and that a "revolutionary culture must situate itself firmly on the terrain of its capitalist antagonist, must not attempt a dramatic leap beyond capitalism in one explosive rupturing moment of release, must work its way through capitalism's language of domination by working cunningly within it, using, appropriating, even speaking through its key mechanisms of repression (Lentricchia, *Criticism and Social Change* 24).

Lentricchia then summarizes, demonstrating his own commitment to literary academic work as legitimate ideological action:

> What Burke's proposal in 1935 to America's intellectual left amounts to is this: the substance, the very ontology of ideology—an issue that Marx and Engels engaged with little clarity, to put it charitably—in a broad but fundamental sense is revealed to us *textually* and therefore must be grasped (read) and attacked (reread, rewritten) in that dimension (*Criticism and Social Change* 24).

At this point, Lentricchia acknowledges what I argue is the overall aim of Burke's rhetoric but which Lentricchia interprets as Burke's major contribution to ideological rather than rhetorical analysis: "Burke concentrates therefore on the linguistic instruments which produce our sense of community, the 'symbols' of 'communal relationship by which a group is bound,' the 'myth' of the collective that is the 'social tool for welding the sense of interrelation'" (24).

The question for me is what differences does it make for Lentricchia to label this attention to textuality, specifically to "the linguistic instruments which produce our sense of community," as ideological rather than rhetorical? What difference does it make that Lentricchia's "community" is limited to one bound by a shared ideology or shared ideologies, rather than a community of all who share language and who are united in our shared differences and conflicting ideologies, understood as the motives and grounds for community, communication, and identification? Burke's community is *animal symbolicum*; the scope and circumference of this community is worldwide. At the same time, and this point is also critical: identification is the body of proof in his rhetoric, but it is not the only proof and action in a world given to hierarchy, power, and domination. Equally important, there is no one way for people to identify with others; we must always everywhere try everything to connect and get along.

Lentricchia concludes this section with a shift to affirm his literary readers' sense of community with him, so that he can revise us into ideological critics through identification with him. He uses Burke in the 1930s to appeal to the heroic revolutionary aspirations in his own audience of literary and cultural critics in the 1980s. He appeals to their hierarchical desires for mastery and leadership in war, not to their desires to identify with and learn from others in order to get along and avoid war:

It was a situation of maximum opportunity for the literary intellectual: a struggle for cultural position was fully underway, and the literary intellectual, with his mastery of the tools of discourse, might have found himself in strategic leadership as a director of rhetorical war (Lentricchia, *Criticism and Social Change* 25).

Rhetorical critics have responded to Lentricchia's challenge here to engage in rhetorical war and to credit that engagement as heroic and responsible ideological action. His book is pivotal in Burke criticism as it marks the beginning of constructions of Burke as a model ideological critic, rather than a deficient one. It also reinforces the conflation or integration of the literary, the rhetorical, and the ideological as all textual, and the textual as ideological.

Lentricchia's Interpretation of Burke's Educational Project

Like Jameson, Lentricchia understands Burke's critical project as educational. He begins "Provocations":

> I can tell you what my book is about, at its polemical core, by citing a distinction of John Dewey's that I first encountered in the amazing meditative labyrinth Kenneth Burke called *Attitudes Toward History*. The distinction is between "education as a function of society" and "society as a function of education" (*Criticism and Social Change* 1).

Lentricchia aligns himself with "Burke who understands that the teacher aims to remake society," without acknowledging the Burke who understands also that the teacher may at times aim to support society.

While Lentricchia is concerned with *what* changes to make, Burke tries to figure out what, why, and how to make certain changes. Again, I am drawing fine lines to distinguish the motives and consequences of their terministic screens and the aims and effects of their "cuts." Lentricchia's model and audience remain literary as he attempts to revise "literary" into "ideological" through Burke's theory of language as symbolic action. He embraces Burke as a literary critic who uses literature as an "instrument for social change," with the following explanation: "The 'literary' for Burke is always embedded in those concerns. As a form of action in the world the literary is fully enmeshed in the social—it is not an imaginative space apart" (Lentricchia, *Criticism and Social Change* 25).

He continues to use Burke to justify his actions and those of other literary intellectuals: "He was telling them that right social action, for a literary intellectual, was preeminently a literary act, because it was grounded in, its effectivity proceeded from, the rhetorical textures, strategies, and structures of discourse" (Lentricchia, *Criticism and Social Change* 26). And he recognizes Burke's methods of using language as dialectical rather than paradoxical or ambiguous: "The distinction and—to the old left—the anomaly of Burke's mind was that it refused both sides of this controversy; Burke simply negated and at the same time preserved the Marxist/formalist controversy in a dialectical maneuver that insisted that the literary was always a form of social action, however rarely it might be recognized as such" (27).

Lentricchia understands Burke's recommendations to his audience at the Writer's Congress as rhetorical, but he focuses on Burke's actions as ideological:

> In effect Burke asks Marxists—and the real value of his question is that it is not limited to that audience—whether or not it is their ambition to become workers: "There are few people who really want to work, let us say, as a human cog in an automobile factory, or as gatherers of vegetables on a big truck farm. Such rigorous ways of life enlist our *sympathies*, but not our *ambitions*. Our ideal is as far as possible to *eliminate* such kinds of work, or to reduce its strenuousness to a minimum." Burke's nice point needs a little filling out: you can't expect, he says, in effect, to his progressive friends, on the one hand, to keep painting these riveting portraits of workers under capitalism, of degradation and alienation—you can't expect people to accept these portraits as the truth, which is your rhetorical desire, after all, and then, on the other hand, at the same time, expect people to want to identify with workers, or become workers, or even enlist their energies of intellect and feeling on behalf of workers. Even though your intentions may be otherwise, the fact is that your representations of workers are being received as representations of "the other." Such portraits, when they do enlist our sympathies, often, at the same time, in ways too subtle to trace, create an effect of repulsion—which is always, after all, the effect of "the other" when perceived from inside the self-rationalizing norm. You must therefore attend to the machinery of representation; you must, as Marx would urge, rethink your representations of workers. You must somehow bring them within, make sure that their fate and ours are bound up with each other (*Criticism and Social Change* 27–28).

As Lentricchia recognizes but does not emphasize or develop further, Burke challenges his own audience to invite their audiences to identify with them, "bring them within, make sure that their fate and ours are bound up with each other" (28). Burke also emphasizes throughout that the writer or speaker must also identify with readers and that the attitude of cooperation in writers and readers and speakers and listeners is critical to identification. Burke teaches by what he says and does in speaking and writing.

Although the differences may seem slight between Burke's motives and emphasis and Lentricchia's, *how* Lentricchia "fill[s] in" Burke's "nice point" shifts focus away from language to the "degradation and alienation" and shifts focus from Burke's claim that the word "worker" won't work to the 'truth' of the riveting portraits. In other words, Lentricchia stresses representation and the movement of the reader to identify with the writer, without the writer changing, because the writer is the one who knows what is right. In contrast, Burke stresses identification as action by all involved. Similarly, Lentricchia does not consider *how* Burke himself speaks and writes as a means of creating identification; he is not concerned with Burke's enthymematic arguments as uncharacteristic of the literary intellectual's mode of persuasion, nor with enthymematic arguments as having broad, public appeal.

Lentricchia remains consistent throughout his text in addressing his familiar audience of literary ideological critics, using the shared language, values, assumptions, and conventions by which they identify with him as an authority. He does not revise his language, his Marxist interpretation, nor his logical method of proof: he does not move to identify with readers, for *what* he offers is right and *how* he offers is conventional.

Burke's Rhetoric and Eagleton's Ideology

We can also track in three works of Terry Eagleton how the literary, rhetorical, and ideological can be converted, transformed, subsumed, and revived for various purposes and contexts. In *Marxism and Literary Criticism* in 1976, he argues for a Marxist criticism of literature "in terms of the historical conditions which produce it" and for this literary criticism to be understood and practiced as part of Marxism, defined as "a scientific theory of human societies and of the practice of transforming them" (vii). He explains that "what that means, rather more concretely, is that the narrative Marxism has to deliver is the story of the struggles of men and women to free themselves from certain forms of exploitation and oppression," and he adds that there is "nothing academic about those struggles, and we forget this at our cost" (Eagleton, *Marxism and Literary Criticism* vii).

In *Literary Theory* in 1983, Eagleton analyzes various theories, locating them historically and ideologically, and in conclusion shifts from literary to political criticism to rhetoric. Although he explains that his intention "is not to counter the literary theories that I have critically examined in this book with a literary theory of my own, which would claim to be more politically acceptable" (Eagleton, *Literary Theory* 204). He expands "literature" into discursive practices in a broad context: "What would be specific to the kind of study I have in mind, however, would be its concern for the kinds of *effects* which discourses produce, and how they produce them" (205). He then, however, identifies this study of how "discourse is structured and organized, and examining what kind of effects these forms and devices produce in particular readers in actual situations" as "probably the oldest form of 'literary criticism' in the world, known as rhetoric" (205). In other words, Eagleton has moved from literary theories to political criticism; revised "literature" and political criticism into the study of "the way discourses are constructed to achieve certain effect; named that study "rhetoric" and then called rhetoric "probably the oldest form of 'literary criticism' in the world" (205).

In 1991 in *Ideology*, rhetoric is not indexed although he uses the term, for example in connection with J. L. Austin's performatives: "the class of speech acts which get something done" and with Althusser's shift from "a *cognitive* to an *affective* theory of ideology" (Eagleton, *Ideology* 19). His purpose in these cases in chapter 1, "What is Ideology?" is primarily to consider issues of false consciousness, falsehoods, and falsifying. This concern with truth is not the direct concern of Burke's rhetoric, which deals in a world of doubt and uncertainty. Later, in "Discourse and Ideology," Eagleton writes:

> All discourse is aimed at the production of certain effects in its recipients, and is launched from some tendentious "subject position"; and to this extend we might conclude with the Greek Sophists that everything we say is really a matter of rhetorical performance within which questions of truth or cognition are strictly subordinate. If this is so, then all language is "ideological," and the category of ideology, expanded to breaking-point, once more collapses. One might add that the production of this effect is precisely part of the ideological intention of those who claim that "everything is rhetorical."
>
> It is, however, a simple sleight-of-hand, or sheer intellectual disingenuousness, to imagine that all language is rhetorical to exactly the same degree (201).

From Burke's perspective, assertions, such as "all language is ideological" or "all language is rhetorical," are assertions not of truths but of metaphors to work with, in order to see things other than they are, and to consider what was and what might be. They are not disingenuous: they are rhetorical.

I am most interested in Eagleton's discussions of Pierre Macherey's notion of *decentred form* in *Marxism and Literary Criticism* and in *Ideology*. Eagleton explains:

> For Macherey, a work is tied to ideology not so much by what it says as by what it does not say. It is in the significant *silences* of a text, in its gaps and absences, that the presence of ideology can be most positively felt. It is these silences which the critic must make "speak." The text is, as it were, ideologically forbidden to say certain things; in trying to tell the truth in his own way, for example, the author finds himself forced to reveal the limits of the ideology within which he writes. He is forced to reveal its gaps and silence, what it is unable to articulate. Because a text contains these gaps and silences, it is always *incomplete*. Far from constituting a rounded, coherent whole, it displays a conflict and contradiction of meaning; and the significance of the work lies in the difference rather than the unity of these meanings (*Ideology* 32).

He explains further: "When Macherey argues that the work is 'incomplete,' however, he does not mean that there is a piece missing which the critic could fill in. On the contrary, it is in the nature of the work to be incomplete, tied as it is to an ideology which silences it at certain point" (35). The "critic's task is not to fill the work in" but instead "to seek out the principle of its conflict of meanings, and to show how this conflict is produced by the work's relation to ideology" (35).

For Eagleton, a text is inherently incomplete for ideological reasons; for Burke, a work is incomplete because people and language are incomplete and ideologies are also for the same reason. Incompleteness for Burke is, however, the motive and grounds for identification. As Eagleton searches for "the principle of its conflict of meanings," Burke focuses on the collaborative actions of writer and reader to create meaning, and meaning for him is action.

Earlier, Eagleton says that ideology for Macherey and Althusser is "more than an amorphous body of free-floating images and ideas; in any society it has a certain structural coherence" (*Marxism and Literary Criticism* 17). He admits that their comments are "at crucial points ambiguous and obscure" but "the relation they propose between literature and ideology is nonetheless deeply suggestive" (19). He explains Macherey's interest in decentered form in terms of ideology but not in terms of rhetoric, as I discuss it in chapter 2 in connection with Burke's revision of the enthymeme into identification.

In *Ideology*, in "Ideological Strategies," he returns to Macherey to explain that for him ideology "is the invisible colour of daily life, too close to the eyeball to be properly objectified, a centreless, apparently limitless medium in which we move like a fish in water, with no more ability than a fish to grasp this elusive environment as a whole" (Eagleton, *Ideology* 46). Later, in "From Adorno to Bourdieu," he again refers to Macherey as he discusses a "final parallel between ideology and psychical disturbance" (135):

> A neurotic pattern of behaviour, in Freud's view, is not simply *expressive* of some underlying problem, but is actually a way of trying to cope with it. It is thus that Freud can speak of neurosis as the confused glimmerings of a kind of solution to whatever is awry. Neurotic behaviour is a *strategy* for tackling, encompassing and "resolving" genuine conflicts, even if it resolves them in an imaginary way. The behaviour is not just a passive reflex of this conflict, but an active, if mystified, form of engagement with it. (135)

Eagleton explains that Etienne Balibar and Macherey "have argued that works of literature do not simply 'take' ideological contradictions, in the raw, as it were, and set about lending them some factitious symbolic resolution" (*Ideology* 135). He adds:

> One might therefore attribute to the language of ideology something of the devices employed by the unconscious, in their respective labour upon their "raw materials": condensation, displacement, elision, transfer of affect, considerations of symbolic representability and so on. And the aim of this labour in both cases is to recast a problem in the form of its potential solution. (135–36)

Despite the connections we can make between Eagleton's concerns here, many of which I explore in chapters 2 and 3 as "strategies for coping" and "equipment for living," his focus is on the writer's work, not on the writer's work to engage readers in collaborating and not on how forms are actions that can generate what Burke calls "formal identification" and "stylistic identification."

Bygrave's Rhetorical/Ideological Critic and His "Manner of Writing

Bygrave situates his 1993 *Kenneth Burke: Rhetoric and Ideology* as a response to Jameson's and Lentricchia's readings of Burke as an ideological critic and as a response to the fact that "in Britain Burke has been hardly read at all"

(8). Bygrave's study is particularly useful to me because he defines and works with the "fraught terms," "rhetoric" and "ideology." He acknowledges how he reads Burke—he "cast[s] him in a role which he would himself refuse, as a historical critic who exemplifies a road not taken for ideological critique" (16). He examines this road but does not associate it with the enthymeme or identification as the body of proof in his rhetoric. He also positions himself as an academic interpreter who appeals primarily through logical arguments rather than by enthymematic proof.

Nevertheless, Bygrave attends to "Burke's own distinctive manner of writing" (7), which, he says, is "interactive and dialectical rather than being reflexive and, ultimately, narcissistic" (16). He takes Burke's work "as exemplary in part for its methodological agility, its demonstration of the possibilities offered by changes in perspective and by analogical reasoning (7). He also attempts to explain Burke's "distinctive manner of writing" as rhetorical in that it is "interactive and dialectical."

While Bygrave admits "ideology is a term on whose usage the only consensus seems to be among those who would reject its use" (2), he defines it in his introduction, distinguishing ideology from rhetoric as he argues that they cannot be separated:

> Most uses of the term contain centrally the sense that ideology is motivated, in however concealed, contradictory or even unconscious a fashion, by a programme of action. It contains implicitly petitions, imperatives, exhortations and other devices which may serve either to legitimate the interests of a dominant group or to challenge those interests in the name of others. An ideology in fact depends on the devices codified as the set of tropes of a rhetoric. This does not mean that rhetoric and ideology are coterminous but it does mean that where ideology becomes apparent in language it can only ever be understood (as opposed to "experienced") through interpretation and that the kind of interpretation best suited to it is that which shows the relation of language to action—that is rhetoric (2).

Bygrave defines rhetoric as "directed at the 'uses' of discourse" and adds that to "consider 'use' is to consider context and effect together" (15). He argues that Burke is both a rhetorical critic and an ideological critic, agreeing with both Jameson *and* Lentricchia, because at the core of his argument is the claim that rhetoric and ideology are not the same but that they cannot be separated—even for analytical, ideological, and rhetorical purposes.

The problem I have with Bygrave's interpretation may seem trivial, but I believe it is significant in its probable consequences. In brief, he suggests that the uses of discourse are always ideological and rhetorical, but unlike Burke he does not weight these terms and concepts for given contexts. He does not accept the explicit claim in his reply to Jameson that is implicit throughout his work: "For any expression of something implies a repression of something else, and any statement that goes only so far is analyzable as serving to forestall a statement that goes farther" (Burke, "Methodological Repression" 401). Different terministic screens orient us differently and yield different consequences.

In the conclusion of his introduction, Bygrave recommends Burke's criticism as a resource for ideological readings, for it supports his definition of the interpreter's task as an act of "reading *into* history." But Bygrave also recommends the resources of Burke's rhetoric to supply what he says is missing in critique today:

> However, he is not so much a missing link in Anglo-American theory as an untapped resource. The final chapter suggests that his rhetoric offers a means of reading history as well as reading *into* history: a means of connecting all sorts of "symbolic action" to ideology and the programme of palpable action which underlies it. Burke offers resources of critique which we need (17).

In his final chapter, "Conclusion: Strategies," Bygrave begins by saying that "[t]his book has argued that Kenneth Burke's kind of interpretation provides cultural studies with an urgent example," and he claims that "Burke offers a methodology which still remains to be exploited" (107). He returns to "some of the negative claims made about it: for example, that it fails to engage with the terms of debate current in any of the disciplines on which it encroaches and that it overvalues metaphor and arguments from analogy at the expense of logic" (107). He admits that Burke's project

> can be charged with being repetitive, with depending on analogy rather than logic, with announcing "principles" derived from analysis as though they had generated the analysis, and perhaps with mistaking American liberalism for "human nature"; but these constitute not failings in the project but some of its most important insights. Rather than being exceptional, aberrant instances of discourse these are the unconscious strategies of discourse itself (108).

Bygrave deals first with strategies, the word "Burke translates from a military to a rhetorical context" (108) and the word, as we have seen earlier, that Jameson objected to earlier. He explains that "we are more comfortable with the notion of a text or discourse having an 'ideology' than with its employing 'strategies' because the former can assign meaning to an author, not agency to an inanimate object" (108). In Burke's rhetoric people use strategies in writing, reading, and living, and choose means of persuasion.

His explanation here is key to distinguishing his views of rhetoric and ideology and their interrelationships to Burke's angles. He says, "[a]lthough strategies may then be attributed to a reader rather than to her text, such an attribution would commit us not to honorific particularity but to hopeless relativism since we could no longer appeal to the text to validate claims we have made about it" (Bygrave 108). Burke does not fear the attribution of strategies or ideologies to a text, a writer, reader, or context, for with each and all he is dealing with people using language. Any of these terms may be useful on particular occasions. Most importantly, the validation of claims about a text are not made solely by reference to the text; people make claims for rhetorical purposes that must stand "pragmatic tests."

Bygrave also refers to "an unconscious suspicion, however it may be consciously denied, that textual meanings originate in and may be foreclosed by the author of a text" (108), but for Burke meanings are created by writers and readers together, acting in concert. Burke does not fear relativism, because no one makes meaning alone: no writer is persuasive without a reader, no reader reads without a writer, and no text means without both writer and reader. What is stable in his rhetoric are acts of identification. What is relative is how, why, when, and where different writers and readers will identify with each other and create meanings together. Most important, what is certain in rhetoric is that meanings must stand "pragmatic tests," not tests of truth.

He comes closer to this rhetorical position than do Jameson, Lentricchia, and many ideological and rhetorical critics today, but, finally, Bygrave expresses his literary and textual biases:

> Provided we accept the validity of arguments by analogy in the first place, "strategies" may then be a good analogy for the description of any reasonably extended piece of language and an exact one for the highly motivated and organized language of literary texts or for the adversarial rhetoric of political ones. The advantage of such a term is that it enables us to see what I have called a "system" or "project" as active. Its disadvantage is that we may be led into a territory in which the duality of text and reader and of the metaphorical and literal may be elided. This, as we have seen, is the territory of theology. Kenneth Burke is however a reader in Babel and is only ever momentarily nostalgic for Eden (109).

On the slippery slope of rhetoric, writers and readers identify temporarily through language, not at the same time or place and not with the same meanings; in this territory, the metaphorical and the literal can be read as differences in kind or degree. Associations and dissociations are variously motivated and have consequences that cannot be guaranteed in advance nor erased after the fact. Therefore, we must hesitate to assess motives and situations, choose among available means, and act in uncertainty and in concert to provide "equipment for living," not dying.

In the final pages of his book, Bygrave turns from Burke as a writer to Burke as "an exemplary reader" (109), although he closes his introduction, as we have seen, with an image of Burke as an "untapped resource" rather than "a missing link in Anglo-American theory": "Burke offers resources of critique which we need" (17). Bygrave attends to how Burke writes extensively in chapter four, but he finally privileges reading over writing and excludes Burke as a resource for *writing* critique. In the conclusion to his final chapter, he does restate his understanding that Burke is a rhetorician and an ideological critic. Although these terms are not synonymous, he says, "Burke demonstrates that to regard rhetoric and ideology as wholly discrete realms is to be in thrall to both" (109). Similarly, he explains that "Burke's own objection to the term ideology being applied to his work is an objection to what he takes to be a single, specialized discourse, the economic, taking priority over an essentialist definition of human beings themselves" (109). Burke is "equally suspicious of a determinate 'history'" (Bygrave 110). Bygrave then turns to rhetoric: "Actually it is 'rhetoric' which is the more troublesome term. In part this is because rhetoric is both practice and the study of that practice, the latter hypostasizes an object of study which is outside itself" (110). For Burke, rhetoric *is* the troublesome term that deals with the troubles of communication and miscommunication.

Bygrave summarizes by saying that the "argument of this book has been that Burke is most exemplary not as an interpreter of 'literary' texts but as a reader of proverbs, of constitutions, of the narrative of 'history' itself" (110). These "local gains" are "part of the bigger gains to be had from the way (often surprising) they can be contextualized": "Reading proverbs leads him to announce a 'sociological criticism'; he moves from the Constitution to constitutions; and he writes not history but historiography" (110).

Burke's rhetoric of identification invites writers and readers to extend current resources of rhetoric to include enthymematic arguments along with logical arguments and extend the horizons of rhetoric beyond the academy. Lentricchia's and Bygrave's readings of Burke make clear that Jameson's judgment about Burke's work in 1978—his "immense critical corpus" has "been utterly without influence in its fundamental lessons"—no longer holds true. They also make clear how reading Burke as a literary, ideological, cultural, or rhetorical critic yields different results. I continue to build on the work of Jameson, Lentricchia, and Bygrave, but I try to heed Burke's advice: "But where problems of terminology are concerned, we must always keep on the move. So, for a windup, let's try a different slant, having in mind both the psychoanalytic and the Dramatistic concepts of 'symbolic action.'" (*LASA* 73–74). The challenge that lies ahead for me in the following chapters is to persuade contemporary readers that Burke's *rhetorical* lessons in identification are useful today in academic and public discourse.

PART II
A LESSON IN WRITING: ATTITUDES AND ACTIONS FOR WRITING AND REWRITING

2 Reading as Revision to Identify: Burke's Rewriting of Aristotle's Enthymeme into Identification

All "metaphorical extension" is an aspect of casuistic stretching. Our proposed methodology to "coach" the transference of words from one category of associations to another, is casuistic. . . . Since language owes its very existence to casuistry, casuistic stretching is beyond all possibility of "control by elimination." The best that can be done is to make its workings apparent by making casuistry *absolute* and *constant*. In Shakespeare, casuistry was absolute and constant. He could make new "metaphorical extensions" at random. He could leap across the categories of association as readily as walking. The mortmain of dead metaphors ("abstractions") that has gripped us since his time has rigidified this original liquidity. All sorts of "academicians" have arisen, even among those who belong to no formal academy. We propose by the casuistry of "planned incongruity" to follow in the conceptual vocabulary the lesson that Shakespeare taught us with his (Burke, *ATH* 230).

The general approach to the poem might be called "pragmatic" in this sense: It assumes that a poem's structure is to be described most accurately by thinking always of the poem's function. It assumes that the poem is designed to "do something" for the poet and his readers, and that we can make the most of relevant observations about its design by considering the poem as the embodiment of this act. In the poet, we might say, the poetizing existed as a physiological function. The poem is its corresponding anatomic structure. And the reader, in participating in the poem, breathes into this anatomic structure a new physiological vitality that resembles, though with a difference, the act of its maker, the resemblance being in the overlap between writer's and reader's situation, the difference being in the fact that these two situations are far from identical.

> The justification for this pragmatic view of the poem resides in the kind of observation that a functional perspective leads us to select, from among an infinite number of its observations about poetic structure. (Burke, *PLF* 89–90)

A Classical Justification for a Contemporary Rhetoric

Aristotle justifies the "art" of rhetoric by the fact that previous rhetoricians had overlooked what he identifies as the body of proof in rhetoric, the enthymeme:

> Now, previous compilers of "Arts" of Rhetoric have provided us with only a small portion of this art, for proofs are the only things in it that come within the province of art; everything else is merely an accessory. And yet they say nothing about enthymemes which are the body of proof, but chiefly devote their attention to matters outside the subject; for the arousing of prejudice, compassion, anger, and similar emotions has no connection with the matter in hand, but is directed only to the dicast (*The Art of Rhetoric* I.1. 3–5).[8]

I want initially to justify this rhetoric of Kenneth Burke by the fact that previous compilers of his rhetoric have overlooked the enthymeme.[9] This is not surprising because what's missing (or almost missing) in his rhetoric is the term *enthymeme*. Although he uses the classical term only twice and both times glancingly, first in *A Rhetoric of Motives* and later in his 1978 "Rhetorics, Poetics, and Philosophy," I argue here that in *Counter-Statement* he revises Aristotle's enthymeme into what he first imagines as a "margin of overlap," names "formal identification" and "stylistic identification," specifies later as "qualitative progression" as opposed to "syllogistic progression," and then claims all as his theory of forms. Although he drops these terms after his first collection, he then continues to develop the images and ideas

---

8. For different translations and commentaries, see Grimaldi 3–4, and Kennedy 29–30.

9. Don M. Burks is the only critic, as far as I know, who makes explicit connections between the enthymeme and identification. See especially "Persuasion, Self-Persuasion, and Rhetorical Discourse," "Dramatic Irony, Collaboration, and Kenneth Burke's Theory of Form," and "Kenneth Burke: The Agro-Bohemian 'Marxoid.'" See also Jean Nienkamp's *Internal Rhetorics: Toward a History and Theory of Self-Persuasion*.

into the action that in *A Rhetoric of Motives* becomes "identification." But identification is not only the subject and organizing principle of Burke's rhetoric: it is also the "body of proof" that he practices.¹⁰

It is a commonplace in Burke criticism that his major contribution to the rhetorical tradition is that he replaces Aristotle's persuasion with identification.¹¹ More accurately, as Burke himself says, he proposes "the term 'identification,' not as a substitute for the traditional approach but as 'an accessory' to the standard lore" (*RM* xiv). Despite critical recognition of the centrality of identification in Burke's rhetoric, there are no extended discussions of his revision of Aristotle's enthymeme into identification, how identification works as subject, organizing principle, and method of proof in his rhetoric, and how it involves both writer and reader in collaborative meaning-making as a way to avoid violence and war.

For many good reasons, discussions of the enthymeme are not central in Burke scholarship. As I mention above, he mentions this term only twice, although he discusses at length many rare figures and tropes. Another reason may be that there have been conflicting definitions and approaches to the enthymeme over the ages, with attention to it as a figure, form, structuring principle, and as action. There have also been disagreements about its characteristics as a figure and form, since one of these has to do with what's missing. To argue that absence is presence is tricky; to argue that what's missing is action by readers with writers is more so. The enthymeme has been defined as a truncated, two-legged, and deficient syllogism with

---

10. George A. Kennedy says that Aristotle uses the enthymeme throughout the *Rhetoric*: "The first sentence of the treatise, with its proposition and supporting reason, is an example of what Aristotle will call an enthymeme. The reader should become sensitive to the constant use of enthymemes throughout the text, often introduced by the particle *gar* (for)" (29n3). He makes no case, however, for the enthymeme as the body of proof in the *Rhetoric*.

11. Barbara A. Beisecker's comment in *Addressing Postmodernity: Kenneth Burke, Rhetoric, and a Theory of Social Change* returned me to the work of Bernard L. Brock and James W. Chesebro: "A bit more recently, critics like Bernard Brock and James Chesebro have argued that the *Rhetoric* is an extension of dramatism ["a method for understanding the social uses of language"] and have interpreted Burke's theory of identification as "the 'key term' instrumental to understanding" rhetorical discourses and events (Brock 94, 95)" (41). They emphasize rhetoric's general epistemic function, while I focus on the collaborative construction of meaning as the body of proof in rhetoric. In addition, I try also to explore how the act of identification changes writer's and reader's identities and the situations involved.

one leg missing. Most recently, the enthymeme has been defined by how it functions.[12]

Other difficulties arise in discussing the enthymeme because what *Aristotle* and the *Rhetoric* mean is also contested. Contemporary scholars understand the *Rhetoric* as fragments, reconstructions, and fictions, perhaps multiply authored in various situations and open to infinite interpretations. Some reject Aristotle and the *Rhetoric* for ideological reasons. Jeffrey Walker provides a history of the enthymeme in *Rhetoric and Poetics in Antiquity* as he argues for the origins of rhetoric in poetry, specifically in the lyric enthymeme, rather than in politics.

Walker provides a rich scholarly and supportive context for my arguments about the enthymeme in this chapter and for my reading of Burke's revisions of Aristotle's enthymeme into identification.[13] Walker constructs the history of rhetoric as "centrally and fundamentally an art of epideictic argumentation/persuasion *that derives originally from the poetic tradition and that extends, in 'applied' versions of itself, to the practical discourses of public and private life*" (*Rhetoric and Poetics* viii). His work challenges

---

12. I am deeply indebted to the work of William M. A. Grimaldi and of scholars in rhetoric who focus on the enthymeme, particularly James C. Raymond's "Enthymemes, Examples, and Rhetorical Method"; Jeffrey Walker's "The Body of Persuasion: A Theory of the Enthymeme" and *Rhetoric and Poetics in Antiquity*, discussed above; Lawrence D. Green's "Enthymematic Invention and Structural Predication," "Aristotelian Rhetoric, Dialectic, and the Traditions of Aristrophos," and "Aristotle's Enthymeme and the Imperfect Syllogism"; John T. Gage's "An Adequate Epistemology for Composition: Classical and Modern Perspectives" and "Teaching the Enthymeme: Invention and Arrangement"; Thomas M. Conley's "The Enthymeme in Perspective" and "*Pathe* and *Pisteis*: Aristotle, Rhet. II.2-11"; Andrea A. Lunsford and Lisa S. Ede's "On Distinctions Between Classical and Modern Rhetoric"; Lloyd F. Bitzer's "Aristotle's Enthymeme Revisited"; Arthur B. Miller and John D. Bee's "Enthymeme: Body and Soul"; and David Blakesley's *The Elements of Dramatism* and "Defining Film Rhetoric: The Case of Hitchcock's Vertigo." Their work on the enthymeme helps me interpret Burke's identification as his revision of the enthymeme, although they do not make this claim and would probably not agree with such casuistic stretching.

13. Burke is not included in Walker's index, but in note 22 on page 346, Walker refers readers to Burke after a brief outline of Perelman and Olbrechts-Tyteca's theory of argumentation: "see also Burke 1969 on 'identification.'" Walker adds a comment to his note that heartens me: "Both theories remain extraordinarily fruitful as basic analytic frameworks and remain in my opinion unsurpassed (but see the more recent work overviewed in van Eemeren et al. 1996). For a recent restatement of this general framework, shifted into the vocabulary of poststructuralist philosophy and 'performativity' theory, see Butler 1993 107, 241" (346).

"the received, standard history of rhetoric" that "typically presumes that 'rhetoric' is and was originally, essentially, an art of practical civic oratory that emerged in the law courts and political assemblies of ancient Greece and Rome, while defining epideictic, literary, and poetic manifestations of this art as 'secondary,' derivative, and inferior" vii). He adds, "(This opposition often takes on a gendered tone as well: practical rhetoric is more manly)" (vii).

More specifically, his work, which realigns rhetoric and poetics and integrates the public and private, locates the enthymeme as the heart and body of proof in rhetoric. In chapter 6 on "Lyric Enthymemes," he explains the "mainstream modern view" of poetry in general and of lyric poetry in particular: "*the essential business of a lyric is to dramatize or express a state of feeling or subjectivity*" (Walker, *Rhetoric and Poetics* 168). His objections are that this view

> tends to presuppose an extraordinarily narrow conception of 'argument' as something like formal syllogistic or 'scientific' reasoning and that, on the other hand, it leaves itself without any means of accounting for how a poetic practice—especially one that wants to be politically or culturally significant—can embody 'thought' or 'feeling' or a mode of subjectivity *persuasively* or can have a real effect on the beliefs and values of an audience that is not already predisposed to think or feel exactly as the poet does and that is free to differ or disagree. (169)

At this point he states his overall argument: "My claim then, is that the ancient notion of 'enthymeme' (*enthymema*) as the distinctively 'rhetorical' form of argument and reasoning, or as what Aristotle called the body of persuasion (*soma tes pisteos*), provides a more adequate means of accounting for lyric argumentation" (Walker, *Rhetoric and Poetics* 169).

He outlines the advantages and disadvantages of "modern interpretation" that "has tended to define the enthymeme as an informal, elliptical syllogism based on probable rather than certain premises and on tacit assumptions shared by the audience and rhetor" (Walker, *Rhetoric and Poetics* 169). He explains the advantages:

> Chief among them is its recognition that the enthymeme, as an elliptical form of argumentation depending on shared assumptions, involves a dialogic, co-creative relationship between the audience and rhetor, in which the audience engages in a kind of "self-persuasion" by completing or constructing for itself the tacit, elided aspects of the enthymeme. (170; my emphasis)

He notes Lloyd Bitzer's 1959 "Aristotle's Enthymeme Revisited" in the *Quarterly Journal of Speech* and John T. Gage's 1984 "An Adequate Epistemology for Composition" in *Classical Rhetoric and Modern Discourse*.

The "chief limitation," he explains, is "that the very concepts of 'rhetorical syllogism' and of rhetoric as the 'counterpart of dialectic' tend to subsume the notion of 'enthymeme' to that of 'syllogism' and thus to 'logic,' or to what 'syllogism' and 'logic' have generally meant in modern, Western culture (Walker, *Rhetoric and Poetics* 170). The problem is that "even when conceived as elliptical, probabilistic argumentation," the enthymeme becomes "assimilated to a fairly rigid notion of 'syllogistic' form" (170). It "tends to be presupposed that a 'valid' enthymeme, however informal or elliptical its reasoning may be, still can be restated in proper syllogistic form" (170).

With the help of Grimaldi, among others, he constructs "a broader, more general notion of 'enthymeme' for which both Aristotelian and non-Aristotelian perspectives offer lines of description" (Walker, *Rhetoric and Poetics* 173). Sophocles, he says, used enthymeme "to mean a piece of heartfelt reasoning" (173). He explains: The term "clearly was linked semantically to the family of terms that included *enthymios* and *enthymeomai* and that ultimately derived from *thymos*, meaning 'heart' or 'mind' or 'spirit' as the seat of emotion, thought, wish, desire, intentionality, or will. In one's *thymos* one considers things, draws inferences, becomes impassioned, forms desires, has intentions, and makes plans" (173). Later, he summarizes:

In sum, the complex notion of thymos embodies and makes available, on one hand, a concept of "heartfelt" interpretation, inference, and emotional response endowed with a sort of rationality that operates quasi-syllogistically from heterogeneous "premises" present to the psyche and, on the other hand, a concept of intentionality as an emotive state that both arises from and shapes a person's "thymatic logic." The point is that this "logic" cannot be reduced or restated as a formal syllogism—at least not in a fully satisfactory way—because it is not strictly prepositional and may include among its "premises" such things as sense perceptions, mental imagery, memories, cognitive schemata, deep-set beliefs and values (ideologies), bodily states, the aesthetic effects of things like music or drugs, and exiting emotional dispositions (the "habits" of response that Aristotle considers to constitute *ethos*), as well as explicit propositions or "ideas" overtly present to the psyche. (Walker, *Rhetoric and Poetics* 174)

In other words, the enthymeme "as an 'in-thymatic' argument appears to involve notions not only of intuitive inference-making (which the term *syllogismos* covers) but also notions of affective force and passional response" (Walker, *Rhetoric and Poetics* 174). The enthymeme seems to draw on the whole person of both the writer and the reader.

Burke locates his rhetoric within the rhetorical tradition and draws on Aristotle and the *Rhetoric* to revise the traditional principles of rhetoric to make them useful for his contemporary audience. As we saw in chapter 1, Burke states clearly in "Methodological Repression and/or Strategies of Containment," his reply to Fredric Jameson's claim that he is reluctant to use the term ideology, that Aristotle's *Rhetoric* is a major resource and influence on his understanding of the relationship between rhetoric and ideology. More important for my purposes here, Burke links identification to Aristotle's *Rhetoric* in *A Rhetoric of Motives*:

> My dealings with the term here form an integral part of my thesis, that, although Aristotle's *Rhetoric* as enviable a text as it ever was, and I still view it as our central text, the term "persuasion" did not cover the ground that I felt should be part of a modern rhetoric. To this end I proposed the term "identification," not as a substitute for the traditional approach but as "an accessory to the standard lore" (*RM* xiv).

And later, as we shall see, he associates identification with Aristotle's enthymeme and with issues of opinion, truth, attitude, and action: "Reasoning based on opinion he calls 'enthymemes,' which are the rhetorical equivalent of the syllogism" (*RM* 56).

In this chapter, I take a roundabout approach to bring up the issue of Burke's revision of Aristotle's enthymeme into identification, rather than to make it "crystal-clear" (*ATH* 86). I follow Burke's lead also in using "metaphorical extension," "casuistic stretching," "planned incongruity," and the drawing and redrawing of lines. I also collapse, substitute, and revise terms and their relationships to argue that, as early as *Counter-Statement*, Burke revises literature into rhetoric,[14] as he addresses how writers appeal to readers to collaborate with them in acts of meaning-making.[15]

---

14. See Jack Selzer's *Kenneth Burke in Greenwich Village: Conversing with the Moderns 1915-1931*, for a thorough and lively portrait of Burke as a man of letters during this time; Ross Wolin's *The Rhetorical Imagination of Kenneth Burke;* and Paul Jay's *The Selected Correspondence of Kenneth Burke and Malcolm Cowley 1915-1981*. All of these provide ample support for reading Burke as a literary aesthete within the modernist symbolist tradition. To their views, I juxtapose my interpretation of Burke as a rhetorician who revises the aesthetic into rhetoric and Cassirer's philosophic theory of symbolic form into a rhetorical theory of symbolic action.

15. Literary theories and theories of reading discuss gaps, gapes, silences, aporias, and abysses and how they challenge traditional subject-object relationships. They sometimes draw on aspects of rhetoric, particularly on figures and tropes, but they do not focus on forms as actions and how the enthymeme requires collaborative

Burke's Counter-Statement to Aristotle: A Retrospective Way In

In 1986, I condensed my 1983 dissertation into an article, "Reading Kenneth Burke: Ways In, Ways Out, Ways Roundabout," for *College English*. I begin the article by focusing on early critical responses to Burke's style as obscuring his meaning and on New Critic's understanding of their task as explaining what Burke means. As I reread and revise my article today in 2020, I realize that I am still trying to explain how and why Burke teaches us to read by participating with him, but now I am also trying to evaluate the usefulness of his ways of reading for today's world by contrasting his lessons in reading, writing, and living with those of other critics.

I begin the article with "Perspectives and Perturbations," to identify how some early literary critics defend Burke by explaining what he means because his works don't meet readers' expectations. For example, Stanley Edgar Hyman says in *The Armed Vision: A Study of the Methods of Modern Literary Criticism* that his works cause a "tremendous shock of novelty" (347). George Knox in *Critical Moments: Kenneth Burke's Categories and Critiques* says, "Burke exploits the Cult of Perhaps," but Knox does not educate his readers in an attitude of perhaps. Instead, he orients us so that we can walk without uncertainty "into Burke's world and feel relatively at home" (Knox xvii). Here Knox is drawing on Burke's analyses of De Gourmont and Mann and on his statement in the 1952 "Preface to the Second Edition" of *Counter-Statement*, where he articulates imagistically his theory of rhetoric. Burke distinguishes between Aristotle's "lightning rod" approach and Plato's "censorship principle," between Plato's "'totalitarian' view of art and thinking" designed to "'suppress' danger,'" and Aristotle's "more complex 'liberal' view" which advocates "purification" by "the draining-off of dangerous charges, as lightning rods are designed, not to 'suppress' danger, but to draw it into harmless channels" (*CS* xii). Burke prefers the more "ho-

---

meaning-making. See Wolfgang Iser's 1978 *The Act of Reading: A Theory of Aesthetic Response* for a historical understanding of reception theories and for his specific interpretation of the formation of a text "as a set of instructions" or "operations" that activate the reader to assemble and construct meaning. See also Frank Lentricchia's 1980 *After the New Criticism* for analyses of various works that relocate meaning in readers or in interactions between writers and readers rather than in authors; Jane P. Tompkins's *Reader-Response Criticism: From Formalism to Post-Structuralism*; and Richard Beach's *Reader-Response Theories: A Teacher's Introduction*. Beach discusses Burke's focus on how audiences identify with a speaker or author and identify with "the text's people, ideas, or institutions" in a search of "social unity" (32). He does not develop Burke's identification as a lesson in reading.

moeopathic notion that we are cleansed of emotional tensions by kinds of art deliberately designed to affect us with these tensions under controlled conditions" (*CS* xii). He chooses the "more complex 'liberal' view" over the "totalitarian" one:

> For short periods, unquestionably, the principle of conditioning, or coordination by censorship, is very effective, particularly now, when people generally have not yet learned how to discount the motivational powers of the new mass media. But it is my contention that a society is protected in the long run only by the more liberal principle. And I had such a condition in mind when I referred, at one point, to "the cultural value of fear, distrust, and hypochondria." I had in mind here the kind of uncertainty, or even uneasiness, that goes with a Cult of Perhaps, and with its corresponding Method (*CS* xii–xiii).

The attitude of uncertainty—the willingness to be unsure and in need of others—is a characteristic of Burke and of both writers and readers in his rhetoric of identification.

William H. Rueckert, Burke's strongest and longest ally, attempts in *Kenneth Burke and the Drama of Human Relations* to "purify" Burke by hacking away the "stylistic and terminological underbrush" which he says is "an irritation, a distraction, the rank of growth of a fecund mind" (5). Rueckert also refers to the "pure art" of Burke's *The White Oxen*, but he does not here develop connections between Burke's own pure art and his arguments in *Counter-Statement* that even pure art tries to persuade readers, if only to keep them reading. While he relates Burke's "qualitative progression" to the writing of T.S. Eliot (Rueckert 22), as Burke does, Rueckert does not here acknowledge that Burke's own qualitative style also puts the reader into "a state of mind which another mind can appropriately follow" (Burke, *CS* 125).

Armin Paul Frank does claim in *Kenneth Burke* that Burke's methods are more than "mere stylistic vagaries":

> With him, verbal figures virtually merge with figures of thought. He proceeds by preferences, on the byways and roundabouts of the mind. He will "with assays of bias/By indirections find directions out." In his own words: he likes to radiate. Even if he criticizes a view, he is reluctant to abandon it. Such a reflexively ironic turn of mind makes for much essential complexity which cannot be hacked away without intrinsic damage. (ii)

Frank seems to understand that figures and tropes invite active responses and that Burke's self-reflexive style, which reveals his mind at work, requires readers who identify with him also to take a roundabout and indirect approach. Frank seems to recognize that Burke does not reject an idea, method, or text once and for all: he criticizes what may not work in a particular instance, realizing that what he finds ineffective in one context may be useful elsewhere.

Frank finds meaning in how Burke writes by associating it with collage, used as a literary technique in the work of Modernist writers, and with De Gourmont's and Flaubert's theories of pure art. He says the "collage technique has value as a 'presentational device and as a heuristic method subject to verification'": "Verification, as Burke sees it, operates through 'recalcitrance'—the strategic alteration of one's arguments when they meet with opposition, their modification for the purpose of communicating one's vision" (Frank 91). He doesn't develop further his conception of the reader's role as a "recalcitrant agent" or how Burke's reader acts as a "*dramatis persona*" (78) in the symbolic action.

In my article in *College English*, I then turn to "three more recent critics" who "do not seek determinate meaning in Burke" but, instead, "use him for their own purposes" (T. Warnock, "Reading Kenneth Burke" 65). Wayne Booth aims to explain Burke to bring him into the mainstream of literary criticism in the 1960s and 1970s. I briefly mention his interpretation of Burke in *Critical Understanding: The Powers and Limits of Pluralism*, where he says that Burke's "whole enterprise is impossibly, outrageously, shockingly ambitious, yet it finally frustrates intellectual ambition by undermining all solutions" (126). I do not include Burke's response, "Dancing with Tears in My Eyes," first published in *Critical Inquiry* in 1974 and later revised and republished in *Critical Understanding*. Burke confesses he feels uncomfortable and scared of himself when Booth forgives him for his incoherence (137).

I also mention Hayden White who in *Tropics of Discourse* credits Burke for his four categories—metonymy, synecdoche, metaphor, and irony—the foundation for White's overall argument about history. I say that I understand White's work as a taxonomy rather than a tropology of discourse because it fails to include Burke's understandings of all tropes as rhetorical actions that engage readers in co-creating meaning (65). And I reduce Frank Lentricchia's arguments in *Criticism and Social Change* by saying that he uses Burke to justify a critic's work within the academy as real action but that "by ignoring Burke's meaning, Lentricchia promotes Marxism as the key term, instead of rhetoric, and he thereby limits the critic's role and power" (65).

My reductive interpretations embarrass me now and yet motivate me still to develop further my understanding of Burke's theory of identification as a lesson in reading, writing, and living. Because the motives and probable consequences of reading to identify differ from those of other reading theories, it provides an alternative, not a replacement, which we may practice and select in given situations.

A Context for Examining Burke's Reading Lesson in *Counter-Statement*

In the second section of my article, "From Symbolism to Symbolic Action to a Rhetorical Theory of Reading," I make assertions I now want to develop more fully. Burke saw in the elliptical quality of Symbolist writing an important alteration in method: "Instead of saying that something was like something else, the symbolist progressed from one thing to the other by ellipsis." But at this earliest stage in his development of method, in *Counter-Statement*, Burke considers the writer's capacity to make connections as a separate issue from the reader's capacity to make connections. When he speaks of connections, he leaves the subject or agent out of his sentence: "Objects are thus linked by their less obvious connectives." (qtd. by Warnock, "Reading Kenneth Burke" 66)

In the article, I ignore the complexities of agency and discuss ellipsis and its "long tradition in the theory of discourse, reaching back to Aristotle's rhetoric and forward to 'reader response' literary criticism" (66). I associate the "missing links of symbolism" with Aristotle's enthymeme, Iser's gaps, Barthes's gapes, and Hugh Kenner's "rhetoric of silence," all of which, I say, "describe similar features of a text which have the effect of engaging the reader's active participation" (66). Instead of developing this claim, I repeat my point that in his first work Burke writes about "the emotional connections in the text and then of the psychology of the audience—without clearly relating the two" (66).

Unable to do more at that time with my cluster of terms from several reader response critics and with issues of agency, I say that "[o]f course, in leaving gaps in his text he is doing precisely what he is describing, and the elliptical quality of *Counter-Statement* becomes part of his argument" (66). I then show how Burke begins teaching his readers how to read his first work in the preface to the first edition when he says he will "elucidate a point of view" which is "somewhat apologetic, negativistic, and even antinomian, as regards everything but art" (*CS* viii). I state that the book's progress is "not strictly syllogistic" but is "qualitative, like any real process of growth, 'a fruition' achieved by the consummation of poet and reader" (45):

> Burke presents a series of essays that the reader links intuitively at first and then by retrospective arrangement. The text itself is like a symbol, a showing forth rather than a telling, and like any symbol it is important chiefly as it affects the reader. (66)

I do not explain how Burke subsumes "syllogistic progression" under "qualitative progression," explaining that all progressions are enthymematic from the perspective of rhetoric."[16]

---

16. Grimaldi corrects the conclusion that "A. is saying effectively in this first chapter that the only true art of rhetoric is concerned purely and simply with the rational demonstration of the problem under discussion" with his claim that "the enthymeme is a rhetorical argument which is organic in character," containing appeals to ethos, pathos, and logos (8–9). Aristotle, he explains, "proceeds through the first two books to develop his treatise around all three proofs: logical, ethical, emotional" (9). He adds that Aristotle "is quite aware, in other words, that one is always speaking to a person who is a complexus of reason, feelings, emotions, and set attitudes"; as he says at B1, 77b 21–24: 'But since rhetoric is directed to judgment . . . it is necessary for the speaker not only to look to the discourse that it be probative and convincing, but also to develop a certain character in himself and in the one deciding an argument'" (9–10). Rhetoric "is a reasoned activity" (15). Grimaldi explains later that "[f]or A. the syllogism is the instrument for demonstrating something by the deductive method"; "the enthymeme is the form of rhetorical argumentation which, as we know from the opening section of this chapter (54a 11–16), previous technographers have failed to discuss" (20–21):

> But in accepting such a difference between rhetorical and logical syllogisms we should not set up a sharp cleavage between the true and the probable as though probability had little or no relation to truth, and then conclude that rhetorical reasoning is not concerned with truth. In a matter of a few lines (55a 21f) A. will define the usefulness of rhetoric on the ground that it helps truth and justice to prevail. It is more likely, therefore, that the clause 55a 14 –18 affirms the close relation between enthymeme and logical syllogism because the intellect constructs both in its effort to arrive at what *is* the truth in a given case, or the *truth as far as it can be discerned*" (23).

Grimaldi's interpretation also affirms that the "function of rhetoric is, not persuasion in itself, but the ability to perceive in any given subject, problem, or situation". . . those elements which are 'suasive'. . . and which make decision possible and reasonable" (32). In other words, "Rhetoric does not make persuasion (i.e., a persuaded mind) the way an artist makes his object. . . . " (32): "For A. *rhetoric creates an attitude in the mind of another by selecting the elements on hand whereby the listener can arrive at his own decision*; see *Top.* 101b 5–10" (32; my emphasis).

I then align Burke first with indeterminists but later with determinists, to show that Burke like his "actual reader fluctuates between these extremes" (*CS* 180). I leave this image of Burke and the reader swinging back and forth between being determinists and indeterminists, with no discussion of rhetoric, agency, choice, purpose, or situation. I fail to see that claims of determinate or indeterminate meaning are rhetorical and metaphorical claims to evaluate in terms of their use rather than truth. I remain caught between conflicting arguments about the life or death of the author, of the self, of subjectivity, of readers, and of meaning, without analyzing these claims also as rhetorical assertions to be assessed in terms of gains and losses in using them. I had not learned the lesson Burke teaches everywhere. When he writes "language as symbolic action," "form *is* the appeal" (*CS* 138), and the "peril of power is monotony" (*CS* 160), he is asserting similes and metaphors meant to be assessed for "social reasons" not to be accepted as truths. He educates us to be active recalcitrant readers of language who use frames of acceptance and rejection. He deals in the realm of rhetoric—of language, doubt, and uncertainty.

I do state in the article that Burke "teaches readers how to read his own text as well others" (68), beginning with *Attitudes Toward History* which operates on the assumption that "getting along with people is one devil of a difficult task, but that, in the last analysis, we should all want to get along with people (and do want to)" (*ATH*, "Introduction" n.p.). I say Burke exploits this model of communication, making himself easy to get along with, invoking the reader's "charity" and requesting his reader's indulgence: "We must ask the reader, if he can, merely to consider it as being on the track of something. We are trying to bring up an issue, rather than to persuade anyone that we can make it crystal-clear" (*ATH* 86). I show how Burke apologizes near the end of *Attitudes Toward History*, so that his readers will accept his book:

> Frankly, we were not sufficiently aware of our procedure until we neared the end of the book (that is, we did not verbalize our implicit method into an explicit methodology). It is probably better so, since an over-exactitude of schematization, maintained throughout, would have wearied writer and reader both. (*ATH* 294)

I did not then connect "getting along" with identification or the implications of both for a rhetoric dedicated to *Ad bellum purificandum*.

Burke's Development of Qualitative Progression Throughout *Counter-Statement*

I state in the article that "[t]he whole of *Counter-Statement*, what it shows as well as what it tells, seems an effort to revise Symbolism to include a rhetorical dimension" (66). I can now revise that into a stronger claim: Through retrospective arrangement, we can see that from the first pages of *Counter-Statement* Burke begins to revise symbolic forms into symbolic actions and to rewrite poetics, aesthetics, literature, and art into rhetoric that aims to persuade readers to collaborate in mutual meaning-making. Although I will discuss the essays in the order they appear in *Counter-Statement*, Burke develops his theories qualitatively rather than syllogistically, and I select and make connections to serve my purposes in constructing Burke's rhetoric of identification.

The Four Adepts (Flaubert, Pater, De Gourmont, and Burke) and How They Engage Readers

Burke begins his first essay, "Three Adepts of 'Pure' Literature," and the development of his theory of form as action by pointing out the contradictions between Flaubert's aspirations to "pure art" and his writing of realistic art. He quotes from two letters by Flaubert as evidence of his desire to produce "pure art" that persuades formally. The first was written in 1852:

"What seems beautiful to me, what I would most like to do, would be a book about nothing, a book without any exterior tie, but sustained by the internal force of its style . . . a book which would have almost no subject, or at least in which the subject would be almost invisible, if that is possible. The most beautiful works are those with the least matter . . . I believe the future of art is in these channels." (qtd. in Burke, *CS* 6)

Burke presents the next, written twenty-four years later by Flaubert to George Sand:

> "I remember what poundings of the heart I experienced, what keen pleasure I felt, on beholding a bare wall of the Acropolis . . . *Eh bien*! I wonder if a book, independently of what it says, might produce the same effect? In the precision of its groupings, the rarity of its materials, the unction, the general harmony—is there not some intrinsic virtue here, . . . something eternal as a principle?" (qtd. in Burke, *CS* 6–7)

Despite his desires, Burke says Flaubert "devoted years on end to the patient accumulation of detail, of those minute accuracies that his disciples look upon as the basis of his intentions (and which he himself, even at a moment of faith in them, called of secondary importance)" (*CS* 7). He adds: "The anomaly of the situation would have wearied any but this ox of art" (*CS* 7).

Burke explains Flaubert's desire to affect his readers through pure art as his challenge, but he credits the national response to Flaubert's novel to the prosecution for obscenity, without developing Flaubert's motive and methods to "arrest his readers in spite of himself":

> There is also the possibility, however, that the pugnacity of Flaubert's material came of an instinctive demand that he arrests his readers in spite of himself. In any case, it is true that he reached his public in just this way. *Madame Bovary* could hardly have set a nation to buzzing over its technical triumphs of form and its microscopic style: this was accomplished by the prosecution for obscenity. (*CS* 4)

As Burke demonstrates that art is not pure because it aims to persuade readers, he also explores how writers use forms as well as content to affect readers. Here Burke begins to explore the relationships between form and information and both as probable means of persuasion in given contexts. Here he also anticipates what he later calls formal or stylistic identification.

He briefly develops another point that will later become critical to his rhetoric. Flaubert's ideal is that art is life, though removed from daily life. He wrote in the genre, however, "wherein one can be rhetorically brilliant only by subterfuge, or by endangering the purity of one's effect" (Burke, *CS* 7). The novel, Burke explains, using his tactic of "weighting" terms, "makes of literature the verbalization of *experience*, the conversion of *life* into diction—whereas Flaubert, with his pronounced interest in the absolute effects of art, would make of literature the *verbalization* of experience, the conversion of life into *diction*" (*CS* 7).

As Burke critiques Flaubert's desires and practices, he is developing his theory of language that credits symbolic action as motivated, situated, and consequential in the world. Reality exists for Burke, but we know and interact with reality through language. Language and reality also create and revise us and our views of both. Burke does not want to, nor can he, remove art from life, turn life into art, or transform art into life. Symbolic action is art and life.

Pater's Art-to-Reveal-Art: Appeals to Readers through Oblique and Layered Approaches

Burke juxtaposes this discussion of Flaubert's "art-to-display-art preferences" and his attempts "to write under an art-to-conceal-art aesthetic" to his analysis of Walter Pater's art-to-reveal-art. He trusts that his readers can make the leap along with him from one adept to another and learn to make the larger leaps between essays and ideas.[17]

Pater, he says, "shaped prose fiction to his purposes" (Burke, *CS* 9), handling matters "obliquely," with a "leisurely approach" (*CS* 11): "Art to Pater was 'not the conveyance of an abstract body of truths,' but 'the critical tracing of . . . conscious artistic structure.' He thought of a sentence as a happening—he prized particularly 'the resolution of an obscure and complex idea into its component parts'" (*CS* 12). Burke summarizes what he admires in Pater: "Other men have sought the values of power and directness; Pater was interested, rather, in laying numerous angles of approach" (*CS* 12).

Pater's art-to-reveal-art was formal action, an event, and his "laying numerous angles of approach" resulted in the power of indirectness—its requirement that readers participate by making sense for themselves. The construction of various angles and approaches does not include explicit connections among the angles for readers to accept; in laying angles, the artist asks readers to establish relationships among seemingly disparate parts for themselves. Burke's recognition of Pater's "numerous angles of approach" later become "perspective by incongruity" and "planned incongruity." Later, in *A Rhetoric of Motives*, Burke explains parenthetically to his readers: "(A direct hit is not likely here. The best one can do is to try different approaches towards the same center, whenever the opportunity arises)" (*RM* 137).

While others promote "the values of power and directness," Burke values the powers of collaboration and indirection to involve readers in creating the meaning they in turn accept. He says Pater's "preference for artifice was consistent" and a "subject was valuable to him in that it offered possibilities

---

17. See Jack Selzer's discussions of the writing and publication of the essays in *Counter-Statement* in *Kenneth Burke in Greenwich Village: Conversing with the Moderns, 1915-1931*; Ross Wolin's discussions of the writing, correspondence, and publication of these essays in *The Rhetorical Imagination of Kenneth Burke*; and correspondence between Burke and Malcolm Cowley about essays in *Counter-Statement* in Paul Jay's *The Selected Correspondence of Kenneth Burke and Malcolm Cowley 1915–1981*. Also, see Timothy W. Crucius's *Kenneth Burke and the Conversation After Philosophy* for a discussion of Burke's post-philosophical understanding that "even the reasoning of the rationalizing human is dependent on nonrational processes" (55), particularly 43–72 and 105–15.

for a show of deftness" (Burke, *CS* 12). Here Burke assumes Pater was interested in the writer's rather than the reader's deftness, but he demonstrates again how a writer's rhetorical intentions emerge. Pater used ideology "for its flavor of beauty, rather than of argument," and he "treated ideas not for their value as statements, but as horizons, situations, developments of plot, in short, as any other element of fiction" (*CS* 14). These statements may be read as negative criticism of Pater and his style, but by the end of *Counter-Statement* we have learned about the power of ideologies as "margins of overlap" by which writer and reader identify and about style as action, scene as motive and action, and plot as appeal.

DE GOURMONT'S LIQUIDITY: DISSOCIATIVE METHODS FOR ART'S SAKE

Burke begins his discussion of the third adept, Remy De Gourmont, by saying he "had much too strong a detestation of democratic standards to be anything but a disciple of Art for Art's Sake" (*CS* 16). Here Burke establishes expectations in readers that he will gradually revise. He next explains that for De Gourmont "[a]rt was 'justified' because art was an appetite—in being desired it found its ample reason for existence" (*CS* 16). It did "not require defense as an instrument of political or social reform. Art was purely and simply a privilege to be prized as a cosmic exception" (*CS* 16–17). His attitude, Burke says, "manifested itself in the experimental nature of both his critical and imaginative writings," and here Burke modifies his former interpretation by adding: "while this theoretical freedom was checked in him, as in every artist, by the desire to communicate, it did contribute to the variability of his work" (*CS* 17).

In the ambiguities and contradictions, Burke finds in De Gourmont, in the symbolists, and in the art-for-art-sake movement the rhetorical aim to communicate. What he values in De Gourmont's writing is the "experimental nature of both his critical and imaginative writings" (Burke, *CS* 17), his "complete lubrication of phrase" (*CS* 17), his "pliant fiction" (*CS* 17), and mainly his powers of "dissociation" (*CS* 22). De Gourmont "lets himself loose with this method, and produces a type of writing which is delightfully exact" (*CS* 23). As Burke explains how De Gourmont writes in "*La Dissociation des Idees*," he explains what he will continue to value and cultivate in his rhetoric—revisions in language and in identity that allow us to see around the edges of our terms, instead of painting ourselves and others into the corner, and revisions that help us avoid becoming "rotten with perfection."

Burke says De Gourmont in his closing "leaves us a list which he has not troubled to examine, but which seems to fall apart by the mere *clarity of juxtaposition*: virtue-recompense; wrong-punishment; God-goodness; crime-remorse; duty-happiness; future-progress" (*CS* 23; my emphasis). Burke regrets that De Gourmont did not carry his dissociative method, "clearly a companion discovery of symbolic," into the realm of literary criticism, but Burke does just that, and more. He also cultivates the dissociative method, as he cultivates ambiguities and contradictions, as motive and means of involving readers in symbolic action. Lists become plots, progressions, syllogisms, narratives, and histories. He revises orders, changing from temporal to logical priorities and back again, all of which readers must order and reorder by making sense of the disparate parts. The "clarity of juxtaposition" becomes "perspective by incongruity," "planned incongruity," collage, and "scissor-work" (Burke, *PLF* 21). Burke continues to associate and dissociate for specific purposes and situations. He finds this principle useful in defining people as individuals and groups, divided and connected.

All of these forms are actions that invite readers to participate. Later he articulates them as the one important alteration in method" of symbolism" (Burke, *CS* 68). Here, however, he explains symbolism in terms of "clusters of association," a method he focuses on in his reading and uses in his writing:

> The method was clearly a companion discovery to symbolism, which sought its effects precisely by utilizing, more programmatically than in any previous movement, the clusters of associations surrounding the important words of a poem or fiction. And such writers as James Joyce and Gertrude Stein are clearly making associative and dissociative processes a pivotal concern of their works. Any technical criticism of our methodological authors of today must concern itself with the further development and schematization of such ideas as De Gourmont was considering. (*CS* 23–24)

> Burke continues in *Counter-Statement* to develop a rhetoric of the symbolist aesthetic, using pliancy, lubricity, and the dissociation and association of terms. He also builds on and revises what he interprets as De Gourmont's rhetorical philosophy, which balances the view of man as animal and man as distinct from animal, and his understanding of the usefulness of ambivalence and a conflict of attitudes:

De Gourmont, with his insistence upon the unimportance of humanity and the importance of man, his conception of the intelligence as a disease or an error along with his enthusiasm over the beauty of a perfectly functioning intelligence, his balance of man as an animal over against man as something distinct from all animals, maintained a conflict of attitudes which gives his work considerable liquidity. Such ambivalence was characteristic. (*CS* 20)

De Gourmont, like the other adepts, "lives most of his life in his head" and "must perform his transgressions on paper" (Burke, CS 24). Burke begins exploring life on the page and life as a rough draft as he develops his theory of language as symbolic action, his definition of man, the act of identification as collaborative meaning-making, and his methods for encouraging readers to identify with him.

"Psychology and Form": The Arousing and Fulfilling of Desires

Burke begins the next essay, "Psychology and Form," explaining how Shakespeare arouses and fulfills expectations in *Hamlet,* so that the audience, identifying with characters on stage, wait consciously and unconsciously for the ghost. At the same time, the dramatist creates a series of situations that move readers to progress qualitatively to connect the various scenes:

> It is time for the ghost. Sounds off-stage, and of course it is not the ghost. It is, rather, the sound of the king's carousal, for the king "keeps wassail." A tricky, and useful, detail. We have been waiting for a ghost, and get, startlingly, a blare of trumpets. And, once the trumpets are silent, we feel how desolate are these three men waiting for a ghost, on a bare "platform," feel it by this sudden juxtaposition of an imagined scene of lights and merriment. But the trumpets announcing a carousal have suggested a subject of conversation. In the darkness Hamlet discusses the excessive drinking of his countrymen. (Burke, *CS* 29)

Burke continues this line of analysis of how Shakespeare leads his audience, arousing and fulfilling expectations and creating turns that require them to connect what went before with the present and with might lie ahead. He steps back to observe what the actors and Shakespeare have done:

> All this time we had been waiting for a ghost, and it comes at the one moment which was not pointing towards it. This ghost, so assiduously prepared for, is yet a surprise. And now that the ghost has come, we are waiting for something further. . . . Here again Shakespeare can feed well upon the use of contrast for his effects. (Burke, *CS* 30)

Burke describes the turns and indirections that surprise, arouse expectations, and keep readers reading.

Having led us through a series of scenes, he finally states what he has done so far: "I have gone into this scene at some length, since it illustrates so perfectly the relationship between psychology and form, and so aptly indicates how the one is to be defined in terms of the other" (Burke, *CS* 30–31). He then explains more fully the argument of this essay that informs his theory of form as it is defined later in "Lexicon Rhetoricae." He uses *Hamlet* here and later as one of his examples of how qualitative progressions engage audiences in the action of making meaning by creating links between parts, across reversals and indirections, and contrasts of various kinds. He uses the terms, such as *desire* and *appetite*, that he will use later in defining his theory of form. His explanation also prepares us for how he defines terms and revises them contextually and how he "weights" them for specific purposes and situations:

> That is, the psychology here is not the psychology of the *hero*, but the psychology of the *audience*. And by that distinction, form would be the psychology of the audience. Or, seen from another angle, form is the creation of an appetite in the mind of the auditor, and the adequate satisfying of that appetite. This satisfaction—so complicated is the human mechanism—at times involves a temporary set of frustrations, but in the end these frustrations prove to be simply a more involved kind of satisfaction, and furthermore serve to make the satisfaction of fulfilment [*sic*] more intense. If, in a work of art, the poet says something, let us say, about a meeting, writes in such a way that we desire to observe that meeting, and then, if he places that meeting before us—that is form. While obviously, that is also the psychology of the audience, since it involves desires and their appeasements. (Burke, *CS* 31)

As Burke explains how Shakespeare's drama involves his audiences, he explains his own actions that involve us. He uses Shakespeare here and elsewhere because of his "metaphorical extensions" and "casuistic stretching," the kinds of symbolic actions that characterize his own rhetoric and the creative and critical works of those who use extensions and stretching, perspective by incongruity, anecdotes, joycings, and other methods to encourage readers to participate. Throughout this essay Burke develops a vocabulary, methods of stylistic identification, and illustrative texts that he will use across the essays to develop his theory of formal identification. His clusters of repeated terms, images, and texts help us connect discussions across chapters and relate ideas that might otherwise seem unrelated. As we make connections, we are creating by enacting the meaning of Burke's rhetoric.

As we have seen, he explores rhetorical strategies in terms of psychology of information and psychology of form with emphasis initially on the writer: "The seeming breach between form and subject-matter, between technique and psychology, which has taken place in the last century is the result, it seems to me, of scientific criteria being unconsciously introduced into matters of purely aesthetic judgment" (Burke, *CS* 31). The "great influx of information has led the artist also to lay his emphasis on the giving of information—with the result that art tends more and more to substitute the psychology of the hero (the subject) for the psychology of the audience" (*CS* 32). He illustrates these contrasting rhetorics by turning to music that "is by its nature least suited to the psychology of information, and has remained closer to the psychology of form" (*CS* 34). He draws a line here between a psychology of information that "depends on "surprise and suspense" and a psychology of form that relies on "formal excellence, or eloquence" (*CS* 37). He then blurs his distinction and privileges formal appeal to refine his definition of eloquence:

> Eloquence is the minimizing of this interest in fact, *per se*, so that the "more or less adequate sequence" of their presentation must be relied on to a much greater extent. Thus, those elements of surprise and suspense are subtilized, carried down into the writing of a line or sentence, until in all its smallest details the work bristles with disclosures, contrasts, restatements with a difference, ellipses, images, aphorism, volume, sound-values, in short all that complex wealth of minutiae which in their line-for-line aspect we call style and in their broader outlines we call form. (*CS* 37–38)

Later in "Lexicon Rhetoricae," Burke builds on this notion of how eloquence, form, and style are actions and how a work "bristles" and thereby involves readers. In "Lexicon," he defines eloquence as "a frequency of Symbolic and formal effects" (*CS* 165) and explains how eloquence motivates readers to make connections: "each line had some image or statement *relying strongly upon our experience outside the work of art*, and in which each image had a pronounced formal saliency" (*CS* 165; my emphasis). This "experience outside the work of art" is the "margin of overlap" between a writer's and reader's experiences, the common ground or scene that makes collaborative meaning-making possible; it is also the reader's prior and immediate experiences in making meaning with others.

Burke illustrates his point in "Psychology and Form," as he will do again in "Lexicon Rhetoricae" with the same language and text: "the turn from the murder scene to the porter scene is a much less literal channel of development," in that *"one quality calls forth the demand for the another,* rather than one tangible incident of plot awaking an interest in some other possible tangible incident of plot" (*CS* 38–39; my emphasis). This "less literal channel of development" becomes "qualitative" progression in "Lexicon," but here he explains further how the turn from the murder scene to the porter scene encourages readers to act:

> To illustrate more fully, if an author managed over a certain number of his pages to produce a feeling of sultriness, or oppression, in the reader, this would unconsciously awaken in the reader the desire for a cold, fresh northwind—and thus some aspect of a northwind would be effective if called forth by some aspect of stuffiness. (*CS* 39)

Instead of the plot moving readers linearly, sequentially, and logically to a conclusion, the poet juxtaposes the murder scene to the porter scene and calls for another quality. His example here is the pub scene in T.S. Eliot's *The Waste Land*, which he also uses later to discuss qualitative progression and formal identification in "Lexicon." He explains the poetic process here more broadly than he will do later: "the vulgar, oppressively trivial conversation in the public house calls forth in the poet a memory of a line from Shakespeare"—"Good-night, ladies, good-night, sweet ladies, good-night, good-night" (Burke, *CS* 39). When the "slobs" are "forced by closing time to leave the saloon," Burke explains that "suddenly the poet, feeling his release, drops into another good-night"—"Goonight Bill. Goonight Lou. Goonight May. Goonight. Ta ta. Goonight. Goonight" (*CS* 39). Burke backtracks and refines the point critical to his theory of form as action, his theory of "formal identification," and to his broader theory of identification:

> But I simply wish to point out here that this transition is a bold juxtaposition of one quality created by another, an association in ideas which, if not logical, is nevertheless emotionally natural. In the case of *Macbeth*, similarly, it would be absurd to say that the audience, after the murder scene, wants a porter scene. But the audience does want the quality which this porter particularizes. (*CS* 39–40)[18]

---

18. Ellipses, created by the arrangement of parts, give access to the motives and actions of writers and readers. These are "watershed moments" or "portals of discovery," to use Joyce's term, that are the basis of Burke's rhetoric of the symbol and his understanding of the rhetoric of T.S. Eliot's poetry built on qualitative progressions. He distinguishes between Eliot the critic and Eliot the poet, saying that Eliot is like the disciples of art-for-art's-sake in being the "preserver of older standards which the bourgeoise themselves were attempting to discredit" (Burke, *CS* 67),

"Eloquence," Burke concludes, "is no mere plaster added to a framework of more stable qualities": "Eloquence is simply the end of art, and is thus its essence. . . . Eloquence is not showiness; it is, rather, the result of that desire at the same time "advocating many requisite alterations of morality" (Burke, *CS* 68). Burke revises through rephrasing one of Eliot's principle theories, that of the objective correlative, making it more consistent, at least from Burke's perspective, with Eliot's poetry and his reliance on disjointed forms, narration, juxtaposition, allusions, and qualitative progressions, all of which invite readers to join into the symbolic action:

> This is not offered as an alternative explanation to Mr. Eliot's. As a matter of fact, I believe that it is little more than Mr. Eliot's explanation rephrased. As stated in *The Sacred Wood* the argument runs: 'The only way of expressing emotion in the form of art is by finding an 'objective correlative'; in other words, a set of objects, a situation, a chain of events which shall be a formula of that *particular* emotion; such that when the external facts, which must terminate in sensory experience, are given, the emotion is immediately evoked. If you examine any of Shakespeare's more successful tragedies, you will find this exact equivalence; you will find that the state of mind of Lady Macbeth walking in her sleep has been communicated to you by a skillful accumulation of imagined sensory impressions; the words of Macbeth on hearing of his wife's death strike us as if, given the sequence of events, these words were automatically released by the last event in the series. The artistic "inevitability" lies in this complete adequacy of the external to the emotion; and this is precisely what is deficient in *Hamlet*. Hamlet (the man) is dominated by an emotion which is inexpressible, because it is in *excess* of the facts as they appear. And the supposed identity of Hamlet with his author is genuine to this point: that Hamlet's bafflement at the absence of objective equivalent to his feelings is a prolongation of the bafflement of his creator in the face of his artistic problem. (*CS* 197-98n4)

Hamlet cannot objectify his "disgust occasioned by his mother," and "Shakespeare tackled a problem which proved to much for him" (Burke, *CS* 198n4). Burke agrees with Eliot that we "cannot ever know" but adds: "We may, however, insist that the trend of subjective writing since Shakespeare's time gives us greater authority for identifying Hamlet as Shakespeare than Mr. Eliot here seems to acknowledge. For it is precisely when a Symbol is created as a parallel to life rather than as a recipe for obtaining certain effects, that such "Hamletic" confusions generally arise (Burke, *CS* 198n4).

My point is that the poetic process described here, a translation from "The Poetic Process" earlier in the collection, emphasizes the artist's channeling emotions into forms and the creative collaborative actions by writer and reader. The artist doesn't tackle what she can control, for she can never completely control, nor can the reader. Burke as rhetorician finds possibilities in the limitations of *animal symbolicum*, in words, and in the world for imagining what all might be, at least temporarily.

in the artist to make a work perfect by adapting it in every minute detail to the racial appetites" (*CS* 41). In other words, eloquence is rhetorical appeal to readers. Throughout this essay, Burke explores ideas, terms, and texts that revise art into rhetoric. He will revise and articulate them more directly but with less complexity in his synoptic "Lexicon Rhetoricae."

Formal Identification in "The Poetic Process"

In "The Poetic Process" Burke discusses explicitly his notion of *formal identification*—how we identify with forms and how we identify with each other through shared forms. He focuses on how the crescendo or climax works to move readers in life, in bodies, and in art, to arouse and fulfill desires and expectations. He later explains how other forms, figures, and tropes, such as qualitative progression and *gradatio,* function qualitatively by inviting readers to make connections temporarily and partially in order to read. And he returns again to how formal identification draws on common biological, natural, and cultural experiences that develop our appetites for them in art. He modifies his earlier point about the crescendo and climax result and explains how the brain responds to the appeal of forms:

> There is in reality no such general thing as a crescendo. What does exist is a multiplicity of individual art-works each of which may be arranged as a whole, or in some parts, in a manner which we distinguish as climactic. And there is also in the human brain the potentiality for reacting favorably to such a climactic arrangement. (Burke, *CS* 45)

The principle of the crescendo has been used repeatedly in art "because we 'think' incrementally," making sense of a "multiplicity of individual artworks." A crescendo "parallels certain psychic and physical processes which are at the roots of our experience" (Burke, *CS* 45). He refers to the "accelerated motion of a falling body, the cycle of a storm, the procedure of the sexual act, the ripening of crops—growth here is not merely a linear progression, but a fruition" (*CS* 45). He reinforces this point through repetition: "And surely, we may say without much fear of startling anyone, that the work of art utilizes climactic arrangement because the human brain has a pronounced potentiality for being arrested, or entertained, by such an arrangement" (*CS* 45).

Burke picks up here on his earlier reference to "racial appetites" and combines biological and cultural appetites, attitudes, and expectations as a way to explain here and later in "Lexicon Rhetoricae" the universal and categorical appeal of forms and the individuation of forms. He is also working towards his definition of man that acknowledges the biological connections that all people share within their separate, individual bodies and that emphasizes people as animals, while distinguishing us from animals because of our symbol-using capacities.

He keeps trying to explain how readers respond to forms and how forms engage readers in action: "innate forms of the mind" that are the "potentialities of appreciation which would seem to be inherent in the very germ-plasm of man," creating "'potentiality' for being interested by certain processes or arrangements,' or the 'feeling for such arrangements of subject-matter as produce crescendo, contrast, comparison, balance, repetition, disclosure, reversal, contraction, expansion, magnification, series, and so on'" (Burke, *CS* 46). He adds "that these 'forms' may be looked upon as minor divisions of the two major 'forms,' unity and diversity" (*CS* 46). In a note, he warns: "Any device for winning the attention, if too often repeated, soon becomes wearisome (*CS* 51).

The poetic process, which by now has become a rhetorical process, begins with the poet/ rhetorician "with his moods to be individuated into subject-matter, and his feeling for technical forms to be individuated by the arrangement of this subject-matter" (Burke, *CS* 52). Self-expression of the artist, "*qua* artist," however, "*is not distinguished by the uttering of emotion, but by the evocation of emotion*" (*CS* 53; my emphasis). In other words, the artist, "at the agonizing point of expressing himself, *discovers himself not only with a message, but also with a desire to produce effects upon his audience*" (*CS* 54; my emphasis). Desiring to affect readers, writers select among the available means of persuasion—symbols, forms, genre, for example—those that they think will probably be effective, and they individuate the common forms. Similarly, readers, motivated to go along with a writer, select among the symbols, forms, and information; individuate them as they are aroused by them; and become convinced by what they create.

Not yet satisfied, Burke begins again: The artist "begins with his emotion, he translates this emotion into a mechanism for arousing emotion in others, and thus his interest in his own emotion transcends into his interest in the treatment" (*CS* 55). Burke's poetic process is rhetorical in that it affects both writers and readers and relates art and life. The symbol for Burke is an abstraction from a situation, an entitlement, a strategy for encompassing a situation—it is action. He closes by again translating the poetic process:

> In closing: We have the original emotion, which is channelized into a symbol. This symbol becomes a generative force, a relationship

to be repeated in varying details, and thus makes for one aspect of technical form. . . . The originating emotion makes for *emotional* consistency within the parts; the symbol demands a *logical* consistency within this emotional consistency. (*CS* 61)

He undermines this direct statement because he is still exploring: He is on the track of something that retrospectively we can name "identification":

> The symbol faces two ways, for in addition to the technical form just mentioned (an "artistic" value) it also applies to life, serving here as a formula for our experiences, charming us by finding some more or less simple principle underlying our emotional complexities. For the symbol here affects us like a work of science, like the magic formula of the savage, like the medicine for an ill. (*CS* 61)

In "The Poetic Process" Burke also emphasizes that "the relationship between beauty and art is like that between logic and philosophy" (*CS* 55). In his developing theory of forms as progressive actions, he juxtaposes the artist's self-expression and "means of evoking emotions" in readers to the philosopher's self-expression and means of persuasion. He considers the following proposition as applicable for both: "*the artist's means are always tending to become ends in themselves*" (*CS* 55–56). He then proceeds to explain the rhetoric of logic:

> The philosopher, as far as possible, erects his convictions into a logically progressive and well-ordered system of thought, because he would rather have such a system than one less well-ordered. So true is this, that at certain stages in the world's history when the content of philosophy has been thin, philosophers were even more meticulous than usual in their devotion to logical pastimes and their manipulation of logical processes. Which is to say that the philosopher does not merely use logic to convince others; he uses logic because he loves logic, so that logic is to him as much an end as a means. Others will aim at conviction by oratory, because they prefer rhetoric as a channel of expression. (*CS* 55)

He will continue to juxtapose logical and qualitative progressions and logical and nonlogical or analogical systems of thought, to assess their effectiveness in various contexts. Even here, Burke presents logic as rhetoric and a means of persuading others; later he will demonstrate how a "logically progressive and well-ordered system of thought" and "one less well-ordered" are different in degree not in kind and both require readers active to participate.

The Critic's Role as Educator: Burke's Lesson on the Status of Art and the Rhetoric of Symbolist Aesthetics

The key passage in the next essay, "The Status of Art," is charged with terms, attitudes, and texts that Burke has been using in the previous essays and will use in later ones. The "slogan of *Art for Art's Sake*" arose, Burke says, "[w]ith the development of technology" when "'usefulness' was coming into prominence as a test of values, so that art's slogan was necessarily phrased to take the criterion of usefulness into account" (*CS* 63). Against the attack that art was "useless," the artist "pitted the challenge that art was important to those to whom art was important" (*CS* 63). Burke explains Kant's proposition, "purposiveness without purpose" as a "formula for the aesthetic" that "had no intention of providing 'a refutation' of art" (*CS* 63). The proposition, however, "could be readily perverted: if the aesthetic had no *purpose* outside itself, the corollary seemed to be that the aesthetic had no *result* outside itself" (*CS* 63). He adds, "Logically there was no cogency in such an argument, but psychologically there was a great deal" (*CS* 63). The association of the "art instinct" with the "play instinct" caused trouble "in an age when 'work' was becoming one of society's basic catchwords" (*CS* 64). Therefore, "a division between artist and bourgeois was emphasized" (*CS* 68).

As Burke explains that this bourgeois-Bohemian conflict "had another unfavorable feature in its alliance with the rise of symbolism," he names the important change in method that Symbolism contained and thereby revises Symbolism into rhetoric. He describes the change simply, using words, attitudes, and actions that he has used before and that he will use later in explaining qualitative progression:

> Symbolism contained one important alteration in method. In emphasizing the emotional connection of ideas and images, it tended to suppress their commoner experimental or "logical" connections. Instead of saying that something was like something else, the symbolist progressed from the one thing to the other by ellipsis. He would not tell us that a toothache is a raging storm—rather, he might advance directly from the mention of a diseased tooth to the account of a foundering ship. Objects are thus linked by their less obvious connectives. This is, of course, an over-simplification of symbolist methods, but it is roughly indicative. (Burke, *CS* 68)

He only implies at this point how the symbolist's actions might implicate the reader, but he does return to the broader literary issue he has been developing—that art, even "pure art" and "art-for-art's-sake," tries to communicate and affect audiences. Art is therefore useful: it meets the criteria of science; its uses are different, however. and therefore valuable.

He then continues to explore his more specific interpretation of the bourgeois/Bohemian conflict by increasing the scope of his analysis to include areas he has already touched on: relationships among criticism, art, and life. The critic's task is to educate people to read and live, but this aim cannot be fulfilled without the recognition that what in life might have "temporal priority" might be presented orally or on the page as having "logical priority." Although he doesn't use these terms here, he explains the differences between creating and interpreting and discursive and narrative forms:

> Whether it is correct or not, however, the fact remains that while the artist was attempting new departures in methodology, he was not matching his imaginative experiments with their equivalents in critical theory. To an extent he was probably uncertain as to the exact critical principles underlying the new tendencies. And taking his cue from the earlier moral conflict between bourgeois and Bohemian, he now widened the conflict to include questions of methods. Far from pleading with his public, the artist heightened his antagonism: hence his readiness to *epater le bourgeois*. Art now took on a distinctly obscurantist trait, not because it was any more "obscure" than previous art (nothing is more obscure than an after-dinner speaker's distinctions between optimism and overoptimism, yet no one is troubled by them) but because the public had not been schooled as to just wherein the clarity of such art was to be sought. (Burke, *CS* 68–69)

The methods of the "pure" art movement, "[c]losely allied with the 'mystification' of the new movement," seemed "negative, retiring, and powerless" and "certain to limit their reading public" (*CS* 69). The lack of critical theory to explain the "imaginative experiments," the moral conflict between bourgeois and Bohemian, and the fact that "the public had not been schooled as to just wherein the clarity of such art was to be sought," all combine to explain the changing status of art:

> Had not the spread of literacy through compulsory education made readers of people who had no genuine interest in literature? Would not this group henceforth form the majority of the reading public? And would not good books pale into insignificance, not because they had fewer readers than in the past (they had more) but because an overwhelming army of readers had been recruited? (*CS* 69–70)

Critical and imaginative works revise readers and the practices of reading and writing. Art teaches people to read texts and the world differently, and the critic's role is to educate people about what and how art teaches.

The critic's task is not impossible because "most of the works fed to the public are purely derivative, and as such can constitute the bridge between the 'rare' writer and the public at large" (Burke, *CS* 70) Through such "derivative processes," the public "com[es] to accept methods which, but a few years ago, were confined to the most 'abstruse'" (*CS* 70). What counts as "abstruse" art, and who counts as "rare" writers, change as the unfamiliar becomes familiar; perhaps more accurately at this point in the development of his rhetoric, art involves and educates readers, so that what seems new grows familiar. The influence of art may be direct or devious: "A single book, were it greatly to influence one man in a position of authority, could thus indirectly alter the course of a nation; and similarly the group that turns to 'minority' art may be a 'pivotal' group" (*CS* 71). And the "role of opposition is by no means negligible in the shaping of society" because the "victory of one 'principle' in history is usually not the vanquishing, but the partial incorporation, of another" (*CS* 71).

One further point that Burke makes in "The Status of Art" is critical to his development of his theory of forms and of the function of qualitative progression to engage readers—the dialectical relationship between a text and its contexts: "[C]ritics influenced by the tenets of evolutionism held that to appreciate a work we must understand the environmental conditions out of which it arose" (*CS* 77). Although Burke says "[t]he point is irrefutable" (*CS* 70), he argues that "even a savant's 'restoration' of the environmental context is not adequate" for understanding (*CS* 78). Burke concludes this discussion by presenting aspects of the poetic process he developed in "Psychology and Form" and in "The Poetic Process." He also introduces a key term and image, *margin of overlap*, signifying identification between writer and reader who draw own shared experiences:

> For in the last analysis, any reader surrounds each word and each act in a work of art with a *unique* set of his own previous experiences (and therefore a unique set of imponderable emotional reactions), *communication existing in the "margin of overlap" between the writer's experience and the reader's*. And while it is dialectically true that two people of totally different experiences must totally fail to communicate, it is also true that there are no two such people, the *margin of overlap* always being considerable (due, if to nothing else, to the fact that man's biologic functions are uniform). Absolute communication between ages is impossible in the same way that

absolute communication between contemporaries is impossible. And conversely, as we communicate approximately though "imprisoned within the walls of our personality," so we communicate approximately though imprisoned within the walls of our age. (*CS* 78–79; second emphasis mine)

Burke closes with a statement that testifies to the enthymematic quality of his own writing that resists perfect solutions and final answers: "We advocate nothing, then, but a return to inconclusiveness" (*CS* 91). With this attitude, in this posture, he readies himself for listening and learning more as he educates his readers to collaborate with others in making meaning together.

Burke's Sympathy with the Abyss: "Thomas Mann and Andre Gide"

Burke returns to close reading of texts in his next essay, "Thomas Mann and Andre Gide." He states directly a purpose he has enacted throughout the collection: "Our primary purpose, however, in establishing this distinction between the conscientious and the corrupt is to destroy it" (*CS* 99). This is a recurrent purpose, as Burke teaches us to distinguish between terms with the understanding that terms define each other and are dialectically interrelated. He plays here with the "psychology of humility" and the "psychology of humiliation" (*CS* 100), as he has with the "psychology of form" and the "psychology of information" earlier. He juxtaposes Mann and Gide, letting the reader make associations and dissociations between the two. More specifically, Burke asks,

> Has not Mann, on the other hand, spoken with fervor of a "sympathy with the abyss," an admitting of the morally chaotic, which he considers not merely the prerogative, but the duty, of the artist? . . . In "the repellent, the diseased, the degenerate" Mann situates the ethical. (*CS* 101)

In the distance between the repellent and the ethical, lies the rhetoric of Mann's art. This recognition recalls Burke's earlier discussion of De Gourmont's abilities to associate and dissociate in order to help readers gain perspective by incongruity, by connecting what appear as opposites and by disconnecting what appear united. He also finds in Mann's art the "cult of conflict, a deliberate entertaining of moral vacillation, which could not permit a rigid standard of judgments" (*CS* 102). Burke asks about Mann and Gide a question we might also ask about him: With their "[i]rony, novelty, experimentalism, vacillation, the cult of conflict," are they "not trying to make us at home in indecision, are they not trying to humanize the state of doubt?" (*CS* 104–05). In general, Burke argues in this essay for art as counter-statement and corrective because it advocates uncertainty rather than certainty and asks readers to accept complexity rather than reductions to simplicity. He again defends art as useful in a world where science and technology flourish and their rhetorics of certainty hold sway.

We can read "Program" as Burke's acceptance of the challenge of not reducing a program of action into programmatic action and forms into formats, formalities, and formulas. Again he challenges easy oppositions:

> It is not true that the aesthetic and the practical are necessarily opposed. The terms of one are readily convertible into the terms of the other. . . . Accordingly, to ask that the aesthetic set itself in opposition to the practical is to ask that the aesthetic be one specific brand of the aesthetic. The present essay asks that the aesthetic ally itself with a Program which might be defined roughly as a modernized version of the earlier bourgeois-Bohemian conflict. (Burke, *CS* 111)

Burke alludes to his earlier discussion of the major alteration in method of symbolism, when the poet progresses qualitatively and thereby invites readers to join the action, and to his discussion of the critic's literacy task to educate people to read what appear to be obscure texts.

Burke includes along with this complex of issues the importance of uncertainty in the face of certainties that "will always arise, impelling men to new intolerances." He again parenthetically reinforces his point: "(Certainty is cheap, it is the easiest thing of which a man is capable. Deprive him of a meal, or bind his arms, or jockey him out of his job—and convictions spring up like Jacks-in-the-box.)" (Burke, *CS* 113). Artists persuade by encouraging readers to participate in the action not by arguing with certainty that they are right.

He finally states what his program does not do and what is in fact not final: "This program would not, let it be repeated, sum up the absolute, unchanging purposes of the aesthetic. It would define the function of the aesthetic as effecting an adjustment to one particular cluster of conditions, at this particular time in history" (Burke, *CS* 121). He does not propose his program or his lesson in reading as an efficient, effective, and programmatic solution for all circumstances. People must act to figure out what works in specific scenes, using the resources of language to imagine possibilities and probable outcomes.

Having progressed recursively and qualitatively throughout *Counter-Statement*, a collection of essays written at different times for different audiences, Burke begins his next essay, "Lexicon Rhetoricae," by defining terms and giving the "gist" of his theory of form as action.

Syllogistic and Qualitative Progressions: Burke's Uses and Abuses of Aristotle in "Lexicon Rhetoricae"

In "Lexicon Rhetoricae" Burke redefines his terms again, drawing from terms, attitudes, and actions that he has developed qualitatively throughout his collection. He begins his synoptic essay with a section subtitled, "The Nature of Form," in which he defines form in literature as an act of "arousing and fulfillment of desires" (Burke, *CS* 124). Throughout the collection, as we have seen, Burke has revised literature and art into rhetoric. Here he states explicitly and succinctly what he has been exploring from the beginning of his collection of essays: "A work has form in so far as one part of it leads a reader to anticipate another part, to be gratified by the sequence" (*CS* 124). While all writing, from the perspective of rhetoric, moves writers and readers to collaborate, how writers lead readers "from there to there" is a matter for analysis.

Burke introduces five aspects of form that are the means for arousing and fulfilling desires through anticipation and gratification: "progressive form (subdivided into syllogistic and qualitative progression), repetitive form, conventional form, and minor or incidental form" (*CS* 124). Part 2 juxtaposes two kinds of progressive form—syllogistic progression and qualitative progression. I want to provide Burke's full definitions of these two terms to show that many of the terms, texts, and attitudes that cluster around "qualitative progression" here are familiar from earlier discussions in *Counter-Statement*. He will use the same ones later in his direct references to the enthymeme and in discussions of identification in *A Rhetoric of Motives*.

Syllogistic and qualitative are both progressive forms. Here again he sets up two terms in opposition, as they define each other by contrast, but then he blurs his distinction to show that, from a rhetorical perspective, all forms function qualitatively and enthymematically, including syllogistic progressions:

> 2. *Syllogistic progression* is the form of a perfectly conducted argument, advancing step by_step. It is the form of a mystery story, where everything falls together, as in a story of ratiocination by Poe. It is the form of a demonstration in Euclid. To go from A to E through stages B, C, and D is to obtain such form. We call it syllogistic because, given certain things, certain things must follow, the premises forcing the conclusion. In so far as the audience,

from its acquaintance with the premises, feels the rightness of the conclusion, the work is formal. The arrows of our desires are turned in a certain direction, and the plot follows the direction of the arrows. The peripety, or reversal of the situation, discussed by Aristotle, is obviously one of the keenest manifestations of syllogistic progression. In the course of a single scene, the poet reverses the audience's expectations—as in the third act of *Julius Caesar*, where Brutus's speech before the mob prepares us for his exoneration, but the speech of Antony immediately after prepares us for his downfall. (*CS* 124)

Burke juxtaposes syllogistic progression to qualitative progression for readers to compare, contrast, and connect:

> 3. Qualitative progression, the other aspect of progressive form, is subtler. Instead of one incident in the plot preparing us for some other possible incident of plot (as Macbeth's murder of Duncan prepares us for the dying of Macbeth), the presence of one quality prepares us for the introduction of another (the grotesque seriousness of the murder scene preparing us for the grotesque buffoonery of the porter scene). In T.S. Eliot's *The Waste Land*, the step from "Ta ta. Goonight. Goonight" to "Good night, ladies, good night, sweet ladies" is a qualitative progression. In Malcolm Cowley's sonnet *Mine No. 6* there is a similar kind of qualitative progression, as we turn from the octave's description of a dismal landscape ("the blackened stumps, the ulcerated hill") to the sestet's "Beauty, perfection, I have loved you fiercely." Such progressions are qualitative rather than syllogistic as they lack the pronounced anticipatory nature of the syllogistic progression. We are prepared less to demand a certain qualitative progression than to recognize its rightness after the event. We are put into a state of mind which another state of mind can appropriately follow. (*CS* 124–25)

Still under the heading, "The Nature of Forms," Burke catalogues other forms—repetitive form, conventional, and minor or incidental forms. Again, having made these distinctions, he merges them as actions by discussing the interrelation of forms and the conflict of forms, before turning to rhythm and rhyme and to "significant form" (*CS* 135). The remainder of the lexicon is divided by subtitles, "The Individuation of Forms," "Patterns of Experience," "Ritual," and "Universality, Permanence, and Perfection," as Burke uses various approaches to extend his theory of formal identification to develop his theory of reading.

In "The Nature of Form," Burke subsumes syllogistic progression under qualitative progression because no step-by-step progress is without gaps, although forms vary in the degree to which the steps are presented explicitly and discreetly, from word to word, from line to line, from image to image, from chapter to chapter, from allusion to referent. Like the crescendo and climax, all forms are composed of parts that we perceive and create as continuous and whole. As we also saw earlier, Burke turns the logical into the qualitative. Readers always create links between steps and parts to make meaning, based on the margin of overlap in their experience, knowledge, assumptions, appetites, attitudes, and expectations. As he incorporates syllogistic into qualitative progression, as different in degree and not in kind, he subsumes logic as well as poetics under rhetoric.

As he has done earlier, Burke links qualitative and syllogistic progressions with narrative and links narrative with logic.

His example of a syllogistic progression is a work of fiction: Poe's mysteries are syllogistic; syllogisms progress "step by step," as in a "mystery story, where everything falls together, as in a story of ratiocination by Poe" (Burke, *CS* 124). He seems to counter this example by explaining syllogistic progression in a more familiar way, as "the form of demonstration in Euclid," where to "go from *A* to *E* through stages *B*, *C*, and *D*, is to obtain such form." But what Burke shows is that Euclid and Poe move from there to there and to some extent rely on readers to make connections. Their progressions must motivate and convince readers to act, because their conclusions are not, in truth, self-evident. In one context, logical progressions are effective; in another qualitative progressions work better; both progressions require, though to different degrees, readers to bridge steps, to supply what's missing, using what they share in common with readers. The movements by Poe and Euclid are called "syllogistic" because, "given certain things, certain things must follow, the premises forcing the conclusion." Even with logical progressions, readers make emotional connections and "recognize its rightness after the event" (*CS* 125).

In other words, the syllogism is a formal construction that is convincing in certain situations when it appears to follow step by step and when it achieves the end for which it was constructed, acceptance. To reinforce this point, Burke writes that the "arrows of our desires are turned in a certain direction, and the plot follows the direction of the arrows." A syllogism is a plot with explicit steps that arouses desires and appetites. A response to logical argument requires initially a frame or attitude, a getting along with the writer of acceptance, even when the argument may finally be rejected.

At this point, Burke turns to Aristotle to reinforce his argument that in rhetoric all forms are qualitative: "The peripety, or reversal of the situation, discussed by Aristotle, is obviously one of the keenest manifestations of syllogistic progression." He cinches his point that syllogistic progressions are art and artifice with an example built on his recognition that all literature tries to do something and that poetics, like rhetoric, aims to persuade: "In the course of a single scene, the poet reverses the audience's expectations—as in the third act of *Julius Caesar*, where Brutus's speech before the mob prepares us for his exoneration, but the speech of Antony immediately after prepares us for his downfall" (Burke, *CS* 124). He has already taught us that turns and juxtapositions in scenes in *Macbeth* are ways Shakespeare involves his audience as actors in his drama.

Here in Burke's rhetoric, as in Aristotle's, there are two means of persuasion, the syllogism and the enthymeme, or syllogistic and qualitative progression. In the act of enthymeme-making, the rhetor chooses between the forms to be persuasive in particular contexts. In Aristotle, the enthymeme is the "body of proof" in rhetoric, and enthymeme-making is the act of selecting the appeal—pathetic, logical, or ethical—that will most likely be persuasive in a particular situation. In rhetoric, appeals to logic are appeals to the enthymematic aspects of all orderings, none of which is complete, final, or perfect. The act of choosing may be primarily a logical choice or an emotional choice, but, ideally, rhetorical choices involve all aspects of a person.

Like Aristotle, Burke focuses first on plot as he distinguishes between syllogistic and qualitative progressions by saying simply that qualitative ones are "subtler":

> Instead of one incident in the plot preparing us for some other possible incident of plot (as Macbeth's murder of Duncan prepares us for the dying of Macbeth), the presence of one quality prepares us for the introduction of another (the grotesque seriousness of the murder scene preparing us for the grotesque buffoonery of the porter scene) (*CS* 124–25).

In addition to plot elements arousing and fulfilling desires, particular qualities arouse and fulfill. In this case, the quality has to do with mood or tone or attitude created by character and action.

In his example, however, identification results from connotations of words, sounds, rhythms, and allusions within and across texts that readers bridge in order to make sense. His example is already familiar, as is his point: "In T. S. Eliot's *The Waste Land*, the step from 'Ta ta. Goonight. Goonight' to 'Good night, ladies, good night, sweet ladies' is a qualitative progression," (Burke, *CS* 125), a "perspective by incongruity" (Burke, *PC* 89), or a "planned incongruity" (Burke, *ATH* 230). Readers must make the connections between the two. Therefore, they cannot be too distant or they produce what the *Rhetoric* refers to as "frigidity." They cannot be too close or they won't produce a sense of wonder and seeing anew.

Burke follows these two familiar examples by a third. A sonnet conveys the subtlety and complexity of qualitative progressions which appeal to all the senses as well as to the intellect. This example emphasizes how qualitative progressions work to "put [readers] into a state of mind which another state of mind can appropriately follow" (Burke, *CS* 125):

> In Malcolm Cowley's sonnet *Mine No. 6* there is a similar kind of qualitative progression, as we turn from the octave's description of a dismal landscape ("the blackened stumps, the ulcerated hill") to the sestet's "Beauty, perfection, I have loved you fiercely." Such progressions are qualitative rather than syllogistic as they lack the pronounced anticipatory nature of the syllogistic progression. We are prepared less to demand a certain qualitative progression than to recognize its rightness after the event. We are put into a state of mind which another mind can appropriately follow. (*CS* 125)

Burke has accomplished his task of revising terms and revising Aristotle for the purposes of developing his rhetoric for the contemporary world. From this point on he assumes that readers will follow his lead in understanding poetics, aesthetics, literature, narrative, and logic, all as rhetorical arts not because his revisions are true but because he has demonstrated their pragmatic use for "social reasons." He will continue to refer to poets, to literature, and to logic, but he will do so assuming the revisions he has made. He will continue to refer to Aristotle and the *Rhetoric*, but as he has reconstructed them. He will assume the enthymematic action in qualitative progressions and his extensions of qualitative progressions to include syllogistic ones, narratives of various kinds, and other sequences in art and life.

BURKE'S EXTENSIONS OF ARISTOTLE'S ENTHYMEMES: OUR DESIRE FOR WHAT IS ABSENT

The opening pages of "Lexicon Rhetoricae" arouse reader's desires and expectations for what will follow in this essay. He revises and weaves together his ideas and images of progress, states of mind, and quality throughout his dictionary, modifying them into Burkean terms as he proceeds: "action," "attitude," and "indirection." He uses familiar methods of distinguishing terms, weighting them, converting them, associating and dissociating them, and he uses repetition throughout to qualify, extend, revise, and emphasize the contextual and contingent dimensions of rhetoric.

For example, Burke says that repetitive form "is the consistent maintaining of a principle under new guises" (*CS* 125), implying that the reader connects the various guises and links "[a] succession of images." Repetition of images, character, identity, attitude, "rhythmic regularity," and rhyme scheme, all lead readers "to feel more or less consciously the principle underlying them" and to require "that this principle be observed in the giving of further details" (*CS* 125).

He finally turns repetitive form or "the restatement of a theme by new details" in literature to repetition basic in daily life—"our only method of 'talking on the subject'" (Burke, *CS* 125). The principle of same but different, or theme and variation, arouse and fulfill expectations, yet expectations are not fulfilled like "a perfectly conducted argument, advancing step by step," nor do they turn "the arrows of our desires" in "a certain direction" (*CS* 124).

In his discussion of minor or incidental forms, Burke blurs and extends his categories to explain how particular figures and tropes function not only as separate forms but also as "formal events in themselves" (*CS* 127):

> When analyzing a work of any length, we may find it bristling with minor or incidental forms—such as metaphor, paradox, disclosure, reversal, contraction, expansion, bathos, apostrophe, series, chiasmus—which may be discussed as formal events in themselves. Their effect partially depends upon their function in the whole, yet they manifest sufficient evidences of episodic distinctness to bear consideration apart from their context. Thus a paradox, by carrying an argument one step forward, may have its use as progressive form; and by continuation of a certain theme may have its use as repetitive form—yet it may be so formally complete in itself that the reader will memorize it as an event valid apart from its setting. (*CS* 127)

From the perspective of poetics, readers may analyze a figure or trope as a static form in terms of its parts and kinds; from the perspective of rhetoric, readers may analyze a figure as action—as a progressive form, an episodic plot, an event.

It is useful to track how Burke in this chapter extends these definitions and actions, particularly how he progresses from the appeal of progressive forms, to the appeal of logical and qualitative forms, to how both engage readers in qualitatively making connections among the various parts to create meaning, and then to how other forms, particularly aspects of music, encourage qualitative action. In a sense, he rounds out the discussion of music and pure art that begins in the opening essay. Here, he explains rhythm and rhyme as repetitive forms and explains their appeal "within the terms already given" (Burke, CS 130). He says that "rhyme usually accentuates the repetitive principle of art" and that "[I]ts appeal is the appeal of progressive form" (CS 130). The reader "'comes to rely' upon the rhythmic design after sufficient 'coordinates of direction' have been received by him; the regularity of the design establishes conditions of response in the body, and the continuance of the design becomes an 'obedience' to these same conditions" (CS 130). Rhythm appeals, he adds, as a conventional form "in so far as specific awareness of the rhythmic pattern is involved in our enjoyment" (CS 130), and "[I]t can sometimes be said to appeal by qualitative progressions, as when the poet, having established a pronounced rhythmic pattern, introduces a variant" (CS 131).

Burke extends the notion of variant, "a relief from the monotony" in discussing prose rhythms where "the nature of the expectancy is much vaguer" (CS 131). He suggests that the "principle by which the *variety* in prose rhythms is guided" is perhaps "a principle of logic" (CS 131), but he shifts from logic to "an intellectual factor" (CS 131–32) in a long discussion in which he tries to work out the role of logic in response. He writes about "rhythmically separating the logically joined" and about "logical groupings," although he summarizes by saying that "we are trying to indicate that the rhythmic variations of prose are not haphazard, that their 'planfulness' (conscious or unconscious) arises from the fact that the differentiations are based upon logical groupings" (CS 133). To simplify without being reductive, he tries again to explain how forms function qualitatively or enthymematically for the writer:

> That is, by logically relating one part of a sentence to another part of the sentence, the prose writer is led to a formal differentiation of the two related parts (or sometimes, which is *au fond* the same thing, he is led to a pronounced parallelism in the treatment of the related parts). The logical grouping of one part with another serves as the guide to the formal treatment of both (as "planful" differentiation can arise only out of sense of correspondence). (CS 133)

In this section, when Burke writes about "logically relating one part of a sentence to another part of the sentence," he presents writing as enthymematic, though in other terms: What the reader does is connect disparate parts, some of which force a conclusion. Within the realm of rhetoric, all connections are enthymematic in that readers collaborate with writers in making meaning, for the differences between syllogistic and qualitative progressions are differences of degree not of kind. Writers choose logically among available means of persuasion which attitudes, terms, and actions will most likely be persuasive, but their selections are necessarily matters of opinion and rhetoric rather than truth.

Burke's Rhetorical Reader

Burke concludes "Lexicon" with a discussion of readers, what motivates us, and what we do. Throughout the collection he has taught us how to read; here he names a range of readers who read for different purposes. He first mentions the "recalcitrant reader": "By the 'margin of persuasion' we refer to the means whereby the author can reduce the recalcitrant reader to acquiescence, the means whereby the Symbol, though remote from the reader, can be made to appeal for reasons intrinsic to the author's intention" (Burke, *CS* 176). The writer "[b]y thoroughness" should be able to overwhelm his reader and thus compel the reader to accept his interpretations:

> For a pattern of experience is an interpretation of life. Life being open to many interpretations, the reader is open to many interpretations. Only the madman or the genius or the temporarily exalted (as the lover, the terrified, or the sick) will have a pattern of experience so pronounced as to close him to the authority of other patterns of experience. (*CS* 176)

Here Burke revises his image of a "margin of overlap" into "margin of persuasion" to argue again that writers can persuade readers because of shared experiences. An "artist's attack can 'wear down' the reader until he accepts the artist's interpretation," and the reader may return after reading to "his own contrary patterns of experience" (*CS* 176–77). But the artist may be less aggressive, even with the recalcitrant reader, since "the normal person has a variety of feelings attached to the same object" and our modes of experience are "fluctuant" (*CS* 177).

Burke next describes the "perfect reader," whose experiences would be identical to the author's, "down to the last detail" (*CS* 179): "Perfection could exist only if the entire range of the reader's and the writer's experience were identical down to the last detail. Universal and permanent perfection could exist only if this range of experiences were identical for all men forever" (*CS* 179).

Because perfection does not exist, Burke names three kinds of readers—the "hysteric," the "connoisseur," and the "actual." The hypothetical "hysteric" reader "will demand in art a Symbol which is 'medicinal' to his situation. He will require one very specific kind of art" (Burke, *CS* 180). The hysteric reader seeks in art a cure or "equipment for living." In contrast:

> In so far as the reader approaches the hypothetical state of the "connoisseur," he is open to all Symbols, but is overwhelmed by none. He will approach art *as art*, thus requiring the maximum of ritualization, verbalization. He will be "will-less," "hunger-less," going to art for nothing but art itself. He will require not one specific kind of art (as the hysteric, who must have only detective stories, or murder stories, or success fiction) but any art profuse in technical happenings. (*CS* 180)

Burke's "actual reader" is "an indeterminate and fluctuant of these two extremes" (*CS* 180); all of his readers identify with art and participate in the creation of meaning. He emphasizes the writer-reader relationship and the importance of shared experiences between them in the act of reading, without repeating explicitly his earlier points about formal and stylistic identification and margins of overlap and margins of persuasion:

> Every word a writer uses depends for its very "meaning" upon the reader's previous experience with the object or situation which this word suggests. That is to say, the word is "charged" by the reader's own experiences, and to this extent the reader is "hysteric." "Madness" is but meaning carried to the extreme. (*CS* 180)

Burke concludes this portion of his extended lesson in reading as a collaborative action by reinforcing three points: Writers and readers must share a "margin of overlap" if we are to communicate, and both must desire to identify. Readers "read" by drawing on our prior knowledge and experiences, particularly our prior experience in reading, writing, and living to make connections to construct meaning. Our immediate experiences in co-creating meaning convince us; we are persuaded by what we have created collaboratively with writers.

Although Burke does not here mention qualitative progression and the emotional connections that readers supply, this passage is a revision of the one discussed earlier, in which emotional responses and identification are linked. As readers of Burke, we chart key terms, clusters of terms, watershed moments, perspective by incongruity, attitudes, and other methods of formal identification, and we draw on our shared experiences to make sense of what we read.

What Goes with What? Burke's Two Explicit Uses of the Term "Enthymeme"

Burke uses the term *enthymeme* in *A Rhetoric of Motives* in 1950, in the context of his discussion of identification, and again in "Rhetoric, Poetics, and Philosophy," a 1978 essay published in *Rhetoric, Poetics, and Philosophy*, a collection edited by Don M. Burks. In both direct uses of the *enthymeme*, Burke makes clear that he "draws the line" between rhetoric, poetics, politics, and philosophy and deals in the realm of rhetoric where doubt and uncertainty rather than truth prevail and where persuasion depends on reasoning from opinion. The fact that he uses the term *enthymeme* only twice emphasizes the two cases because he refers often to other figures and tropes, particularly the four master tropes—metaphor, synecdoche, metonymy, and irony—and even to ones as rare as epanaphora, homoeoteleuton, and asyndeton (Burke, *RM* 59).

Many critics tend to use Burke's "master" tropes for their purposes, but Don M. Burks directly addresses the enthymeme in Burke's rhetoric. In "Dramatic Irony, Collaboration, and Kenneth Burke's Theory of Form," published in *Pre/Text* in 1985, he observes that Burke is "preoccupied" with "what may loosely be called a theory of enthymematic collaboration" (261) that is "consonant with Bitzer's interpretation of Aristotle's concept of the enthymeme" (263).

I draw on Burks's insights in this essay and read it along with his earlier essay, "Persuasion, Self-Persuasion and Rhetorical Discourse," published in *Philosophy and Rhetoric* in 1970, although Burks does not relate the two essays directly nor does he mention Burke or identification in the 1970 essay. Reading these two essays together, however, helps me build on Burks's work to refine and extend my argument that the enthymeme is the body of proof in Burke's rhetoric and that the action of the enthymeme, collaborative meaning-making, persuades because readers accept that which they have helped to create.

Burks begins "Persuasion, Self-Persuasion, and Rhetorical Discourse" by responding to Richard Zaner's discussion of essays in *Philosophy, Rhetoric, and Argumentation*, edited by Natanson and Johnstone in 1965. It is problematic to Burks that Zaner attributes the distinction between "persuade" and "convince" to Natanson, since, he says, Natanson "frequently uses them or terms very similar to them, in an unusual way" ("Persuasion" 109). Burks explains that traditionally "'argument to persuade' refers to situations where both 'logical' and 'psychological' appeals are used, whereas in 'argument to convince' 'logical' appeals are chiefly used" (109). For Natanson, Burks says, "the 'rhetoric of persuading' refers to argument where self is risked as distinguished from the 'rhetoric of convincing,' where self is not risked" (109–10). Drawing on Edward Z. Rowell's 1932 "Prolegomena to Argumentation," Burks suggests that Natanson's distinction "may best be thought of as one between "attitude establishing" and "knowledge-establishing" (109). He returns to Natanson to speculate that he "uses Johnstone's thesis regarding risk, his thesis that 'the point of argument is not to provide effective control over others,' but to introduce all the participants of arguments in 'a situation of risk in which open-mindedness and tolerance are possible'" (110). He quotes Natanson in "The Claims of Immediacy" to explain that the "rhetoric of persuading" involves the "commitment of the self to the full implications of a philosophical debate" (qtd. by Burks, "Persuasion" 110).

Burks summarizes Natanson's "rhetoric of persuasion" that involves the "risking of self for both speaker and listener" as they engage in "*mutual* persuasion" ("Persuasion" 111). Although Natanson does not refer to "self-persuasion," Burks explains that in "Rhetoric and Philosophical Argumentation" he treats persuasion on page 153 "as a dialectical transformation of the self through indirect argumentation" (111). Burks's thesis is "that just as there is an internal or self-dialectic so there is self-persuasion, and as internal dialectic is analogous to dialectic with others, so self-persuasion is analogous to dialectic with others" (112).

At this point, with Burks's help, I want to enter the door that Burke opened for me in 1983 when I asked him at his kitchen table why he never discussed the enthymeme more than he did in the two direct yet brief references. He replied, "I should have done more with that," leaving space for me to supply what I find missing in his rhetoric. I also want to respond here to his repeated question, "How do you get from there to there," by answering, "Enthymematically." I offer my collaborative reading with Burke as an interpretation to consider, with the spirit Burke recommends and enacts in "Rhetoric—Old and New":

> For, if identification includes the realm of transcendence, it has, by the some [sic] token, brought us into the realm of transformation, or dialectic. A rhetorician, I take it, is like one voice in a dialogue. Put several such voices together, with each voicing its own special assertion, let them act upon one another in co-operative competition and you get a dialectic, that, properly developed, can lead to the views transcending the limitations of each. (63)

The Context for Burke's First Use of "Enthymeme" in *A Rhetoric of Motives*

Burke first uses the term enthymeme in his discussion of identification in "Traditional Principles of Rhetoric," in part 2 of *A Rhetoric of Motives*. He never explicitly develops the association between identification and the enthymeme, but for me it is a silence waiting to be voiced.

I begin with part 1, "The Range of Rhetoric," and its final chapter "Realistic Function of Rhetoric." Here Burke prepares us for what is to come by linking identification, persuasion, and stylistic identification. He acknowledges that critics will select among these forms for particular purposes and audiences:

> As for the relation between "identification" and "persuasion": we might well keep it in mind that a speaker persuades an audience by the use of *stylistic identifications*; his act of persuasion may be for the purpose of causing the audience to identify itself with the speaker's interests; and the speaker draws on identification of interests to establish rapport between himself and his audience. So, there is no chance of our keeping apart the meanings of persuasion, identification, ("consubstantiality") and communication (the nature of rhetoric as "addressed"). *But, in given instances, one or another of these elements may serve best for extending a line of analysis in some particular direction.* (Burke, *RM* 46; my emphasis)

In this summary, Burke consolidates what he has been developing throughout Part I to provide the context for his revisions of the traditional principles of rhetoric in Part II. He will continue drawing and extending lines of analyses for his purposes. He will also continue to emphasize and generate with his readers what he here calls "stylistic identification" but what he examines as the "appeal of forms" in *Counter-Statement* (Burke, *CS* 318). He will distinguish between terms that define each other and cannot therefore be strictly kept apart, such as "persuasion" and "identification"; but he will also demonstrate how terms can be read as different in kind or degree, for different contexts. He will substitute terms for each other at times, such as *identification* and *consubstantiality* to make a particular point temporarily and experimentally to discover and assess the gains and losses of such moves. He will continue to weight and counter-weight terms, exploiting the pliancy in our uses of terms and in our attitudes.

He begins Part II, "Traditional Principles of Rhetoric," with "Persuasion," in which he provides a brief history of the term. He modifies that history, however, by saying that the rhetorician, through choices that create stylistic identification, moves audiences not only to physical action but also to changes in attitude. He repeats here much of what he has argued in *Counter-Statement*, and he again stresses an attitude of uncertainty—"would permit," "might be classed," and "are considered for":

> Yet often we could with more accuracy speak of persuasion "to attitude," rather than persuasion to out-and-out action. Persuasion involves choice, will; it is directed to a man only insofar as he is *free*. This is good to remember, in these days of dictatorship and near-dictatorship. Only insofar as men are potentially free, must the spellbinder seek to persuade them. Insofar as they *must* do something, rhetoric is unnecessary, its work being done by the nature of things. . . . Insofar as a choice of *action* is restricted, rhetoric seeks rather to have a formative effect upon *attitude*. . . . Thus, in Cicero and Augustine there is a shift between the words "move" (*movere*) and "bend" (*flectere*) to name the ultimate function of rhetoric. This shift corresponds to a distinction between act and attitude (attitude being an incipient act, a leaning or inclination). Thus the notion of persuasion to *attitude* would permit the application of rhetorical terms to purely *poetic* structures; the study of lyrical devices might be classed under the head of rhetoric, *when these devices are considered for their power to induce or communicate states of mind to readers, even though the kinds of assent evoked have no overt, practical outcome.* (Burke, *RM* 50; second emphasis mine)

Here Burke reinforces and revises the traditional principles of rhetoric. He accepts the view that rhetoric operates in the realm of doubt and uncertainty, but he emphasizes that rhetoric is possible only when people are free to choose and there are possibilities for change. In this way, he recontextualizes rhetoric from Aristotle's time and expands the notion of persuasion to out-and-out action to include persuasion in attitudes and states of mind. He credits mental actions, as well as physical actions, all as having consequences in the world.

His aim is to make rhetoric useful in the contemporary world and to extend the range of rhetoric and what counts as action, in order to promote the vision of change that motivates his work, *ad bellum purificandum*, through acts of identification by people using language. He has already demonstrated to us, as early as *Counter-Statement*, how to apply rhetorical terms to poetic structures. He has taught and enacted how poetic forms understood as rhetorical actions engage readers in acts of meaning-making. All forms are poetic in that they are imaginative and not referentially true: all forms are persuasive for those very reasons because writers and readers identify and are convinced by their collaborative experience and by what they have in part created.

It is not enough to understand worlds, identities, and languages as socially constructed by people, nor is it enough to understand that our words and worlds construct us. We must, in Burke's world, understand all constructions as rhetorical, variously motivated, situated, and consequential, including our own.

In this section, Burke explains again, but with a difference, how stylistic or formal identification persuades. He extends the uses of language in poetry to the uses of language in all forms and genres. He turns forms, genres, styles, and art in general into rhetorical actions, expanding the scope and circumference of rhetoric to include both the study of and the uses of persuasion within and across texts and contexts. He undercuts conclusiveness and comprehensiveness through his attitude of uncertainty and recognition that his own claim is not right but rhetoric.

Burke accepts Aristotle's view that rhetoric has general application, dealing with generally accepted principles and commonplaces and not with any one definite class of subjects. He also credits by adopting Aristotle's distinctions between rhetoric, poetics, politics, and other knowledges and his subordination of other terms and fields of knowledge within an arts of rhetoric: "Aristotle rigorously divided knowledge into compartments whenever possible, his *Art of Rhetoric* includes much that falls under the separate headings of psychology, ethics, politics, poetics, logic, and history" (*RM* 51). What distinguishes rhetoric, Aristotle demonstrates, is the body of proof, the enthymeme; what distinguishes rhetoric, as Burke demonstrates, is identification.

Burke also uses Aristotle to reinforce his view of the relationships among rhetoric, truth, and opinion. He says that for Aristotle the "characteristically rhetorical statement involves 'commonplaces' that lie outside any scientific specialty; and in proportion as the rhetorician deals with special subject matter, his proofs move away from the rhetorical and toward the scientific" (*RM* 51). He divides persuasion into appeals to reason and appeals to emotion, but he then presents them as dialectically related, in that they define each other by opposition but can be understood productively as differences in degree not in kind. Rhetors choose logically among various means of persuasion; in rhetoric, all appeals are enthymematic. They require writers and readers to identify because people and language are imperfect yet hierarchical and knowledge is uncertain, incomplete, temporary, and context-dependent. Readers connect disparate parts of the syllogism and the enthymeme, although the parts are less disparate in the syllogism than in the enthymeme:

As for "persuasion" itself: one can imagine including purely logical demonstration as part of it; or one might distinguish between appeals to reason and appeals to emotion, sentiment, ignorance, prejudice, and the like, reserving the notion of "persuasion" for these less orderly kinds of "proof." (Here again we encroach upon the term "dialectic." Augustine seems to follow the Stoic usage, in treating dialectic as the logical groundwork underlying rhetoric; dialectic would thus treat of the ultimate scenic reality that sets the criteria for rhetorical persuasion). (*RM* 51)

Burke puzzles with issues that still preoccupy rhetoricians: What does it mean to say rhetoric is the counterpart of dialectic? What are the motives, uses, and probable consequences of this assertion? What is the place of logical reasoning in rhetoric? How might it be helpful and harmful to understand logical reasoning as reasoning from opinion, in certain circumstances? What sense does it make and what are the gains and losses of understanding logic as a basis for the rhetor's choices between the orderly or logical proof and the "less orderly kinds of proof," ethical and pathetic proof? How can rhetoric have general application and yet be flexible enough to deal effectively within particular contexts? For him, these are questions and issues to explore because they raise the ambiguities and contradictions of life, language, and animal symbolicum. These are the spaces of rhetoric.

Having not gotten it right and not expecting to do so once and for all, Burke continues to explore, assess, and revise the traditional principles of rhetoric. He closes in on the "body of proof" in rhetoric as he explains: "The Greek word, *peitho*, comes from the same root as the Latin word for 'faith.' Accordingly, Aristotle's term for rhetorical 'proof' is the related word, *pistis*" (Burke, *RM 51–52*). He does not use the term *enthymeme* here, though he circles round it to challenge again the traditional hierarchy of scientific proof over rhetorical proof by linking *pistis* to faith and rhetoric. He distinguishes faith and rhetoric from logical reasoning before considering them similar in that both are social or cooperative reasoning. He extends Aristotle and his own line of argument even further by distinguishing between the active form of persuasion and the passive form of obedience:

> In his vocabulary, it names an *inferior* kind of proof, as compared with scientific demonstration (*apodeixis*). (See *Institutio Oratoria*, Book V, Chapter X). But it is, ironically, the word which, in Greek ecclesiastical literature, came to designate the *highest* order of Christian knowledge, "faith" or "belief" as contrasted with "reason." While the active form of *peitho* means "to persuade," its middle and passive forms mean "to obey."

But the corresponding Latin word, suadere, comes from the same roots as "suavity," "assuage," and "sweet." (*RM* 52)

He admits that "following these leads, one may want to narrow the scope of persuasion to such meanings as 'ingratiation' and 'delight,'" but he adds that "the ability of rhetoric to ingratiate is considered secondary, as a mere device for gaining good will, holding the attention, or deflecting the attention in preparation for more urgent purposes" (*RM* 52). Aristotle, he says, "looks upon rhetoric as a medium that 'proves opposites'" and "gives what amounts to a handbook on a manly art of self-defense" (*RM* 52). He tracks the "'agonistic' emphasis" in Cicero, the weaker emphasis in Quintilian's "educational emphasis," Augustine's concern in *De Doctrina Christiana* with "cajoling of an audience" rather than with "the routing of opponents" (*RM* 53).

He returns to "rhetoric as a means of proving opposites" to examine the relations between rhetoric and dialectic and offers a "rough approximate" of the matter:

> Bring several *rhetoricians* together, let their speeches contribute to the maturing of one another by the give and take of question and answer, and you have the *dialectic* of a Platonic dialogue. But ideally the dialogue seeks to attain a higher order of truth, as the speakers, in competing with one another, cooperate towards an end transcending their individual positions. Here is the paradigm of the dialectical process for "reconciling opposites" in a "higher synthesis." (Burke, *RM* 53,)

Once again, Burke has led us to an understanding that he then modifies. We have followed his mind at work and linked rhetoricians and practices across the ages with him. We are implicated in the conclusions which we reach and then question if not undermine. In this case, Burke qualifies his previous claims:

> But note that, in the Platonic scheme, such dialectic enterprise starts from *opinion*. The Socratic "midwifery" (maieutic) was thus designed to discover truth, by beginning with opinion and subjecting it to systematic criticism. Also, the process was purely verbal; hence in Aristotle's view it would be an art, not a science, since each science has its own particular extraverbal subject matter. The Socratic method was better suited for such linguistic enterprises as the dialectical search for "ideas" of justice, truth, beauty, and so on than for the accumulating of knowledge derived from empirical observation and laboratory experiment. Dialectic of this sort was

concerned with "ideology" in the primary sense of the term: the study of ideas and of their relations to one another. But above all, note that, in its very search for "truth," it began with "opinion," and thus in a sense was *grounded* in opinion. The point is worth remembering because the verbal "counterpart" of dialectic, rhetoric, was likewise said to deal with "opinion," though without the systematic attempt to transcend this level. (*RM* 53–54)

Here again Burke restores and revises rhetoric by claiming that rhetoric is the "verbal 'counterpart' of dialectic" and that it "deal[s] with 'opinion,' though without the systematic attempt to transcend this level" (*RM* 54). But he keeps on trying, not sure he has made his point persuasive to himself and to others: "But we think that the relation between 'truth' and the kind of opinion with which rhetoric operates is often misunderstood" (*RM* 54). The terms and ideas in the following are familiar from earlier works: And the classical texts do not seem to bring out the point we have in mind, namely:

> The kind of opinion with which rhetoric deals, in its role of inducement to action, is not opinion *as contrasted with truth*. There is the invitation to look at the matter thus antithetically, once we have put the two terms (opinion and truth) together as a dialectical pair. But actually, many of the "opinions" upon which persuasion relies fall outside the test of truth in the strictly scientific, T-F, yes-or-no sense. (*RM* 54)

For Burke, terms define each other, not a reality beyond, and they can be used dialectically as well as antithetically. He extends the dialectical relationships between two terms, here between *truth* and *opinion*, through *action*, to include the dialectical relationships between other terms, for example between *mind* and *world*, *self* and *other*, and *cooperation* and *competition*. What curbs his metaphorical extension and casuistic stretching is a test of the collective:

> The critic's tests, whereby he gets his own pattern of selectivity, choosing to stress some distinctions and to neglect other possible distinctions, is the pragmatic test of use. Facing a myriad of possible distinctions, he should focus on those that he considers important for social reasons. Roughly, in the present state of the world we should group these about the "revolutionary" emphasis, involved in the treatment of art with primary reference to symbols of authority, their acceptance and rejection. The critic thus becomes propagandist and craftsman simultaneously; he serves a didactic purpose in that he constantly reaffirms, in varying subject matter,

the necessary tactics of transition; and he gives proper attention to the formal organization of poetry in that such an approach reveals the basic strategy of poetic symbolism (ritual, "secular prayer," dramatic change of identity, etc.). (Burke, *ATH* 200)

Having reached a resting place rather than a conclusion, Burke continues his revisions of the traditional principles of rhetoric, explaining that "many of the 'opinions' upon which persuasion relies fall outside the test of truth" (Burke, *RM* 54). He refines the terms: truth in the "strictly scientific, T-F, yes-or-no sense" and opinion in an ethical sense that "clearly falls on the bias across the matter of 'truth' in the strictly scientific sense" (*RM* 54). He examines this muddled distinction further: "'opinion' (opinion in the moral order of *action*, rather than in the 'scenic' order of truth)," and he explains that "the rhetorician, as such, need operate only on this principle" (*RM* 55). He concludes this section with a reference to identification, the title of the next section: "If, in the opinion of a given audience, a certain kind of conduct is admirable, then a speaker might persuade the audience by using ideas and images that *identify* his cause with that kind of conduct" (*RM* 55; my emphasis).

Having established uncertainty as the realm of rhetoric, his purpose in the next section is to identify further what is necessarily certain in persuasion: the enthymeme as the body of proof.

Burke's Direct Hit on the Enthymeme

Having redefined rhetoric, proof, truth, opinion, and persuasion, Burke is ready to begin the next section, "Identification." He begins by focusing on shared *qualities* as the basis for identification in Aristotle's *Rhetoric*:

> "It is not hard," says Aristotle, in his *Rhetoric*, quoting Socrates, "to praise Athenians among Athenians." He has been cataloguing those traits which an audience generally considers the components of virtue. . . . And he has been saying: For purposes of praise or blame, the rhetorician will assume that qualities closely resembling any of these qualities are identical with them. . . . Part of the quotation appears in Book I. It is quoted again, entire, in Book III, where he has been discussing the speaker's appeal to friendship or compassion. And he continues: When winding up a speech in praise of someone, we "must make the hearer believe that he shares in the praise, either personally, or through his family or profession, or somehow. (Burke, *RM* 55)

Here Burke focuses on identification based on qualities shared—valued or rejected—by writers and readers. Elsewhere he discusses identification based on property, concrete objects, common concerns, languages, and experiences. His use of the term *quality* and its variations remains throughout his rhetoric, from *qualitative progression* in *Counter-Statement* to "the qualitative difference between the symbol and the symbolized" in *The Rhetoric of Religion* (*RM* 16).

To ground his discussion at this point, Burke explains "perhaps the simplest case of persuasion":

> "You persuade a man only insofar as you can talk his language by speech, gesture, tonality, order, image, attitude, idea, *identifying* your ways with his" (*RM* 55).

Although persuasion through language is hardly simple, a shared language creates grounds for identification. In a typical move, Burke undercuts or minimizes the importance of this major point about identification by extending its meaning; but as he extends and minimizes it, he is, in fact, locking in agreement about identification as the most available means we have for getting along with each other.

He then shifts qualitatively rather than logically to flattery as "a special case of persuasion in general" that can "safely serve as a paradigm if we systematically widen its meaning, to see behind it the conditions of identification or consubstantiality in general" (Burke, *RM* 55). To flatter is to identify your ways with another and to create a connection whereby the other identifies with you. The orator gives 'signs' of such consubstantiality by deference to an audience's 'opinions'" and thus "earns the audience's good will" (*RM* 55–56).

He next makes explicit the notion that both writer and reader move to action and change in order to identify with each other: "True, the rhetorician may have to change an audience's opinion in one respect; but he can succeed only insofar as he yields to that audience's opinions in other respects" (Burke, *RM* 56). Identification must be two-way. Neither writer nor reader has absolute control or power for both must come to terms in order to communicate. While identification depends on divisions between us and our desires to communicate, identification also depends on our willingness to understand divisions and differences as scenes for connection. This is as true in the actions of writing, reading, speaking, and listening as it is in daily conversation and exchange.

In this context where Burke uses Aristotle's *Rhetoric* to emphasize that the rhetor's task is to select among available means of persuasion, he selects the term enthymeme for the first time:

Reasoning based on opinion he calls "enthymemes," which are the rhetorical equivalent of the syllogism. And arguments from example (which is the rhetorical equivalent for induction) are likewise to be framed in accordance with his various lists of opinions. (*RM* 56)

Like Aristotle, Burke juxtaposes the enthymeme to the syllogism but refers to both as rhetorical acts of reasoning and as acts of reasoning from opinion. Unlike Aristotle, Burke shifts immediately away from the "enthymeme" in a long parenthetical aside on the "'permanence' of such 'places' or topics, when stated at Aristotle's level of generalization (*RM* 56).

In sum, Burke uses Aristotle to revise and reconfigure the traditional principles of rhetoric—relationships between opinion and truth and between the enthymeme and the syllogism; relationships among the three appeals; and distinctions between rhetoric and science and poetry and politics. More specifically, he uses Aristotle's understanding of the enthymeme as a figure, form, structuring principle, and action to engage readers, so that they become complicit and convinced. Burke's first lesson in reading is that what's missing in all texts motivates writers and readers to identify; what's missing in all texts becomes the basis of rhetorical proof and persuasion. His second lesson teaches us that identification can be based on almost anything and that it is temporary and partial rather than permanent and consubstantial.

BURKE'S EXTENSIONS OF ARISTOTLE'S ENTHYMEME IN *A RHETORIC OF MOTIVES*

After his brief mention of the enthymeme in *A Rhetoric of Motives*, Burke follows Aristotle's lead in the *Rhetoric* by extending the figure and action. Aristotle demonstrates how the metaphor, simile, proverb, maxim, and other figure and tropes function enthymematically to involve readers. Burke extends identification to "pun-logic," "specious and sophistical arguments," and to other ways of turning, transforming, exaggerating, defining, selecting, and dividing up (*RM* 57). He associates how identification, an act of invention, relates and changes participants and their situations:

> Though the translation of one's wishes into terms of an audience's opinions would clearly be an instance of identification, this last list of purely formal devices for rhetorical invention takes us farther afield. However, it seems to be a fact that, the more urgent the oratory, the greater the profusion and vitality of the formal devices.

So, they must be *functional*, and not mere "embellishments." And processes of "identification" would seem to figure here, as follows:

> Longinus refers *to that kind of elation wherein the audience feels as though it were not merely receiving, but were itself creatively participating in the poet's or speaker's assertion. Could we not say that, in such cases, the audience is exalted by the assertion because it has the feel of collaborating in the assertion?* (*RM* 57–58; my emphasis)

Through "an attitude of collaborative expectancy" (*RM* 58) and through formal identification, people are persuaded by their own acts of meaning-making. Burke collaborates with his own readers as he explains his point further. He teaches directly and through demonstration that invites us to participate:

> At least, we know that many purely formal patterns can readily awaken an attitude of collaborative expectancy in us . . . . *Once you grasp the trend of the form, it invites participation regardless of the subject matter. Formally, you will find yourself swinging along* with the succession of antitheses, even though you may not agree with the proposition that is being presented in this form. (*RM* 58; my emphasis)

Burke continues to explain the swinging along, the dancing of attitudes, and the linking of qualities, all as actions at the heart of rhetorical persuasion: "Or it may even be an opponent's proposition which you resent—yet for the duration of the statement itself you might '*help him out' to the extent of yielding to the formal development*, surrendering to its symmetry as such"(*RM* 58; my emphasis). All readers identify to some degree, even through their resistances and revisions.

In the continuation of the previous quote, Burke uses terms, images, and attitudes that he uses in *Counter-Statement* and later to develop his rhetoric of "getting along" and identification:

> Of course, the more violent your original resistance to the proposition, the weaker will be your degree of "surrender" by "collaborating" with the form. But in cases where a decision is still to be reached, *a yielding to the form prepares for assent to the matter identified with it*. Thus, you are drawn to the form, not in your capacity as a partisan, but because of some "universal" appeal in it. And this attitude of assent may then be transferred to the matter which happens to be associated with the form. (*RM* 58; my emphasis)

The persuasiveness of enthymematic proof is not in the reader's or the writer's completion of the form but in the writer's and reader's collaborative acts, at least briefly, until the negative sets in. Collaboration is not complete, and participants aren't equal. Meaning is not mutually created by writer and reader at the same time or in the same place. Meaning is action.

Burke specifies what he has been discussing generally in *A Rhetoric of Motives* by turning to a particular form, a *gradatio*, and repeating parts of earlier discussions throughout *Counter-Statement*. *Gradatio* is a progressive form that leads readers to take steps and thereby accept conclusions by connecting them. Burke selects an example of a *gradatio* about persuasion and politics to illustrate formal or poetic identification as action that leads to further collective political action:

> But recall a *gradatio* of political import, much in the news during the "Berlin crisis" of 1948: "Who controls Berlin, controls Germany; who controls Germany controls Europe; who controls Europe controls the world." As a proposition, it may or may not be true. And even if it is true, unless people are thoroughly imperialistic, they may not want to control the world. *But regardless of these doubts about it as a proposition, by the time you arrive at the second of its three stages, you feel how it is destined to develop—and on the level of purely formal assent you would collaborate to round out its symmetry by spontaneously willing its completion and perfection as an utterance. Add, now, the psychosis of nationalism, and assent on the formal level invites assent to the proposition as doctrine.* (RM 58–59; my emphasis)

The gradient series, a cumulative progressive form, is a qualitative form which readers go along with and thereby give formal assent to the conclusion all along the way. Collaborative expectancy leads to acceptance of meaning co-created. A gradient progressive form calls for writer-reader identification. The rhetor gauges how close together and how far apart the steps or distances need to be to create a sense of seeing anew, of learning, of wonder. In Aristotle's terms, if the steps are too close or too distant, readers experience "frigidity" instead of *kairos*, the temporary sense of order and wholeness before the negative sets in.

Burke concludes this section on identification by widening the scope of his analysis to include Quintilian's discussions of tropes and figures in the eighth and ninth books of *Institutio Oratoria*. He explains that "the invitation to purely formal assent (regardless of content) is much greater in some cases than others" (Burke, *RM* 59), and he gives a typical disclaimer to guarantee our assent:

> It is not our purpose here to analyze the lot in detail. We need but say enough to establish the principle, and to indicate why the expressing of a proposition in one or another of these rhetorical forms would involve "identification," first by inducing the author to participate in the form, as a "universal" locus of appeal, and next by trying to include a partisan statement within this same pale of assent. (*RM* 59)

The principle that Burke affirms is the traditional principle of rhetoric in Aristotle, the enthymeme as the body of proof, but he does so in his own term, identification. Identification persuades because writers are willing to induce readers to "participate in the form" (Burke, *RM* 59), to "creatively participate in the poet's or speaker's assertion" (*RM* 58), "to swing[ing] along" (*RM* 58), and "to grasp the trend of the form" (*RM* 58). Identification persuades because readers are willing to "get along" with writers.

Burke's Other Explicit Use of the "Enthymeme" in "Rhetoric, Poetics, and Philosophy"

In his other explicit use of the term enthymeme, in "Rhetoric, Poetics, and Philosophy," Burke specifies some of the associations that cluster around the term for him, some of which are familiar from his earlier discussions in *Counter-Statement* and in *A Rhetoric of Motives*:

> Similarly, with regard to rhetoric, I take it that not truth but opinion is the surest ground for persuasion—and Aristotle seems to have implied considerations of that sort when distinguishing between enthymeme and syllogism. Often, though not always, truth helps—yet many questions are called "rhetorical" precisely because there is no "truth" to which one can refer. (*RM* 16)

In this essay, Burke explains the cuts that he and Aristotle make between rhetoric and poetics and between "truth," "probability," "opinion," "syllogism," and "enthymeme." He assumes his earlier definitions and uses of these terms. He associates his terms, actions, and attitudes with Aristotle's, specifically with his distinction between logical and rhetorical proof. Burke says Aristotle implied "considerations of that sort when distinguishing between enthymeme and syllogism." For both, the enthymeme is appropriate for matters of opinion and persuasion, although "'[o]pinion' in this ethical sense clearly falls on the bias across the matter of 'truth' in the strictly scientific sense" (*RM* 54). What is assumed in rhetoric is that enthymeme-making is reasoning from opinion about which kind of appeal will most likely work. Rhetoricians use logic to choose among appeals, and they select logic when it will more likely persuade than other appeals. In rhetoric, logical, ethical, and pathetic appeals are all acts of uncertainty, not truth.

Again, with Aristotle's help, Burke juxtaposes the enthymeme and the syllogism and opinion and truth as dialectically rather than antithetically related. He acknowledges that the truth often helps to persuade, even in matters of opinion. While he distinguishes between the syllogism and the enthymeme as structures, he emphasizes that both persuade through the collaborative creation of meaning. The risk and challenge of rhetoric is that writers and readers construct meaning in uncertainty, knowing that what we create is partial, changing, and motivated and therefore the uncertain motives and grounds for further rhetorical acts.

3 A Burkean Reading of Fish's Tale of Freud's Analysis of the Wolf-Man's Account: The Long-Lasting Effects of Sisterly Persuasion

> Or again: insofar as our sophisticated trout avoided food of a certain shape or color because the bait that nearly hooked him happened to be of this description, his inadequate interpretation could be called the result of a trained incapacity. Veblen generally restricts the concept to the case of the businessmen who, through long training in competitive finance, have so built their scheme of orientation about this kind of effort and ambition that they cannot see serious possibilities in any other system of production and distribution. (Burke, *PC* 7)

> People may be unfitted by being fit in an unfit fitness. (Burke, *PC* 10)

> Such shifts of interpretation make for totally different pictures of reality, since they focus the attention upon different orders of relationship. We learn to single out certain relationships in accordance with the particular linguistic texture into which we are born, though we may privately manipulate this linguistic texture to formulate still other relationships. When we do so, we invent new terms, or apply our old vocabulary in new ways, attempting to socialize our position by so manipulating the linguistic equipment of our group that our particular additions or alterations can be shown to fit into the old texture. We try to point out new relationships as meaningful—we interpret situations differently; in the subjective sphere, we invent new accounts of motive. Since both the old and the new motives are linguistically constructed, and since language is a communicative medium, the present discussion has taken us from orientation, through motivation, to communication. (Burke, *PC* 36)

Introducing What's Missing to Withhold Something Else

Stanley Fish exposes the rhetoric in Freud's scientific account of the Wolf-Man in "Withholding the Missing Portion: Psychoanalysis and Rhetoric," the last essay in his 1989 collection, *Doing What Comes Naturally: Change, Rhetoric, and the Practice of Theory in Literary and Legal Studies*. He argues that Freud's science is persuasion that serves Freud as much if not more than it serves the patient, because at every turn Freud moves to "preserve masculine self-esteem" (Fish, "Psychoanalysis and Rhetoric" 536): "Freud can present himself as a disinterested researcher and at the same time work to extend his control until it finally includes everything: the details of the analysis, the behavior of the patient, and the performance of the reader" (534).

Like Burke, Fish understands that identification is necessary to persuasion.[19] Unlike Burke, Fish relies primarily on logical appeals that invite

---

19. Throughout this chapter, I distinguish between Burke's and Fish's understandings of rhetoric, literature, and the relationships between rhetoric and poetics. See Olson for his reading of Fish's "belief in the centrality of rhetoric," which Olson defines in terms of "the specific local, contingent context—to the rhetorical situation at play—to explain how something works" (3). In response to Olson's interview question about Burke's influence, Fish says he's "read Burke only sporadically and only occasionally" but that he's been influenced indirectly in many ways, for example through Richard Lanham and Frank Lentricchia (96).

I believe that Fish might classify Burke as a "boutique multiculturalist," who, according to Olson, assumes "a universal human nature—a universal, trans-cultural human identity that is more fundamental than any specific manifestation of human identity colored by some particular cultural practice or attribute" (54). What's universal for Burke is summarized in his definition of "animal symbolicum," a choice that is limited and therefore useful. The boutique multiculturalist is "but one manifestation" of the "liberal rationalist tradition" (55) who assumes "that an individual can and should bracket or set aside deeply held beliefs for the good of others (even when those deeply held convictions are central to the person's religious or entire belief system), and they in effect prescribe that the individual stop short of implementing those beliefs" (55). Burke slips, however, into the category of "strong multiculturalists who value difference for its own sake, not as the surface sign of some more fundamental human nature" and whose "first principle" is "not rationality or some extra-cultural fundamental humanness but tolerance" (55). Difference for Burke, as we have seen, is the motive and grounds for communication and identification.

Getting along is not a matter of tolerance but survival: it is an attitude and action to strive for but one which human beings must accept they cannot always reach. See Fish's "Why We Can't All Just Get Along."

readers to identify with him and his authority and to accept his conclusions as right. However, Burke's rhetoric recognizes distinctions between syllogistic progressions and enthymematic or qualitative progressions as differences in degree not in kind. From this rhetorical perspective, Fish's arguments are not perfectly logical or air-tight and his control is not complete. He needs readers who will fill in the gaps and bridge steps, albeit tiny ones, in his argument, so that they are also persuaded by what they in part construct.

All writers, including Fish, Freud, Burke, and me, are "attempting to socialize our positions by manipulating the linguistic equipment of our group." We are all beneficiaries and victims of our training and orientations. Our terministic screens, our discursive communities, our training, all educate us to focus on by focusing off. Our orientations also influence our conclusions; our orientations and our conclusions are partial, contingent, and situated. We can learn to see "beyond the corners" of our own screens by revision strategies such as perspective by incongruity and through acts of identification by which we revise ourselves and our situations in order to get along with others. Without recognizing the limitations of our positions and of language, we aim to persuade by being right. On the other hand, what's presented as right, complete, and true remains most persuasive, even in a rhetorical world.

I focus here on Stanley Fish's reading of Freud's analysis of the Wolf-Man because he is a literary critic who understands not only the rhetoric of fictions but also the rhetoric of his own discourse. He writes syllogistically in order to be persuasive, but he also uses other strategies in his writing that indicate his desire to move readers to identify with him, to want to be like him. His is a rhetoric of apparent control, supported by a rhetoric of collaboration. I also focus on his reading of Freud's analysis of the Wolf-Man for other reasons: I was so taken by it on my first reading that I wanted to understand why. I wanted to track how Fish moves from certainty to "the oxymoronic state of constant wavering" ("Psychoanalysis and Rhetoric") in his last paragraph. I was also curious about the history of the essay, the succession of scenes in which it was presented and published, and the revisions made for the various audiences and contexts. Mainly, I was also struck by what for me was a glaring absence in Fish's and Freud's analysis but con-

---

What is most important for my argument is Fish's conversion of different ways of knowing into different styles in his response to Olson's question about the feminist distinction between male and female epistemologies: And those different styles will have difference effects, although, again, contingent on particular situations ("Why We Can't All Just Get Along"). It's not always the case. Fish includes Richard Lanham and Frank Lentricchia. Throughout this chapter, I distinguish between Burke's and Fish's understandings and uses of rhetoric.

tinually present in the Wolf-Man's, his sister Anna. I found what Burke and Fish taught me to look for, the missing portion, the magic potion, the "differing sister."[20]

The Missing Premise; or, May the Devil Take the Hindmost

I wrote the following notes after reading Fish's "Withholding the Missing Portion: Power, Meaning, and Persuasion in Freud's *The Wolf-Man*," published in 1987 in *The Linguistics of Writing: Arguments between Language and Literature*, the proceedings of the 1986 conference, "The Linguistics of Writing." I wrote the notes before reading Fish's revised and re-titled "Withholding the Missing Portion: Psychoanalysis and Rhetoric," in his 1989 book, *Doing What Comes Naturally*:

I have a few measly facts to present: Freud had five sisters. Until he was ten, when his brother was born, "he was surrounded by women—his mother, his Nannie, and his five sisters" (Freeman and Stream 25). His first sister, Anna, was born when he was two and a half. Freud's third and last daughter and his sixth child was named Anna. The Wolf-Man's older sister, seldom identified

---

20. My association of the enthymeme with Anna, the Wolf-Man's absent sister, developed over time through my work with Burke's revisions of Aristotle. As I said in note 1 in chapter 2, Jeffrey Walker's recent *Rhetoric and Poetics in Antiquity* provides a useful discussion of the enthymeme for my purposes, particularly his discussions of the following: (1) his recognition of the "co-creative relationship between the audience and rhetor, in which the audience engages in a kind of 'self-persuasion' by completing or constructing for itself the tacit, elided aspects of the enthymeme" (170; my emphasis); (2) the "generally circulating and sophistic notions that Aristotle presupposes and leaves largely tacit in the *Rhetoric*," as well as what he adds (172–73); (3) the association of the thymos with heart, mind, spirit, thought, wish, desire, intentionality, or will, and his extension of the enthymeme beyond the view of it as an incomplete syllogism or logical form (173); (4) his construction from sophistic, pre-Aristotelian theory the enthymeme "conceived as a figure of discourse, or a discursive feature, meant to produce what might be called an 'enthymematic moment' in an audience's experience of a rhetor's discourse" and its link to "concerns with style, and linked as well to notions of *kairos* or 'the opportune' in any given discursive situation" (175); and (5) the association between the syllogism as a manly form and *the enthymeme as the "differing sister"* (171; my emphasis). In this chapter, I argue that Anna speaks enthymematically or whole-heartedly to the Wolf-Man throughout his life.

by anyone but him by her name, was also Anna. She died at nineteen, having poisoned herself with mercury.

Freud tried to dominate his material, as well as his patient and his patient readers, but he couldn't keep it up. He protests too much and, ironically, encourages readers to step in and help him out. The Wolf-Man tried to learn to control himself and act as he was supposed to act through decades of analysis, but he couldn't resist the seductive and long-lasting rhetoric of his dead sister, Anna. He got his name, made his livelihood, and attained immortality because he accepted the diagnosis of sisterly persuasion and his response to it as an illness and a denial of his masculinity.

So did Freud for that matter

Did Freud and the Wolf-Man identify with each other as partners in the crime of responding to and using sisterly persuasion? They were surely partners in the crime of denying that they did so. We all understand Freud and the Wolf-Man as tropes, as master tropes, and we all understand Freud and the Wolf-Man as cultural tropes, as entitlements, abstractions from situations, as something other than they are.

The long-term persuasiveness of Stanley Fish results from his spell-binding logic and from his less obvious enthymematic rhetoric that encourages his readers, despite all evidence to the contrary, to tell his tales with him. Like Freud, the subject of his penetrating analysis and air-tight logic, Fish ignores Anna's seductive rhetoric, but he knows and uses the power of the unstated, the withheld, the surprise, the left out, the absent; he knows the effects of the silenced and the dead.

Fish is a master trope too, and like all figures and tropes he spawns fissures that give breathing room for his readers to act.

In 1991 I was preparing a paper to give as a candidate for the position of Director of Composition at the University of Arizona. When I read Fish's article in *Doing What Comes Naturally*, I immediately put aside the draft I was working on, reread my notes written earlier, and decided to reread Fish, Freud, and the Wolf-Man. I knew where I wanted to go and what I wanted to find, what Burke had taught me to look for, the withheld, the missing portion, that which I contribute. I didn't know how to get there. I also knew I was taking a risk to give a paper on literary and psychological theories as a candidate for a position in composition, but I wanted to use Burke to talk about the *rhetoric* of such theories of reading and the place of the enthymeme and identification in them.

I decided to read Fish's tale by following in his footsteps, at the risk of committing the "imitative fallacy" that he warns himself against in his rewriting of Freud. I liked the idea of tracking Fish tracking Freud tracking the Wolf-Man, all of us picking up the crumbs left by the sister. I knew I didn't want to end up with Fish's view of rhetoric nor with his interpretation of the rhetoric of Freud and the Wolf-Man. At some point I would veer from his route to take my own roundabout, indirect, and uncertain path through the woods to Anna.

I gave a version of the paper I presented at the University of Arizona at a later Conference on College Composition and Communication, but I put both versions aside. Critical work on Burke since 1991 motivates the following, as do two responses to my talk in Tucson. A Renaissance scholar seated in the back raised his hand to ask jokingly, "So Aristotle was a feminist?" At the time I laughed, but revisionist histories of rhetoric, including those by Jeffrey Walker, James Kastely, William Covino, Janet M. Atwill, Victor Vitanza, Susan Jarratt, Cheryl Glenn, Andrea Lunsford, Lisa Ede, and others, help me respond now to my colleague's question. A cultural critic warned me against playful and self-reflexive qualities in academic discourse, citing responses to an early article on the trickster. The research and writing in rhetoric and other disciplines that challenge traditional academic discourse also inform my current response.

I now understand that I am using not only what Burke says in writing but also what he does. I am applying his lesson in reading as identification to compare and contrast the motives and consequences of his theory to other theories and practices. Identification is inextricable from his theories of form, stylistic identification, revision, the comic corrective, and the negative, all of which he understands as strategies for coping and equipment for living.[21]

---

21. Walker adds more to assert the centrality of the enthymeme in antiquity and to offer a crucial insight: "In other words, an appeal to the emotion, or any other attempt at proof or persuasion, or any attempt to 'cap' an argumentative passage with a striking declaration, can have no effect (or cannot have the desired effect) unless it functions enthymematically, and it cannot function enthymematically unless it is grounded in 'thymatic,' quasi-syllogistic process of inference and interpretation that makes it seem intelligible, reasonable, and therefore persuasive *at that moment, within the circumstances*, to the rhetor's audience" (*Rhetoric and Poetics in Antiquity* 183). He explains that the "form of the enthymeme is not the enthymeme itself" and that "an enthymeme will generally not be perceivable, memorable, or energetically operative in an audience's consciousness, unless given specific form and so *made present and even memorable* by the rhetor's enthymematic gesture. And that is the crucial insight" (183).

A Burkean Reading of Fish's Tale of Freud's Account of the Wolf-Man

Fish begins various published versions of his essay on the missing portion of Freud's analysis of the Wolf-Man by referring to yet another conference, creating a long paper trail documenting contexts and revisions to support his interpretation. His introductory paragraph arouses desire in his audience by establishing the issues, attitudes, ethos, and actions that will inform his argument and by locating us in the 1958 conference through the present tense:

> I was led to this paper by two moments in the proceedings of the 1958 Style in Language Conference; they are moments in which the topic of persuasion is allowed to surface and then is immediately suppressed. The first such moment coincides with the only substantive mention of Freud at the conference. Roger Brown is discussing the resistance of cognitive psychologists to psychoanalytic procedure in which, it is feared, "anything can mean anything." (Fish, "Psychoanalysis and Rhetoric" 524)

At this point, Fish inserts endnote one. In the back of the book, he cites *Style in Language*, page 385, edited by Thomas A. Sebeok. He then acknowledges the collaboration that underwrites his essay: "Much of what follows was worked out in a series of team-taught classes with Michael Fried" (Fish, "Psychoanalysis and Rhetoric" 591). He admits, "Although it is always difficult to determine who contributed what in such situations," he takes responsibility: "I think it is fair to say anything unpersuasive or insufficiently nuanced is wholly mine" (591n1). He adds that a "very much shorter version of this paper appeared in the *Times Literary Supplement*, August 29, 1986" (591).

Having noted the on-going collaboration and revisions of his work, Fish continues his introduction by describing from his own perspective what happened on two occasions at the conference, one involving Roger Brown and the other I. A. Richards. Fish first interprets Brown's response to the resistance to psychoanalytic procedure as a defense: "one must take into account the fact that its results are often persuasive, and if they are persuasive there must be good reason" (Fish, "Psychoanalysis and Rhetoric 525). He summarizes, again not letting Brown speak for himself:

> The reason, he suspects, is that psychoanalytic *evidence, while not falling obviously into the linear and logical forms with which we are familiar*, must nevertheless be speaking to the criteria by which we

> determine validity, so that at a certain point it must be the case that the accumulation of evidence reaches a level which satisfies those criteria and at that point persuasion occurs. (525–26; my emphasis)

Fish admits that Brown's argument "acknowledges persuasion" but that "it does so by robbing it of any independent force" ("Psychoanalysis and Rhetoric" 525).

Fish has set the stage or rewritten the conference in order to state his claim: "Persuasion ceases to be a scandal if it is the programmed consequence of a mechanical calculation. A persuasion so defined is thoroughly domesticated and ceases to be a threat to the formal projects of linguistics and cognitive psychology" ("Psychoanalysis and Rheotric" 525). For Brown as scientist, persuasion results automatically from the accumulation of evidence that meets a set of criteria; for Fish, persuasion results also if not primarily apart from "mechanical calculation" and "accumulation of evidence." We are set for Fish to demonstrate, using Freud, that persuasion is programmed but calculated consciously and unconsciously not to appear so.

Fish then summarizes, again in his own words, I.A. Richard's remark about rhetoric:

> The second moment at which the conference defends itself against the threat of persuasion occurs at the very end, after the last paper, in a discussion between the participants, a discussion *one finds, if one finds it at all, in exceedingly small print. There, hidden from view lest it infect the entire volume, is a brief consideration of rhetoric.* The topic is introduced by I. A. Richards, who declares that the questions so often debated at the conference, the questions of value and meaning, are finally rhetorical; it is a matter, he says, of the context of discourse and, as Isocrates observes, good discourse is discourse that works. ("Psychoanalysis and Rheotric" 525–26; my emphasis)

At this moment, Fish shifts from his seemingly objective description to a surprisingly bold, present-tense interpretation of the scene: "The response is literally terror" ("Psychoanalysis and Rhetoric" 526). But he steps back to let C. E. Osgood protest, though not directly, "that if the rhetorical view is accepted, then even advertising can be thought of as good discourse, in fact as the best discourse" (526).

He also allows W. K. Wimsatt to add, in part in his own words, "if rhetorical standards have any relevance, it is only with reference to productions like 'the speeches of Hitler during the last war'" (Fish, "Psychoanalysis and Rheotric" 526). Fish then heightens the drama of the scene he has conjured for us with a touch of the comic corrective: "Confronted with the choice of standing either with Hitler or with Wimsatt, Richards does the right thing, and in a supremely rhetorical moment withdraws from the defense of rhetoric. 'Mr. Wimsatt and I,' he says, 'are not in disagreement.'" (526)

Without further ado, Fish exits the scene he constructed to walk center stage into another situation of his own creation. Having already established reader expectations about his purpose, while at the same time withholding it, he delays again moving directly into his argument. But it is clear that he will proceed to find and defend rhetoric everywhere, and he will do so by obviously employing the rhetoric of the logical argument: "the linear and logical forms with which we are familiar" (Fish, "Psychoanalysis and Rheotric" 525). He will also invite readers to identify with him as the man above others who articulates the truth—not rhetoric—and who is in control.

Having identified what was missing or almost missing yet ever present at the 1958 conference—rhetoric—Fish proceeds to examine what he finds missing, contradictory, and incomplete in Freud's *The History of an Infantile Neurosis*—also rhetoric—to convince his readers that Freud's science is a fiction and to explain how the rhetoric of his fiction works. In turn, I will examine what's less obvious in Fish's analysis—enthymematic proof—to persuade readers that Fish's linear and logical rhetoric is in part a camouflage for another method of proof. Since literature and logic are rhetorical for Fish, he pushes the conventions of academic discourse, "with which we are familiar," so that his work avoids being "the programmed consequence of a mechanical calculation" and is persuasive in a somewhat scandalous way that threatens but still sustains the conventions of literary criticism. Fish reads all texts as persuasive literature, but he "draws the line" and privileges poetics and aesthetics over rhetoric.

A Sense of the Beginning as an Ending: There's No Way to Withhold or Tell All

In case we are satisfied that we know where we are going and what we will find, Fish begins another conclusion, again dividing his subject into two parts and keeping his new cast of characters off stage. He remains dead center, reporting what they have said and done, but not for long. He finally lets a character speak for himself: the Wolf-Man does so more dramatically and persuasively than Fish himself does at any point in his essay:

> I have two epigraphs for this essay. The first is from James Strachey's editor's introduction to his translation of Freud's *Complete Introductory Lectures*. Freud, he says was "never rhetorical" and was entirely

opposed to laying down his view in an authoritarian fashion. ("Psychoanalysis and Rheotric" 526)

We already know that Fish disagrees with the editor's first point. Freud's rhetoric is the subject of this essay. We suspect, because of what Fish has already taught us, that Freud's opposition to "laying down his view in an authoritarian fashion" is his resistance to logical argument. We also suspect that Fish's authority results primarily from his logical arguments.

Here Fish inserts his second epigraph, identifying the text to which he refers and giving his readers a brief break before beginning his analytical attack on Freud:

> The second part is a report by the Wolf-Man of what he thought to himself shortly after he met Freud for the first time: "this man is a Jewish swindler, he wants to use me from behind and shit on my head." This paper is dedicated to the proposition that the Wolf-Man got it right. ("Psychoanalysis and Rheotric" 526)

My chapter is dedicated to the same proposition—"that the Wolf-Man got it right"—but not in his comment about Freud. The Wolf-Man got it right in his reported memories and stories about his sister Anna and her influence on him throughout his life.[22] My paper is also dedicated to the proposition that Fish's analytical approach to Freud only appears air-tight ("Everything fits," as Freud exclaims repeatedly in his undoing of Dora). It is also dedicated to the proposition that at this point Fish begins to make a similar move on Freud and begins his undoing of him through penetrating, linear analysis.

---

22. See James L. Kastely's excellent final chapter in *Rethinking the Rhetorical Tradition*," "Rhetoric and Ideology," on Burke's rhetoric of class: "The 'invidious' aspects of class arise from the nature of man not as a 'class animal,' but as a 'classifying animal'" (229). Class is "a formal motive in language," and it is "the natural occurrence for symbol-using creatures" (29). Kastely says that Burke's insight in the following "allows a Burkean analysis a greater flexibility and power than a Marxist analysis":

> Class will be the natural form in which symbol-using animals see their world. If one combines the formal motive to class with the formal motive to hierarchy, oppression becomes a natural occurrence for symbol-using creatures. It is part of our fallenness—injustice need not be understood as a consequence of language itself. (229)

Fish's Terms: Key Terms are Not Always Intended to Open Doors

Fish begins different versions of his essay with the following long opening paragraph in which he locates the key terms of two conferences, *rhetoric* and *open*, to unlock the door to Freud. He first discusses persuasion and then shifts to rhetoric when he has readers in the palm of his hand.

When reading the version in *The Linguistics of Writing: Arguments Between Language and Literature*, the volume of proceedings of the 1986 conference on the same subject, I practiced what I had learned from Fish and turned to the back of the volume in search of "extremely small print," as he had done in the volume of the proceedings from the 1958 Style in Language Conference. There was no small print. I began reading back to front until I found something that caught my eye, something unusual, a question-and-answer format piece featuring Jacques Derrida titled "Some Questions and Responses." I knew right away I had found what I was looking for, or, more accurately, what Burke's rhetoric had taught me to look for and what Fish himself had sought, that which was missing, hidden, implicit, displaced, or silenced.

Chapter 16 begins with a paragraph explaining the conversational, unpolished, and incomplete aspects of the material: It is a "minimally-edited record of responses given by Jacques Derrida, in a necessarily improvisatory fashion, to a number of questions on topics concerning the main area of the Linguistics of Writing Conference and the relation of his [Derrida's] work to it" (qtd. in Derrida, "Some Questions and Answers." 252). The editors note that "Derrida began by pointing out that he could not possibly give full answers to such questions in an hour, and that we would have to give some of his responses the forms of the ellipsis, the aphorism, the thesis without premises or demonstration" (252). In other words, the four editors, including Colin MacCabe, a major character in the drama that follows, had left the work of making connections and smoothing out the elliptical discourse to readers, in keeping with Derrida's request and in keeping with enthymematic proof.

I began reading the questions and answers, still back to front, until I heard Fish speaking (or, rather, read a "record" of Fish speaking) near the end of the exchange. I figured he would still be talking about persuasion and rhetoric and somehow surprise his audience. He begins with a rhetorical move, familiar at conferences. He praises and encompasses in order to blame, correct, and get the upper hand, but he does so with a twist that is, but should not be by this point, unexpected. Like many before him at conferences and other ceremonial events, Fish uses epideictic rhetoric of praise to bury Derrida, along with notions of openness:

> What you've done here today is absolutely remarkable and I'm very grateful for it. You've made one mistake. But in another part of your discourse you corrected that mistake, so I am merely teasing out from your own discourse its final clarification. (qtd. in Derrida, "Some Questions and Answers." (263)

This serves as a prelude to his second key term, a terribly negative one, *open*. Fish aims to dissociate openness from deconstruction and to dissociate open and indeterminate arguments from closed, determinate ones. In Burke's terms, he aims to dissociate rhetoric and persuasion from the "soul of rhetoric," the enthymeme. Instead, he associates persuasion with syllogistic proof. Fish is compelled also to separate notions of openness—of free play and decontextualized language—from both hope and despair:

> It seems to me that what Colin MacCabe was saying is that many hoped that the lessons of deconstruction would lead to (to use a phrase that you've used) an "opening up," and then one can place in the position of what is to be opened up many things—like the study of literature, and things that persons would consider even more significant than the study of literature. I, however, see no *necessary* relationship (there may be a political and institutional relationship, and indeed there has been, demonstrably) between the lesson of deconstruction, if we can speak of them, and any kind of opening whatsoever. (qtd. in Derrida, "Some Questions and Answers." 263)

Fish thus announces the key term of this conference that terrorizes him, *open*. With Burke's guidance, we can connect *open* to the term of terror for others at the style conference, *rhetoric*, and to the body of proof in rhetoric, the enthymeme or identification.

Preferring openness, I turn forward two pages to find MacCabe's comment about how deconstruction, "at least in the Anglo-Saxon context, has been used not to open up the literary curriculum but as a last way of going back and *saving* that literary curriculum" (qtd. in Derrida, "Some Questions and Answers." 261). As Derrida warned, his responses take the "form of the ellipsis, the aphorism, the thesis without premises or demonstration," and he "avoid[s] questions and answers" (252). The form of the enthymeme characterizes the session overall, but it is also the subject of Derrida's reply to MacCabe:

> I totally agree with that. Deconstruction, if such a thing exists, should open up, and I have often insisted on that point. If in a certain phrase of its elaborations it first has the "bad effect" you are describing (but here one would have to be very careful: there are things which are to be saved in the so called "literary curriculum"), *nevertheless I think it's strategically necessary to go back to the library and read in a different way. This is necessary provided that you don't get stuck in this phase. If on the contrary you miss this phase, then you will reproduce the old thing, the old ways of reading, so you have strategically to do many things at the same time.* But I totally agree with your expectation, and your hope. I did my best, especially in France, to insist on this necessity. (261–62; my emphasis)

Here Derrida shifts from "the literary curriculum" to practices of reading and to reading differently. He concludes by agreeing with MacCabe's point about hope, but he continues after Roger Sell asks, "Would you then say that all changes in human thought in the past have been, in some sense or other, covertly, or patently even, deconstructive?" (qtd in Derrida, "Some Questions and Answers." 262):

> Are you referring to changes in kind or changes in degree? Of course, it would be absurd to say everything changes by way of deconstruction. But if there is change this means that there is somewhere a structural logic which makes it possible. This has to do with deconstruction. For instance, if you take a philosophical system or a social structure, it has in itself, I would say, the "principle" of its own opening, dislocation, disintegration. If you read anything—Plato, Descartes, or a social system—you can find somewhere something inadequate which accounts for its own deconstruction. So anything which changes has to do with this possibility in a given system, the possibility of being opened up, dislocated, dissociated, has to do with the principle of internal dissociation. (Just a parenthesis on that point, apostrophizing Stanley Fish, who associated mastery with closure: I would say that mastery often consists in opening, not in closing, that there is a certain amount of mastery in opening the closure, in opening the system, in leaving it open; and this is a strategic ruse of masters, not to close and to show consistently why you cannot close, the system; *to show the principle of dissociation*, the principle of deconstruction, *within* every set, every system, every structure). (262–63; first emphasis mine)

"[T]he inner possibility of deconstruction which is present everywhere" is the possibility of dissociation that Burke develops throughout *Counter-Statement*, most explicitly in discussions of Remy De Gourmont (*CS* 19–28). Here, Derrida replaces mastery and closure, which Fish links, with mastery and opening up. While Fish admits the political and institutional reasons for opening—the canon and more—he ignores the rhetorical reasons for opening that encourages readers to actively participate in meaning-making and meaning-remaking. Burke's first essay "Adepts of 'Pure' Literature" in his first collection leads readers to understand the "dissociative method" as "a companion discovery of symbolism" (*CS* 23). Ellipses move readers to act; they are an example of formal identification that requires writer and reader to collaborate with each other. In the second essay, "Psychology and Form," he explores eloquence and form in the smallest details of style—disclosures, contrasts, restatements with a difference, ellipses, images, aphorisms, volume, sound-values—and in larger formal structures (*CS* 37–38).

Burke extends enthymematic action further, as Aristotle does. He discusses how plot moves readers to connect specific details, disparate parts, and reversals. As we saw in chapter 2, he explains that in *Macbeth* "the turn from the murder scene to the porter scene is a much less literal channel of development," as "the presence of one quality calls forth the demand for another, rather than one tangible incident of plot awaking an interest in some other possible tangible incident of plot" (Burke, *CS* 38–39). He presents the good-night scene in *The Waste Land* as an example of what he later identifies as "qualitative progression" in contrast to "syllogistic progression," but he explains:

> But I simply wish to point out here that this transition is a bold juxtaposition of one quality created by another, an association in ideas which, if not logical, is nevertheless emotionally natural. In the case of *Macbeth*, similarly, it would be absurd to say that the audience, after the murder scene, wants a porter scene. But the audience does want the quality which this porter particularizes. (*CS* 39–40)

While syllogistic and qualitative or enthymematic progressions may be established as differences in kind, Burke presents them also as differences in degree. He and Derrida exploit the possibilities of the abyss *within* any closed set, every system, every structure.[23] Reading enthymematically is a way of reading differently that allows for persuasion and change.

---

23. See Derrida's "Structure, Sign, and Play in the Discourse of the Human Sciences" (1970) for a discussion of the ways that a closed structure also permits freeplay inside its total form.

Fish defends himself against Derrida's apostrophizing of him by asking implicitly, "Don't you agree with me that you were wrong?" I feel surprise if not terror as Fish corrects Derrida for his one mistake in his otherwise remarkable performance and as Fish excuses Derrida because he corrected himself later. Fish admits that he has heard if not learned the lessons Derrida teaches that "opening up" is "always going on" and that mastery does not necessarily entail closure, but his words belie his acts of incorporating and revising Derrida in order to put final closure on openness:

> And here I found in another part of your answer this insight: you said that deconstruction is not an enterprise but in so far as we want to use the word for a moment, a symptom. Opening up, as far as I can tell, is something that's always going on; which is to acknowledge the lesson you just read to me about mastery and closure. Opening up is always what is going on, but despite the hopes that I think I detected in Colin MacCabe's question, opening up is what can never be engineered. (qtd in Derrida, "Some Questions and Responses." 263)

Although Fish hurries on to discuss two kinds of responses to Derrida's kind of discourse, I want to stop briefly to agree with Fish that openness cannot be "engineered," that is, without abuse or violence. In the same way that persuasion is not, as he stated in the opening of his article, "the name of a mechanism that is triggered when a level of statistical probability has been reached" (Fish, "Power, Meaning, and Persuasion" 155), openness cannot be engineered. It has to do with people (writers and readers) agreeing to identify with each other through the margin of overlap in their shared language, knowledge, and experience. The art of rhetoric is not exact because people and situations change in a world of doubt and uncertainty. The *bricoleur*, in contrast to the engineer, is the one who, like Finnegan and other rhetoricians, makes do, using the tools at hand, patching together, aware that structures created are not perfectly air-tight, correct, and invincible but are workable, as long as others are willing to pitch in and do their share.

Meanwhile, Fish proceeds confidently, no longer asking a question or making a comment but taking the floor to make his own point to the broader listening and later reading audiences. He explains that there have been two responses "to the kind of discourse that Jacques Derrida has so eloquently given us" (qtd. in Derrida, "Some Questions and Responses." 263). He names, claims, and explains them:

> One I have called Theory Fear, and you have spoken of it today, that is the fear that if we listen to people like Derrida we will lose

> our hold on rationality, chaos will come again, and we will never be able to say anything because anything could be said and will therefore have no bite. That is wrong for the reasons which you have given. The opposite mistake is what I've called Theory Hope: the hope that we have now in effect learned that the certainties that we enjoy and the knowledge to which we would testify do not have their sources in some independent mechanism, in some Logos; and that, armed with this lesson, we can proceed to perform all kinds of new epistemological feats. I think that also is a mistake. (qtd. in Derrida, "Some Questions and Responses." 264)

Theory fear results from the fear of losing rationality and order forever—that "anything can mean anything" (Fish, "Power, Meaning, and Persuasion" 155)—while theory hope results from the belief that human beings can move beyond irrationality and chaos once and for all. Earlier Fish associates the notion that "anything can mean anything" with rhetoric and persuasion, but here he draws the lines in such a way that he presents people other than himself as having theory fear or theory hope or swinging back and forth endlessly or perhaps "oxymoronically" between the two. Confronted with the choice of standing either with the hopeful or the fearful, Derrida, like Richards before him, does the right thing. He withdraws from his defense of openness and shifts the terms from *theory* to *pathos* and turns Fish's statement back on him:

> Yes, I agree. As you will realize, I'm not optimistic in the way you describe, so the pathos—if there is such a thing—of deconstruction is double. For me too sometimes it's the pathos of "opening up": we'll change things, we'll transform, reform, invent—and sometimes it happens. There is another pathos, and this is exactly the opposite. No, nothing new, no. We'll follow deconstruction, but deconstruction is not something new; on the contrary it's a memory, it's another experience and practice of memory. So, I agree with you on that point. What disturbs me is the reference to consciousness, to deconstruction as essentially a way of transforming our analysis of consciousness. On the contrary, the problem of consciousness is a very local and marginal problem for deconstruction. So why do you insist on consciousness? (Derrida. "Some Questions and Responses." 264)

Fish says "this would get us into a long discussion of notions like intention, which always bring out the worst in everyone" (qtd. in Derrida, "Some Questions and Answers" 264), but he imagines briefly that if there were to be a discussion he would reassert the "inescapability of intention" and protest "against statements, not so much yours but some statements that have occasionally been attributed to Paul de Man, to the effect that meanings are always in excess of intention, etc." (264).

Attridge immediately asks, "Would you like a last comment of any kind?" (qtd. in Derrida, "Some Questions and Responses" 264). Derrida responds with an apology that reinforces what he has been saying: "I'm sorry for not having answered so many questions, both written questions and implied questions in the explicit questions. I just want to thank you for your patience" (264).

In contrast, Fish practices a rhetoric of control. Meanings are not in excess of intention: he knows what he is doing. He does not draw from the range of rhetorics or from the range of theories. He implies that his theories of hope and fear, and perhaps all theories, are reflections of reality, rather than constructions for rhetorical purposes. He suggests they are therefore responded to appropriately as either right or wrong rather than as "means of persuasion" available for critics to choose among in given contexts. His notion of interpretive community has been criticized because it suggests that communities are intact and stable rather than contact zones, to use Pratt's terms, where languages, rules, and identities are up for grabs by people who are trying not to win or lose but to survive.

Whose Rhetoric Is This Anyway? The Wolf-Man Creates His Dreams

In the final paragraph of his introduction, Fish quotes Strachey's translation of the thoughts the Wolf-Man reported he had after his initial encounter with Freud: "this man is a Jewish swindler, he wants to use me from behind and shit on my head" (Power, Meaning, and Persuasion 156). The body of Fish's essay also opens with the Wolf-Man's words, this time with words quoted in Muriel Gardner's edition of *The Wolf-Man by the Wolf-Man* in 1971. Here Fish uses double quotes: "I dreamt that it was night and that I was lying in bed. Suddenly the window opened of its own accord, and I was terrified to see that some white wolves were sitting on the big walnut tree in front of the window." (qtd. by Fish, "Psychoanalysis and Rhetoric" 526)

Fish reports on Freud's explanation that the Wolf-Man "recalled the dream at a 'very early stage in the analysis' but that its interpretation was a task that dragged on over several years 'without notable success'" ("Psychoanalysis and Rhetoric" 526). He says, "the breakthrough, as it is reported, came in an instant and apparently without preparation": "One day the patient began to continue with the interpretation of the dream" because he thought the part about the open window "was not completely explained" (526). The Wolf-Man explained that the window's opening "must mean" that "my eyes suddenly opened" (qtd. by Fish, "Psychoanalysis and Rhetoric" 526). Freud explains that until this time his "charge" had "remained entrenched behind an attitude of obliging apathy" and refused to "take an independent share in the work" (qtd. by Fish, "Psychoanalysis and Rhetoric" 527).

He argues that the Wolf-Man's "It *must* mean" was "not an act of recollection but of construction" (qtd. by Fish, "Psychoanalysis and Rhetoric" 526). Freud trained the Wolf-Man to make this interpretation that he had been seeking. Freud, according to Fish, was saying "'do as you like, it makes no difference to me,'" when what Freud was meaning was "'if you do not do as I like and do it at the time I specify, you will lose the satisfaction of pleasing me to whom I know you are to be attached by the strongest bonds because I forged them'" (527). Fish puts in quotation marks these constructed statements that he attributes to Freud. He concludes confidently, "The coercion could not be more obvious" (527).

Except for these two passages and a few short quotes, the remainder of Fish's article is his interpretation of the rhetoric of Freud's science. The Wolf-Man is silent, and the "talking cure" seems to be taken by Freud and Fish, not the patient. The central actor in Fish's construction is Fish himself, and, as Fish explains, the central figure in the Freudian drama is the psychoanalyst himself. Both subordinate another "original author," the Wolf-Man, and both ignore another "original author," Anna, who is silenced by both.

Throughout Fish's logical argument he reveals Freud's arguments as constructed so that conclusions "will be accepted as the conclusions of an inevitable and independent logic" ("Psychoanalysis and Rhetoric" 536), without admitting that the same holds true for his logical arguments. According to Fish, the psychoanalytic process is a learning process in which the patient learns to do, or not do, as the doctor orders. According to him, the "fallacy of imitative form" is the foundation of psychotherapy. In other words, Freud's science is rhetoric and, more specifically, a rhetoric of training or education if not dominance and coercion. Fish implies that the writing process is different. Writing for Fish does not seem to be a process that teaches readers to read; writing does not teach readers to participate in the creation of meaning with writers and to accept conclusions because they have in part created them.

To support his claim that Freud taught the Wolf-Man how to interpret his history, Fish demonstrates throughout his article that Freud repeats a pattern of saying what his patient didn't know and couldn't say but then, as a result of a "breakthrough" or "cure," can say:

> The pattern is always the same: the claim of independence—for analysis, for the patient's share, for the "materials"—is made in the context of an account that powerfully subverts it, and then it is made again. Each claim is a disclaimer on the part of the analyst of the control he is everywhere exercising; and his effort to deny his effort extends to a denial that he is exerting any influence on himself: "Readers may rest assured that I myself am only reporting what I came upon as an independent experience, uninfluenced by my expectation (p. 158)." ("Psychoanalysis and Rhetoric" 528)

What Freud is really saying, according to Fish, is "Put yourself in my hands because my hands are not mine, but merely the instruments of truth" (528).

By this point, on page 4 of Fish's analysis of Freud's analysis, we are already in Fish's hands, though "not [his], but merely the instruments of truth" (qtd. in Fish, "Psychoanalysis and Rhetoric" 528). Unlike Freud, Fish never acknowledges that he does not have complete control over us and our interpretations, and nowhere in his own account does he admit to the rhetoric of his arguments. He puts his "Cards-face-up-on-the-table" (Burke, *ATH* 260) in the beginning by saying he is looking for rhetoric, but he plays his cards close to his chest from then on. He analyzes the persuasiveness of Freud's texts, without acknowledging the rhetoric of his own and without acknowledging the reader's share.

Fish's rhetoric is not, however, as simple as that.

Fish announces: "the question that arises is one of motive. Why is Freud doing this? Is it simply a matter of desire for personal power?" ("Psychoanalysis and Rhetoric" 529). These are rhetorical questions that call not for an answer but for readers to turn them back on Fish: "What are his motives for doing what he's doing, exposing the rhetoric of Freud's case history through his own rhetoric presented as logical reasoning? Is it simply a matter of a desire for personal power? For control? These are also rhetorical questions that call not for an answer but for readers to turn back on me: "What are my motives for wanting to recognize the rhetorical power of Fish's analytical tale while warning that a rhetoric of control is not the only game in town, though it often seems that way? What are my motives for arguing that all claims and conclusions are partial, temporary, and rhetorical, including my own?

Like Freud, Fish knows where he is heading and knows what he wants to find: he will lead us directly to the surprise, although we should never be surprised by sins of any kind, particularly not of rhetoric, pride, and persuasion. And we should never forget that we are attracted by them. Fish taught that reading lesson years before and keeps trading on it because it is a hard lesson to learn. As Burke says, we are "goaded by the spirit of hierarchy (or moved by the sense of order) and rotten with perfection" (*LASA* 16). We identify with what we understand as power and knowledge that differentiates us from other *animal symbolicum*.

THE TRUTH WILL OUT: OR WILL IT?

As he begins part 2, Fish speaks directly to his readers about Freud's case history:

> Those of you who know the text already may have realized that to this point I have been dealing primarily with the very brief first chapter and the opening paragraph of chapter 2, some five pages out of more than one hundred. And yet, in a sense, most of the work—which is the work of denying that there has been or will be any work—has already been done, for although we have yet to hear a single detail either of the patient's history or of his therapy, we are already so much under Freud's influence that when the details do finally appear, they will fall into the place he has prepared for them. In the following pages Freud will repeatedly urge us, in effect, to take up "our independent share" in the work, but that independence has long since been taken from us. ("Psychoanalysis and Rhetoric" 533)

On page nine, of his twenty-nine-page article, Fish makes his point that Freud has done the work of the article within the first five pages. His readers haven't yet received details about the missing portion—in fact we've been convinced Fish has already told us everything—but Fish's work of exposing the rhetoric of Freud and denying his own rhetoric of control and of collaboration, has also already been accomplished. We are already so much "under his influence" that our responses will mainly be dependent, if not determined. Fish is teaching us by example to read not only Freud but also his own text.

As he rounds out Freud's arguments, he insists that every apparent doubt or questioning by Freud is really an exercise in control. Even though he claims that Freud has such a tight hold on us that readers have no say in the discourse, his own essay is evidence to the contrary, for he revises the scientific account into rhetoric. He breaks Freud's tight hold on truth to claim truth for himself, and he demonstrates his own control of readers, rhetoric, and truth.

The Play's the Thing: Syllogistic and/ or Qualitative Progressions

Fish broadens his scope (without loosening his hold) to place his judgments of Freud in a larger context to include Peter Brooks's reading of the Wolf-Man's account in his *Reading for the Plot: Design and Intention in Narrative*.[24] For a time, Brooks replaces Freud as Fish's foil, father, or fool, but again not before he praises him:

> In Brooks'sreading the Wolf-Man's case is a "radically modernist" text, a "structure of indeterminacy" and "undecidability" which "perilously destabilizes belief in explanatory histories as exhaustive accounts whose authority derives from the force of closure (*Reading for the Plot* 279, 275, 277). Freud's heroism, according to Brooks, consists precisely in resisting closure, in forgoing the satisfaction of crafting a "coherent, finished, enclosed, and authoritative narrative (*Reading for the Plot* 277). (Fish, "Psychoanalysis and Rhetoric" 534)

As if he is neutral on matters of closure, coherence, and authority, Fish says again what he does not mean or mean all together: "This is an attractive thesis, but it has absolutely nothing to do with the text we have been reading" ("Psychoanalysis and Rhetoric" 534). His statement is obviously untrue in that readers already know that matters of closure and control have everything to do with Fish and his reading of Freud.

Although Brooks focuses on plot, he ignores the rhetorical dimensions of plot, even though he refers to Aristotle. As mentioned in chapter 2, Aristotle's discussions of plot in the *Rhetoric* and the *Poetics* are points of overlap between the two texts. From a rhetorical perspective he analyzes how plot affects readers; from the perspective of poetics he discusses parts and kinds of plots. Brooks ignores what Fish identifies as the rhetoric of Freud's science how he controls both the Wolf-Man and his readers. In short, Fish

---

24. For studies of Freud and Burke, see Ellen Quandahl's "'More than Lessons in How to Read': Burke, Freud, and the Resources of Symbolic Transformation" and Marshall W. Alcorn Jr.'s *Narcissism and the Literary Libido: Rhetoric, Text, and Subjectivity*. For discussions of Freud's notions of identification, see Alcorn's *Narcissism*; Rene Girard's *Violence and the Sacred* and Judith *Butler's Gender Trouble: Feminism and the Subversion of Identity*.

disagrees with Brooks's a-rhetorical interpretation. More typical of a poetics rather than a rhetorical approach, Brooks identifies repetition and turns of plot without reading them as means of persuading readers. He does note that readers have to connect repetitions and note their differences, but he doesn't examine the effects of this involvement on their roles or actions as readers.

Instead, Brooks locates Freud's work first as a narrative within the nineteenth-century narrative tradition, in which the "process of telling" questions the narrative mode:

> Like the two great representative novels of European Modernism that I have evoked [Thomas Mann's *The Magic Mountain* and Marcel Proust's *Recherche*], the story of the Wolf Man contains within it the outline of a "standard" nineteenth-century narrative—the story of a coherent individual in society and within history—yet, again like these novels, so complicated and undermined by the process of its telling that the apparent premises of the nineteenth-century narrative mode are put into question. In a manner yet more radical than Mann's or even Proust's—perhaps more nearly approaching Faulkner's—Freud's case history involves a new questioning of how life stories go together, how narrative units combine in significant sequence, where cause and effect are to be sought, and how meaning is related to narration. (268)

Brooks also identifies the Wolf-Man account with the nineteenth-century detective, "which claims that all action is motivated, causally enchained, and eventually comprehensible as such to the perceptive observer" (269). He explains that it is the Wolf Man who in his memoirs "provides the explicit link between Holmes's search for explanation and Freud's" (269), but he adds that Freud "was fully aware of the analogies between psychoanalytic investigation and detective work": "Faced with fragmentary evidence, clues scattered within present reality, he who would explain must reach back to a story in the past which accounts for how the present took on its configuration" (270). This "link" is challenged, however, because in the case of the Wolf-Man "Freud will discover 'detection' and its narrative to be extraordinarily more complex and problematic, like the plots of modernist fiction, and indeed inextricably bound up with the fictional" (270).

Having set up his argument, Brooks states his thesis directly: "I want to consider how the narrativity of the structure of explanation deployed in this nonfictional genre, the case history, necessarily implicates the question of fictions through the very plotting of that narrativity and what this implies about the nature of modernist narrative understanding" (271).

Brooks argues that Freud's exposition cannot be "simple or linear" because his "goal can only be reached through a return to beginnings" and because he "encounters not only a problem in investigation but also a problem of exposition, of writing" (272). Freud "confesses" he must "combine different stories and methods of presentation (p. 13)" (Brooks 272). Brooks notes Freud's frequent statements about problems of exposition and explanation in order to classify and differentiate among them—such as "the limitations encountered in 'forcing a structure which is itself in many dimensions' onto a two-dimensional place (p. 72)" (273), having to "tell, both 'at once' and 'in order,' the story of a person, the story of an illness, the story of an investigation, the story of an explanation" (273), and the dream "from childhood, restaged near the beginning of the analysis but fully elucidated only toward its end" (273–74). He is not, however, interested in what the methods of exposition do to engage readers enthymematically.

Brooks identifies "one of the most daring moments of Freud's thought, and one of his most heroic gestures as a writer":

> He could have achieved a more coherent, finished, enclosed, and authoritative narrative by sticking by his arguments of 1914–1915, never adding the bracketed passages. Or, given his second thoughts of 1918, he could have struck out parts of the earlier argument and substituted for them his later reflections. What is remarkable is that, having discovered his point of origin, that which made sense of the dream, the neurosis, and his own account of them, Freud then felt obliged to retrace the story, offering another and much less evidential (and "eventimential') kind of origin, to tell another version of the plot, superimposed on the other as a kind of palimpsest, a layered text that offers differing versions of the same story. A narrative explanation that doubles back on itself to question that origin and indeed to displace the whole question of origins, to suggest another kind of referentiality, in that all tales may lead back not so much to events as to other tales, to man as a structure of the fictions he tells about himself. (277)

For Brooks, the primary significance of Freud's plot line is that it "perilously destabilizes belief in explanatory histories as exhaustive accounts whose authority derives from the force of closure, from the capacity to say: here is where it began, here is what it became" (277). He does not stop here. He relates the disparate parts to "the problematic relation of the seemingly undirected individual existence to large transindividual orders—orders that might explain, organize, justify, if only one were certain of their status, if only one could reinvest them with the explanatory power of sacred myth"

(279). He does not explore how such orders involve readers in meaning-making and persuasion.

Brooks does explain, however, that the modernist thirst for myth, for explanatory and justificatory master plots, which we find not only in Joyce, Mann, and Faulkner, but also in Yeats, Eliot, Gide, Kafka, Giraudoux and so many others, is suggested in Freud's comment that a person "catches hold of this phylogenetic experience where his own experience fails him. He fills in the gaps in individual truth with prehistoric truth (p. 97)." (280)

Brooks says that the case of the Wolf Man "resembles more the tenuous solutions to uncertain problems presented by *Heart of Darkness* or a number of tales of Jorge Luis Borges. He turns to how a text works, explaining Freud's understanding that "causation can work backward as well as forward" and "chronological sequence may not settle the issue of cause," for "the way a story is ordered does not necessarily correspond to the way it *works*" (Brooks 280). He explains that "narrative order, sequence as a logical enchainment of actions and outcomes, must be considered less a solution than part of the problem of narrative explanation" (280–81). He acknowledges the point that Burke makes about logical and temporal priorities and Poe's philosophy of composition—the poet explains how he composed in hindsight, by retrospective arrangement, to make his text appear logical and seamless:

> Thus, the way a story is ordered does not necessarily correspond to the way it *works*. Indeed, narrative order, sequence as logical enchainment of actions and outcomes, must be considered less a solution that part of the problem of narrative explanation. How we narrate a life—even our own life to ourselves—is at least a double process, the attempt to incorporate within an orderly narrative the more devious, persistent, and powerful plot whose logic is dictated by desire. (280–81)

He also acknowledges that "causality must be thought of in a context of probability, complementarity, and uncertainty" and that the "closure demanded by narrative understanding—the closure without which it can have no coherent plot—is always provisional, as-if, a necessary fiction" (281). These are the terms of Burke's rhetoric, but Brooks does not examine how they affect audiences by engaging them in collaborative meaning-making.

This brief juxtaposition of Freud's reading, Brooks'sreading, and Fish's readings of Freud and Brooks dramatizes the differences and the similarities in their approaches to texts—to history and to fiction. As Fish identifies Freud as the "master rhetorician who hides from others and from himself the true nature of his activities"—"he keeps the secret by publishing it, by discovering at the heart of the patient's fantasy the very conflicts that he himself has been acting out in his relationships with the patient, the analysis, the reader, and his critics" ("Psychoanalysis and Rhetoric" 540)—he describes what all writers do to varying degrees, consciously and unconsciously, to engage readers. Fish also demonstrates how he out masters the master Freud, whom he in part created.

But the "true story" of Fish, like that of Freud, is "the story of domination and submission" (Fish, "Psychoanalysis and Rhetoric" 540), an account of only one kind of persuasion. As Fish reveals the rhetoric of Freud, he "tries to keep the secret by publishing it." He, too, is "driven [in his writing] by the obsessions he uncovers, by the continual need to control, to convince, and to seduce in endless vacillation with the equally powerful need to disclaim any traces of influence and to present himself as the passive conduit of [logical] forces that exist independently of him" (540).

Fish also outdoes Brooks and replaces his explanation that Freud is heroic in delaying and defeating closure by continuing to open up possible readings by constructing, deconstructing, and reconstructing origins. He argues, instead, that Freud "simply cannot help himself" and repeats closure in order "to master again" (540). Fish too repeats closure in each of the sections of his essay, and he has the final say about Freud, Brooks, Brown, Osgood, Wimsatt, I. A. Richards, MacCabe, Derrida, and others. Neither Fish nor Brooks recognizes the value of open or enthymematic arguments.

In Defense of Sisterly Persuasion: A Rewriting of Fish's Tale and Freud's Story

Although Brooks never mentions the Wolf Man's sister in the body of his text, he does in note 2 of chapter 10, "Fictions of the Wolf Man: Freud and Narrative Understanding":

> While it is evident that the Wolf Man remained a compulsive personality who was never entirely free from obsessions and delusions, whose erotic life remained marked by his "sister complex" (determining that his choice of women involve the need to degrade), and who never completely resolved the transference relation to Freud, it also seems clear that he managed to negotiate a reasonable normal existence. (352n2)

This note comes after Brooks "lay[s] out briefly the salient points of personal and general history" (265), a narrative that focuses primarily on the Wolf Man's relationship with Therese, the nurse he met in a sanatorium and later married. He explains how the couple lived a "petit- bourgeois existence" until it was "shattered" by Therese's suicide (266).

Brooks then makes an abrupt shift in his narrative from this personal story of a married man and his wife to a character and subplot that he weaves throughout the chapter. Instead of exploring the suicides of the Wolf-Man's wife and his sister, he replaces the story of the man and wife of little means with one of the aristocratic young man. He focuses on the more dramatic and large-scale cultural destruction, against which the Wolf-Man becomes like others of his class and generation as represented in fiction, rather than the subject and object of psychological and rhetorical study: When he first came to Freud in 1910, the Wolf Man was emblematic of one aspect of European high bourgeois culture in its finest flowering: the morbid narcissism of its most sensitive and artistic soul those debris of capitalist and imperialist grandeur who perhaps in some measure legitimized empire building and public affairs through the implicit equation of their incapacity to participate with sickness. (267)

Brooks links the Wolf Man to "the decadent des Esseintes, hero of Huysman's *A Rebours*" and to a "whole line of valetudinarian heroes reaching back to Villiers de l'Isle-Adam's Axel, who said '"Live? Our servants will do that for us"' (267). He dramatizes the "cast of characters that moves through his years in the German sanatoria—French princesses, Russian counts, merchants from Hamburg, an occasional spinster from Boston," and associates them with characters in Mann's *The Magic Mountain*, a "microcosm of European civilization on the brink of its destruction in the Great War" (267). Within this background, he says, the Wolf Man's "pursuit of Therese has much of the grotesque pathos of Hans Castorp's courtship of Clavdia Chauchat" (267). Theresa, as well as other women in the Wolf Man's life, become fictions.

"A Bit of Sleight of Hand": Preserving Masculine Self-Esteem Against Threats of Passivity, Femininity, and Persuasion

Although Fish discusses persuasion and seduction throughout his article, he confronts the seduction scene directly in part II when he states, "That is the business of chapter 3, 'The Seduction and Its Immediate Consequences'" ("Psychoanalysis and Rhetoric" 535). But the business that interests him is how Freud seduces the Wolf-Man and the reader as he "monitor[s] the flow of information and point[s] to the object that is to be understood" (535). He recognizes that the "seduction in question is (or appears to be) the seduction of the Wolf-Man by his sister; but it is less important as an event than as a component in a structure of explanation that will serve as a model for the explanatory acts that will soon follow. The occasion is a succession of dreams 'concerned with aggressive actions on the boy's part against his sister or against the governess and with energetic reproofs and punishments on account of them" (535–36).

His arguments build to Freud's report that "firm interpretation of these dreams seemed unavailable," but at one point "the explanation came at a single blow, when the patient suddenly called to mind the fact that, when he was still very small, his sister had seduced him into sexual practices (p. 164)" (Fish, "Psychoanalysis and Rhetoric" 536). But the sister's seduction is neither the climax nor the conclusion of Fish's argument. He dismisses Freud's report as "a bit of sleight of hand" because "the patient's recollection is not the explanation" and rather than coming suddenly the "explanation emerges as the result of interpretive work done by Freud but never seen by us" (536). Although the event happens "offstage," Fish explains that "what we are presented with is its result, offered as if it were self-evident and self-generating" (536). The "event" for Fish and Freud is not Anna's act of persuasion but her act interpreted as a threat to masculinity. In this way, Fish identifies Freud with the Wolf-Man in their fears and threats to their "masculine self-esteem":

These dreams, Freud says, "were meant to efface the memory of an event which later on seemed offensive to the patient's masculine self-esteem, and they reached this end by putting an imagery and desirable converse in the place of the historical truth" (p.164).That is to say, the patient's masculine self-esteem was threatened by the fact that his sister, not he, was the aggressor seducer, and this threat is defended against in the dream material by reversing their respective positions. (536)Freud's "apparently arbitrary inversions" are, according to Fish, "a precise and concise direction to both the patient and the reader, providing them with a method for dealing with the material they will soon meet and telling them in advance what will result when that method is applied" (536). In Freud's discussion of this dream material, the sister is recognized then dismissed. Fish analyzes Freud's control over the patient and the patient reader through "precise and concise direction" (536). Analysis and logical arguments silence sisterly and sexual persuasion.

According to Fish, the "real seduction in this chapter (which is accomplished at this moment and in a single blow) is the seduction not of the patient by his sister, but of both the patient and the reader by *Freud, who will now be able to produce interpretive conclusions in the confidence that they will be accepted as the conclusions of an inevitable and independent logic*" ("Psychoanalysis and Rhetoric" 536; my emphasis). Fish displaces Anna's seduction in order to claim Freud's interpretive act as the "real seduction." He follows Freud in "a bit of a sleight of hand" or an act of penetrating logic, equal to if not superior to any which Freud performs. He dispenses with the sister's persuasive powers and the consequences of them on her brother, Freud, and on himself. They defend themselves against the "threat of passivity and femininity" to their "masculine self- esteem." (536).

Fish defends himself, his own masculine self-esteem, by replacing Freud as the central actor in the drama whose role is to present interpretations that others have been prepared for and that will be accepted as "conclusions of an inevitable and independent logic" ("Psychoanalysis and Rhetoric" 536). He defends himself by acting as if his interpretation of Freud's interpretation is real, as if he is Axel "Live? Our servants [our words] will do that for us." But it is not only Freud's or Fish's logic and words that persuade us. They prepare us for conclusions in part by withholding and then supplying us with what we need, so that we make connections and fill in the gaps. They teach us that their interpretations are real and true, the "conclusions of an inevitable and independent logic," and minimize the significance of their readers' work.

A Missing Potion

Near the end of his analysis, Fish supplies the earlier missing portion, the primal scene, that piece of rhetoric, that "scene of persuasion" ("Psychoanalysis and Rhetoric" 547), which appears to him to complete the puzzle he has, in fact, constructed. To do so, he must set aside the other puzzle, constructed by Freud in collaboration with his readers, that makes a place for and thereby creates what's missing and which readers with Freud must supply. According to Fish, "The real story of the case is the story of persuasion, and we will be able to read it only when we tear our eyes away from the supposedly deeper story of the boy who had a dream" (537). Fish asks us to join him in stepping back or focusing off the object of Freud's analysis in order to focus on what Fish's analysis requires.

As his strongest piece of evidence that Freud is "so confident in his authority that he can increase it by (apparently) questioning it" (Fish, "Psychoanalysis and Rhetoric" 538), Fish points out what Freud admits to before he introduces the missing portion, the "scene of violent motion" (538). Freud confesses that he has been wrong and that he is not certain he is now right, but he will continue, aware that he might lose the relationship with his readers that his scientific authority and rightness initially created but which he now hopes his uncertainty will sustain, though with a difference: "'I have now reached the point,' he says, 'at which I must abandon the support I have hitherto had from the course of the analysis. I am afraid it will also be the point at which the reader's belief will abandon me' (pp. 180–81)" (538).

Fish notes that Freud's "tone here is playful as Freud amuses himself by raising as specters two dangers he has already avoided" ("Psychoanalysis and Rhetoric" 538). Fish adds jovially: "Presumably it is because of gestures like this one that Brooks is moved to characterize Freud's text as open and nonauthoritative, but I trust that *my* reader will immediately see this as the gesture of someone who is so confident in his authority that he can increase it by (apparently) questioning it" (538). As Fish explains the two dangers Freud has already avoided, we reflect on the dangers avoided by Fish that allow us to read his gesture as that of someone so confident in *his* authority that he can apparently question it by sharing it with readers now closely aligned with him.

The first danger avoided by Freud (and Fish) is "the danger that might follow were he to abandon the support of the analysis," but, as Fish explains, that danger isn't real since the analysis by Freud (and by Fish) "has been entirely determined by him" ("Psychoanalysis and Rhetoric" 538). If Freud abandons the support of the analysis, he, according to Fish, "merely exchanges one rhetorically established support for another" (538). The same holds true at this point for Fish, as he "exchanges one rhetorically established support for another," shifting from persuading readers to identify with his authority, a rhetoric of logic, to persuading readers to identify with him now as collaborator. He trusts us enough, or, rather, he trusts his own teaching enough by now to allow us to act, not, however, independent of his will but, rather, as the "child of his will, accepting as evidence only what he certifies." We can apply what Fish claims about Freud and his readers to Fish and his readers, including ourselves, even as we make a little room for critique:

> To abandon him at this point would be to abandon the constraints and desires that make us, as readers, what we are. By raising the possibility, Freud only tightens the bonds by which we are attached to him and makes us all the more eager to receive the key revelation at his hands. (539)

Fish subtly shifts here to "I" and to the key revelation at *his* hands, not at Freud's: "I give it to you now: 'What sprang into activity that night out of the chaos of the dreamer's unconscious memory-traces was the picture of copulation between his parents, copulation in circumstances which were not entirely usual and were especially favourable for observation' (p. 181)" (539). Fish continues to explain, to give it to us, as he states how Freud aroused our desires and appetites that require what he offers. Explanatory power is getting readers to "understand" and thereby "become [a] partner in the construction of the story; rhetorical power is moving and encouraging others to move to collaborative meaning-making so that what is co-created persuades both participants:

> The credibility of this revelation is not a function of its probability—we have had many demonstrations of how improbable it is that any such event ever took place—but of its explanatory power. *It satisfies the need Freud has created in us to understand, and by understanding to become his partner in the construction of the story.* As at so many places in the text, what Freud presents here for our judgment is quite literally irresistible; for resistance would require an independence we have already surrendered. In return for that independence we are given the opportunity to nod in agreement—to say, "It *must* mean"—as Freud, newly constructed primal scene in hand, solves every puzzle the case had seemed to order. (539; first emphasis mine)

Fish explains that the "secret content of the patient's behavior, expressed indirectly in his symptoms and fantasies, and brought triumphantly by Freud to the light of day" is the "picture of someone who alternates between passive and aggressive behavior, now assuming the dominant position of the male aggressor, now submitting in feminine fashion to forces that overwhelm him" ("Psychoanalysis and Rhetoric" 539–40). The "drama of its disclosing," however, serves to deflect our attention from a secret deeper still, the secret that has (paradoxically) been on display since the opening paragraphs—the secret that the true story of dominance and submission is the story of Freud's performance here and now, the story of a master rhetorician who hides from others and from himself the true nature of his activities.

Once more Freud contrives to keep the secret by publishing it, by discovering at the heart of the *patient's* fantasy the very conflicts that he himself has been acting out in his relationships with the patient, the analysis, the reader, and his critics. In all these relationships he is driven by the obsessions he uncovers, by the continual need to control, to convince, and to seduce in endless vacillation with the equally powerful need to disclaim any traces of influence and to present himself as the passive conduit of forces that exist independently of him. He simply cannot help himself, and even when his double story is fully told, he has recourse to mechanism that opens it again, not, as Brooks would have it, in order to delay or defeat closure, but in order to *repeat* it, and thereby to be master again. (Fish, "Psychoanalysis and Rhetoric" 540)

What to Do with Secrets Paradoxically on Display?

I, too, cannot help myself and need the help of others to tell the story of dominance and submission that I want to tell, not one of endless vacillation that results from obsessive needs to dominate and control, but one of choosing in specific contexts among means of persuading through mastery and means of persuading through cooperation or, in Fish's words, one of "exchanging one rhetorically established support for another." This too results from obsessive needs to dominate and submit, to maintain my feminine self-esteem and my masculine self-esteem and any other means possibly available to me, in order to persuade others to seek, develop, and assess ways of "getting along" with each other to avoid war and the kill.

It is here in his essay that Fish shifts, as he explains how Freud does, from one rhetorical orientation—persuasion through appeals to logic and authority—to another—persuasion through appeals to shared experiences in co-creating meaning. No less, though less often, than Freud, Fish identifies with his readers and encourages us to identify with him. We align ourselves with Fish to focus on Freud's rhetoric and to focus off Fish's somewhat open and nonauthoritative gesture. Like the Freud he presents to us, Fish is confident enough now in his own authority that he can increase it by apparently sharing it.

Until this point, when Fish includes me as one of *his* readers, unknowingly whether consciously or not, his language has been so forcefully logical that it has made me want to submit and give up my work. But Fish's emotional pursuit of Freud encourages me to keep reading Fish's rhetoric about Freud's rhetoric and about their relationship to each other and to the Wolf-Man.

I find a chapter about an "allegory of persuasion" and a crucial piece of information that was withheld but then passed along, the patient's stool. Instead of surprise, I feel the satisfaction of what I have been seeking or rather have been taught to seek. Anal eroticism is the new topic, along with mental blockages and activity of the bowel that "'like a hysterically affected organ'" begins "'to join in the conversation' (p. 218)" (Fish, "Psychoanalysis and Rhetoric" 541). The missing portion is the stool, and the missing action that interrupted the parents' intercourse is the passing of the stool.

In the middle of this analysis, Fish explains: "We commit no fallacy of imitative form by pointing out what hardly needs pointing out, that Freud enacts precisely what he reports; the position he is in is the squatting position of defecation, and it is he who, at a crucial juncture and to dramatic effect, passes a stool that he has long held back" ("Psychoanalysis and Rhetoric" 542). Not content, Fish adds: "What is even more remarkable is that immediately after engaging in this behavior, Freud produces (almost as another piece of stool) an analysis of it. In anal-erotic behavior, he tells us, a person sacrifices or makes a gift of 'a portion of his own body which he is ready to part with, but only for the sake of someone he loves' (p. 223)" (542–43). Still not satisfied with Freud's words, Fish speaks for himself:

> In other words, one who is fixed in the anal phase experiences pleasure as control, a control he achieves by the calculated withholding and releasing of feces. What the anal erotic seeks is to capture and absorb the other by the stimulation and gratifying of desire; what he seeks, in short, is power, and he gains it at the moment when his excretions become the focus and even the content of the other's attention. However accurate this is as an account of anal eroticism, it is a perfect account of the act of persuasion, which is, I would argue, the primal act for which the anal erotic is only a metaphor. It is persuasion that Freud has been practicing in this case on a massive scale, and the "instinct for mastery" of which persuasion is the expression finds its fulfillment here when the reader accepts from Freud that piece of deferred information that completes the structure of his own understanding.
>
> Once that acceptance has been made, the reader belongs to Freud as much as any lover belongs to the beloved. By giving up a portion of himself Freud is not diminished but enlarged, since what he gets back is the surrender of the reader's will which now becomes an extension of his own. The reader, on his part, receives a moment of pleasure—the pleasure of seeing the pieces of the puzzle finally fitting together—but Freud reserves to himself the much greater pleasure of total mastery. It is a pleasure that is intensely erotic, full of "sexual excitement" (p. 223) that is said to mark the *patient's* passing of a stool; it is a pleasure that is anal, phallic, and even oral, affording the multiple satisfactions of domination, penetration, and engulfment. It is, in a word, the pleasure of persuasion. ("Psychoanalysis and Rhetoric" 543)

While Fish's assertion, that the pleasure of total mastery is the pleasure of persuasion, may be metaphorical or otherwise, it is hyperbolic, as mastery is total only for a time and mastery's "moment" of the pleasures of "domination, penetration, and engulfment" are also and obviously limited. Even the "completion of the structure of understanding" is temporary, partial, and motivated, as is persuasion of all kinds, even enthymematic or that of the "differing sister."

In Burke's rhetoric, the fallacy of imitative form is not simply a fallacy: it is both the recognition of limitations in ourselves and in language and the willingness to cooperate with others in creating meaning through language. We see and do what our terms, attitudes, and actions allow. We can also choose to see around our limited perspectives by learning to revise our terms, cultivate attitudes of acceptance and the comic corrective, and to identify with others by giving up a little or a lot and encouraging others to do so also, with the purpose getting along together. Imitation is not only a form of flattery but also a form of stylistic or formal identification, the act of experiencing how another thinks and writes. It is an attempt to persuade by what is said and done.

Identification, qualitative progression, and enthymematic proof rely on experiential proof, in that writers and readers are convinced by what they in part create. It is not right but rhetorical; it is the method of proof in matters of doubt and uncertainty when people must come to terms in order to act collectively. The terministic screen of Burkean rhetoric transforms, as we have seen, logical proof into enthymematic proof, different in degree rather than in kind. A writer selects logical arguments in particular contexts because they are judged to be probably persuasive, with the attitude that her arguments and conclusions are partial, temporary, and uncertain. And this makes all the difference in identification.

Persuasion through Control and Closure and Persuasion Through Control and Openness

In the next section of his essay, Fish turns to issues of openness and opening up. He refers to Freud's view that "when the child's own experience fails him, he 'fills in the gaps in individual truth with prehistoric truth'" ("Psychoanalysis and Rhetoric" 544). Fish again challenges Brooks'sclaim that Freud is "heroic" in his willingness to "open up what his text would seem to have closed" (544), by saying that such opening is only "the opportunity to perform closure once again, and to perform it in conditions that have the appearance of being particularly difficult" (544): "What Brooks sees as a breaching of Freud's authority is a confident exercise of that authority which now feels its strength to such an extent that it can allow itself to be challenged with impunity"(544)

Such a claim can be assessed but not verified; and neither can the motives and consequences of such claims because, like all claims and conclusions, they are limited. Fish practices and values persuasion through dominance and control, and he advocates response of the critically accepting kind. He also, as we have seen, invites readers at times to respond by collaboratively creating meaning. There is no mechanical way to measure acceptance or collaboration; we always have to "draw lines" in given contexts. There are "alternative accounts of the primal scene's origin, but the question of origin is beside the point once the scene has been made real for both the patient and the reader" ("Psychoanalysis and Rhetoric" 544). As Fish says Freud puts it, "what is important is the 'profound conviction of the reality of these scenes' (p. 195), and once that conviction has been secured, it can tolerate any number of speculations without being shaken" (544).

What seems to be at stake for Fish is the writer's and reader's "profound conviction of the reality," rather than writer's and reader's recognition of the unstable and uncertain grounds for action. He reads his audience correctly, as he enacts a rhetoric of certainty persuasive to those in his interpretive community.

Displaced Agencies and the Drawing of Lines; Or, The Fetishes of Footnotes and the Persuasiveness of Subordination

Fish concludes part 3 of his essay by saying that the primal scene "emerges triumphant as both the end of the story and its self-authenticating origin" but that the "true content of the primal scene is the story of its making," and "[a]t bottom the primal scene is the scene of persuasion" ("Psychoanalysis and Rhetoric" 547). Having just explained that the "investment of work and the yield of that work—certainty, conviction, knowledge—are simply too great to risk losing and comprise a resistance stronger even than the resistance that had to be overcome before they could be accomplished" (546), Fish does not risk losing. He presents his claims as truths to accept, even within this essay on rhetoric.

But Fish is a rhetorician who also knows other means of persuading, and in conclusion he exploits these with equal skill. Having, in fact, persuaded his readers, he knows that we, like Freud's audience, "will be unwilling and indeed unable to undo it" ("Psychoanalysis and Rhetoric" 546). Because he has reinforced the fallacy of imitative form, we know better than to focus on how he has, in fact, undone Freud. Fish claims without reference that it "is the definition of a rhetorical object that it is entirely constructed and stands without external support," but he says "we could just as well say that it becomes reality, that insofar as it has been installed at the center of a structure of conviction it acquires the status of that which goes without saying and that against which nothing can be said" (547). It becomes, in his words, "something *beyond rhetoric*" (547).

The secret we have also learned from him is that what appears to be "beyond rhetoric" is rhetoric. Fish seems to be increasing his persuasiveness by sharing it with readers, not by extending control or relinquishing it. We understand the rhetoric of his own arguments and choose to act on them, or not. Fish begins again by explaining that Freud does not know that the primal scene is a scene of persuasion. If he does know, he compartmentalizes or displaces in order for it not "to paralyze him and render his performance impossible" (Fish, "Psychoanalysis and Rhetoric" 547).

Again, as Fish explains what Freud does, he seems to explain his own motives and methods: "And what does one do with loose ends, with related but peripheral bits of information? Why, one puts them in a footnote, and that is exactly what Freud does in 1923, once again managing to hide in plain sight the truth he cannot confront" ("Psychoanalysis and Rhetoric" 548). Obviously, Fish feels that the issue of openness is not yet closed, or he takes another opportunity to assert his control over loose ends and matters not quite settled.

Paradoxically, he does what he has said Freud does. He continues to exert his control, as in note 11 the final page of his essay:

> To say that the primal scene is always a scene of persuasion is to say that it is a scene of closure; a scene marked by the achievement of a seamless coherence in which an explanation has been found for every detail; an explanation whose authority inheres precisely in its power to be wholly convincing, to secure belief. This is not to say that Freud's text cannot be opened, only that it is not his intention to open it. This is certainly the intention of Derrida, Lacan, Brooks, Lukacher, Hertz, and all the other "oppositional" readers who have recently been so busy. It is their project to interrogate the text from an angle that brings to the surface what its operations necessarily exclude; but the undoubted success of that project says nothing about the Freudian text but, rather, it says only that if one submits the text to an interpretive pressure different from the interpretive pressure that produced it in the first place, it will become a different text. There is no natural bar to such an exercise (no text in and of itself) which can be repeated ad infinitum; but to repeat it is to prove nothing except that it can be done; once it is done in the service of a thesis *about* the text it becomes a form of closure itself. ("Psychoanalysis and Rhetoric" 593n11)

I agree in part: It is an interpretation worth assessing that interpretive pressures create different texts. It is also an interpretation worth assessing that we cannot produce interpretive pressures different from the pressures that produced a work in the first place. It is an interpretation worth assessing that there is no "natural bar to such an exercise (no text in and of itself)" and that it can be repeated ad infinitum.

Another interpretation worth assessing is that interpretations no matter how logical ever prove anything fully, finally, forever, and therefore we don't need to fear repetition ad infinitum or groundlessness, because this is the way of the world of rhetoric. It is an interpretation worth assessing that matters are never opened or closed but that such assertions of metaphors may be useful or not and may nevertheless have far-reaching and long-lasting consequences. It is an interpretation worth considering that interpretations have always had to stand people's test of the pragmatic and the "'collective revelation' of testing and discussion" (Burke, *PLF* 4), even when they have been acclaimed and accepted as true.

Fish continues note 11: "Either Brooks and his party are demonstrating something about language—that it is infinitely capable of being appropriated—or he is asserting that something is true of *this* text. If he is doing the first, I have no quarrel with him, although at this late date, I find the point uninteresting; if he is doing the second, I think that he is just wrong" ("Psychoanalysis and Rhetoric" 593n11). To say, "I find the point uninteresting" stops conversation, even though the point is that language "is infinitely capable of being appropriated." What Fish continues to find interesting is the subject of his final footnote:

> The issue here is whether or not having realized that we are always and already in a situation, we are now in a better position to operate in the situations we occupy Those who answer in the affirmative commit what I call anti-foundationalist theory hope, the mistake of thinking that a general awareness of groundlessness leads one to question and distrust the (interpretive) grounds of one's discourse. This distrust could only be performed if one could move to some other (i.e., noninterpretive) grounds from the vantage point of which distrust could be experienced, but that move is precluded by the anti-foundationalist insight itself. (593n13)

Fish again effectively skews the issue by setting up oppositions and therefore parameters within which he restricts the terms for his purposes. He focuses on "groundlessness" and "distrust" instead of on the uncertainties of rhetoric as the grounds for action. Unlike Burke, Fish does not seek ambivalences, ambiguities, and contradictions as sites of rhetoric.

Fish's rhetoric relies on shared assumptions, knowledge, beliefs, and values to convince readers, but he conceals the collaborative nature of his rhetoric and reveals himself as dominant, independent, and in control. Although he makes every effort to persuade readers to accept what he offers, his arguments are not air-tight: The Wolf-Man's sister remains apart from his analysis because she doesn't fit.

Appealing to Readers through What's Absent and Therefore Inviting

Although Anna is a main character in a chapter of Freud's analysis and central throughout the Wolf-Man's own account, Freud represses the significance of her seductive and long-lasting rhetoric, even as he acknowledges her vitality and force. He explains that the Wolf-Man was not the only child; he had a sister, about two years older, "lively, gifted, precociously naughty, who was also to play an important part of his life" (Freud 159). Later he says that "they" used to say of the Wolf-Man that "he ought to have been the girl and his elder sister the boy (160), but he does not specify his reference or develop this point. He leaves it hanging, noting, instead, that Anna showed her brother a picture of a wolf, standing upright on two legs, which scared him, and she did it to torment him" (161).

Even though Anna showed her brother a drawing of a wolf standing upright, and this is the posture in his famous drawing of his dream with a tree of wolves, Freud identifies the wolf with the Wolf-Man's father, not with Anna and her potent powers. He also identifies the Wolf-Man with his father, even though he acknowledges that both father and son seemed to prefer the sister over the other: "His father," Freud reports, "had an unmistakable preference for his sister, and he (the Wolf-Man) felt very much slighted by this" (163). Freud ignores this preference, what motivates it, and what the likely consequences of it are for the father, mother, son, and daughter.

At one point, Freud breaks off his history to admire the sister: "As a child she was boyish and unmanageable, but she then entered upon a brilliant intellectual development and distinguished herself by her acute and realistic powers of mind" (165). He concludes that the sister's seduction led him to a passive sexual role with her, with his Nanya, and with his father and other men (172). Freud recognizes her persistent influence on the Wolf-Man, but he cannot consider the sister as the origin or explanation of his problems within his scientific study. He cannot credit a young woman's persuasiveness as convincing evidence in his day.

Fish remains silent about sisterly persuasion and about how gender and culture influence Freud's rhetoric and his own. He does not question Freud's understanding of her as a reversal of what Freud hears from her brother. He does not bother himself with such hearsay. Both Freud and Fish seem to understand masculine and feminine as binary terms that reflect biological and cultural realities. They also seem to understand the terms "passive" and "aggressive" as discrete characteristics and to associate them with one gender or the other, particularly in sexual and textual discourse. Despite his arguments to the contrary, Fish chooses the certainty.

The Wolf-Man Speaks Her Name, Seldom to Be Heard

In Muriel Gardiner's translation of "The Memoirs of the Wolf-Man," in *The Wolf-Man by the Wolf-Man: The Double Story of Freud's Most Famous Case*, the Wolf-Man gives a prime place to Anna and her influence over him throughout his life, not only in their youthful "sexual practices" when he was three and she was five. He describes how Anna teased him by saying she would draw a "nice picture of a pretty little girl," but she drew instead a drawing of "a wolf standing on his hind legs with his jaws wide open, about to swallow Little Red Riding Hood" (Gardiner 7). He explains that his rage in connection with the wolf "was not so much my fear of the wolf as my disappointment and anger at Anna for teasing me" (7). He says that "in her early childhood" she "behaved less like a little girl than like a naughty boy" (7), and he reports on a particularly difficult occasion when the governess refused, in opposition to the father, to let Anna go to a party in a boy's costume. Her behavior changed toward him even before they left the first estate when he was five: "[S]he began to play the older sister, teaching the little brother. She taught me, for instance, to tell time, and told me that the earth is actually a sphere" (7). And when their parents left, which was often, he and Anna were companions.

In a particularly telling anecdote, the Wolf-Man says that he and his sister liked to draw and that he "found Anna's way of drawing the little round leaves particularly attractive and interesting." He "soon gave up tree-drawing" because he didn't want to imitate her (Gardiner 9). We know, however, that he returned to tree-drawing and to wolves standing upright when he drew the dream of the tree with five wolves for Freud. This tree has no leaves, no "little round leaves particularly attractive and interesting." The tree is bare except for the figures in white calling to him, as she called him in life and from death. Anna remains alive in his memoirs, even though she committed suicide at twenty-one, when he was nineteen:

We later learned that my sister had taken poison. Following this she had suffered severe pains for two days, but nevertheless she had not told anybody what she had done. Only when the pain had become unbearable did she ask for the doctor. When he arrived, she showed him the little bottle which had contained mercury and which had the warning label of a skull on the outside. . . . Now after attempting suicide she wanted to go on living. (23)

THE MAGIC OF NAMING: ANNA

Nicolas Abraham and Maria Torok are the only critics I found who argue for the importance of the Wolf-Man's relationship with Anna and how he associates her with women throughout his life. They are also the only critics who argue enthymematically, involving reading, or perhaps more accurately incorporating readers into their psychological, linguistic, and poetic creation of meaning. In *The Wolf Man's Magic Word: A Cryptonymy*, they remove Anna from the crypt that is the mind and imagination of the Wolf-Man where he kept her alive in death. They return her through their story of yet another primal scene and through the word "tieret," "reconstructed from a visual image (of the floor scrubber), that is, a masturbatory or sublimated fantasy" (Abraham and Torok 83).

But Abraham and Torok create a scene to explain the scene of the sister's seduction of her brother, for it lacks the necessary explanatory power to persuade readers. They encompass sisterly persuasion within the father's seduction of his daughter, viewed by the son whose primary focus is on the father, even when he acts in response to his sister. They choose the Oedipal relationship once again, adding to the series of such accounts from Fish and Freud. Anna is important for them only in her relationships to men, her father and her brother, and they translate the Wolf-Man's words about his sister into other words in order to find what's secret, alive in death. Once again Anna is not persuasive, despite her long-lasting effect on her brother.

More specifically, Abraham and Torok develop layers on layers of interpretation as if they are carefully removing layers. They depend on reversals, inversions, conversions, and associations rather than on logical arguments. Their approach, a "cryptonymy," reads Freud's and the Wolf-Man's accounts as inventions of the conscious and unconscious mind. They interpret across the various languages of the Wolf-Man's world, Russian, English, and German, and explore the ramifications and individuations of symbols. They seek what is missing and hidden, the "silent word," which they create with readers willing to get along and go along with them.

In chapter 8, "The Wolf Man's Cryptonymy," they explain "psychoanalytic listening" as a "special way of treating language" (Abraham and Torok 79). They define symbols as "data that are missing an as yet undetermined part, but that can, in principle, be determined" through psychoanalytic listening that aims "to find the symbol's complement, recovering it from indeterminacy" (79). "From the beginnings of psychoanalysis to the present," they say, "theoretical efforts have been aimed at finding rules that will permit us to find rules that will permit us to find the unknown missing complement, in other words, the fragment that 'symbolizes with'—or, we might say, that 'co-symbolizes'" (79). Given that a form of speech "resists the search for a co-symbol and defeats every attempt at completion," the "discovery may require breaking the usual rules of listening" (79).

Abraham and Torok challenge the rules of science and the rules of psychoanalysis, as, from a Burkean perspective, they move into the realm of rhetoric where the practices of listening are always motivated, partial, temporary, and contingent, in other words, acts of collaborative meaning-making. They also say that the "idea of symbol implies a symbolizable entity and a basic pre-symbolic unity whose dissolution occasioned the formation of the Unconscious" and explain that, when confronted with the enigma that the patient "carries a jigsaw puzzle whose pieces are as largely unknown as is their mode of assembly," they "join these recovered partial components with their hypothetically missing half, that is, with their co-symbolic complement—which has itself been reconstructed in accordance with known rules" (Abraham and Torok 79). They admit that the "jigsaw puzzle is, of course, only an image and therefore deceptive, but it does reflect reasonably well" their efforts to "retrace the broken symbol's lines of fracture" (80). They call "the twists and turns of this intra-symbolic line the 'walls of the crypt.'" The walls were created from the dialogue between the mother and the nurse: they were meant to continue functioning as lines of fracture indefinitely" (80).

As we saw earlier, Fish gives an extended explanation of Freud's technique of "open concealment" ("Power, Meaning, and Persuasion" 166) and relates it to Freud's explanation of anal-eroticism and associates this with persuasion. We can also relate it to Abraham and Torok's more poetic method of creating.

They ask: "Should we perhaps seek the reason for this privileged form of hiding in rhymes in the Wolf Man's cryptic identification with his older, seductive sister, with the 'beloved poetess' of their father? Or is this characteristic typical of the fetishistic crypt?" (Abraham and Torok 80–81). They explain that their answer is included "in a list of words (about forty) that reproduce the initial traumatic dialogue," and once again we find buried in the appendix, "The Wolf Man's Verbarium," not a simple answer but another puzzle for readers to create, with the following warning:

> For the sake of clarity and orientation in this study (*and certainly not with the intent of providing some additional proof for our claims*), we have drawn up the following repertory of the Wolf Man's words and their respective speeches. We give the list without regard to any linguistic or taxonomic criteria, *lifting it as is directly from notes taken along the way.* (Abraham and Torok; my emphasis)

Fish, as we have seen, also addresses the pleasures of words and persuasion but of another sort: What the anal erotic seeks is the pleasure of control, a control he achieves by the calculated withholding of the feces. What the anal erotic seeks is to capture and absorb the other by the stimulation and gratifying of desire; what he seeks, in short, is power, and he gains it at the moment when his excretions become the focus and even the content of the other's attentions. However accurate this is an account of anal eroticism, it is a perfect account of the act of persuasion, which is, I would argue, the primal act for which the anal-erotic is only a metaphor. The reader, on his part, receives the moment of pleasure—the pleasure of seeing the pieces of the puzzle finally fitting together—but Freud reserves to himself the much greater pleasure of total mastery. (Fish, "Psychoanalysis and Rhetoric" 543)

The pleasure that Fish describes here so graphically suggests to me the pleasure of syllogistic progression, when the writer dominates both the material and the reader and wants to use the reader "from behind and shit on [his] head" ("Psychoanalysis and Rhetoric" 526). It is the pleasure of constructing a supposedly air-tight structure with a logical hold on the reader, a coercive move, which certainly can be persuasive at times but which can also be rejected, always or at times when possible, because it is an act of textual persuasion through force. In Fish's tale the reader's pleasure as recipient is subordinate to the writer's "greater pleasure of total mastery." Such mastery may be called and experienced as persuasion and even love, but it is not the only form of persuasion or love.[6] It is not identification.

Derrida's Interpretation: Translation, Transference, Incorporation, Identification

In the foreword to *The Wolf Man's Magic Word*, in "*Topoi* [*Les Lieux*]," Derrida prepares readers for the "cryptonomy" by defining a crypt not as a "natural place [*lieu*] but as a rhetorical scene, "the striking history of an artifice, *an architecture*, an artifice: of a place comprehended within another but rigorously separate from it, isolated from general space by partitions, an enclosure, an enclave" (Foreword xiv). Topoi is place as well as space defined by what it is not. It is form as action: The "crypt enclave," Derrida says, "produces a cleft in space," in which there is a "safe: sealed, and thus internal to itself, a secret interior within the public square, but, by the same token, outside it, external to the interior" (xiv).

Derrida's attention to form as action does not extend, as it does for Burke, to form as action by writers and readers. Instead, he explains: "What is at stake here is what takes place secretly, or takes a secret place, in order to keep itself *safe* somewhere in a self" (Foreword xiv). What is at stake for whom? Who keeps "itself *safe* somewhere in a self"?

Here Derrida dissociates interpretive actions from people, although he does associate deconstructive actions with himself and with Abraham and Torok and dissociates their actions from more traditional criticism: "Cryptological interpretation" is "not a form of hermeneutics"; "it begins with a reconnaissance of the territory [*lieux*] (Foreword xv). Further, "the crypt itself is built by violence" (xv), and the "break-in technique" of deconstruction includes "locating the crack or the lock, choosing the angle of a partition, and forcing entry" (xv). The violence of forced interpretive entry begins with a crack or lock to be opened. This action mirrors the violence or series of violent acts that created the crypt, the structure of partitions and parts that constructs the space for that which is buried to be kept alive and brought to light through analysis.

These symbolic acts are read as physically forced entries into territories, topoi, spaces, and scenes, but such violence is not enough. Additional scenes must be created to intensify both the forced entry and the incorporation, but such persuasion is still not enough. What we are left with is an enthymeme that functions to engage us not in violence but in the possibility for collaboration:

> The Wolf Man would have had to have incorporated within him, in his Self, his older sister; his sister as seduced by the father and trying to repeat the same scene with her brother. And by the same token, the Wolf Man, the brother, would also have had to have incorporated the father's place, the paternal penis confused with his own. . . . The seduction scene alone is not sufficient. What is needed, still mute, is the contradiction springing from the incorporation itself. It ceaselessly opposes two stiff, incompatible forces, erect against each other: "deadly pleasure" and "two contradictory demands: that the Father's penis should neither *come* [*ne jouisse*] nor

go [*ni ne perisse*]." Without this contradiction within desire, nothing would be comprehensible" (Derrida, Foreword xv)

This scenic, sexual, psychological interpretation results from the conviction, as well as from the assembled evidence, that the sister's seduction of her brother "is not sufficient": it would have to have had more. And paradoxically, what is missing because it is provided by the ceaseless opposition of "two stiff, incompatible forces, erect against each other" is the space of rhetoric, the scene of contradiction within desire.

In Abraham and Torok's "cryptological interpretation" and in Derrida's foreword address far more, I am clearly selecting support for my construction of Burke's theory of reading as an act of identification or rhetorical proof. I am also leaving out what I can't deal with at this point. For example, Derrida examines "the hypothesis of the cryptic cleft" against "a whole theory of the symbol (which had been in the process of elaboration for more than fifteen years)" by the time *The Magic Word* was finished (Foreword xix). He explains in a long passage, with emphasis on the psychological, the self, the conscious, and the unconscious, and without emphasis on the rhetorical, that which is created in uncertainty to make do and persuade:

> The "fractured symbol" marked with "indetermination" by the absence of its other part, of its unconscious "cosymbol," can undergo a supplementary break: no longer the break that affects the original of the presymbolic order and that gives rise to the unconscious, but the break that would "fragment the symbolic raw material" until it constituted a subject particularly resistant to analysis, a subject carrying within him a "puzzle of shards about which we would know nothing: neither how to put it together nor how to recognize most of the pieces." The cryptic fortress protects this analysis resister by provoking the symbolic break. It fractures the symbol into angular pieces, arranges internal (intrasymbolic) partitions, cavities, corridors, niches, zigzag labyrinths, and craggy fortifications. Always "anfractuosities," since they are the effects of breakages: Such are the "partitions of the crypt." Thenceforth the wall to pass through will be not only that of the Unconscious (as is the case with the *single* word-thing or repressed co-symbol) but the angular partition within the Self. That is the "supplementary" hypothesis. It requires (as in the blackness and rarefied air of all crypts the image of a night light, its flame flickering with the slightest draft) that some sort of lucidity light up the inner partition of the splintered symbol. Within the crypt, in the Self, a "lucid, reflecting instance" enlightens the crossing of the divided wall and oversees the disguises,

"each fragment being conscious to itself and unconscious to the 'noncrypt' (what is outside the crypt)"... these are the particularities that govern the intrasymbolic and not socymbolic [i.e., belonging in the Unconscious] relations of the *word*." (xix–xx)

Derrida's deconstructionist analysis and Abraham and Torok's "cryptological interpretation" allow Anna to emerge and play a part, but like Freud and Fish they do not grant her explanatory power. Her seduction of her brother is simply not enough for them.

Readers and Writers: (Dis)Trusting to A Catalogue of Rhetoric

Derrida's description of "cryptonymic translation" suggests attitudes, terms, and actions that Burke associates with rhetorical figures and tropes, qualitative progressions, and identification as proof:

> It is as though the cryptonymic translation, playing with the allosemes and their synonyms (always more numerous in their open series than is indicated by a dictionary), swerves off at an angle *in order to throw the reader off the track and make its itinerary unreadable. An art of chicanery: judicial pettifogging or sophistic ratiocination, but also [chicane = maze] a topographical strategem multiplying simulated barriers, hidden doors, obligatory detours, abrupt changes of direction [sens], all the trials and errors of a game of solitaire meant both to seduce and to discourage, to fascinate, and fatigue.*
>
> It is because of the angular, zigzagging procedure of this cryptonomy, and especially because the allosemic pathways in this strange relay race pass though nonsemantic associations, purely phonetic contamination, it is because these associations in themselves constitute words or parts of words that act like visible and/or audible bodies or things, that *the authors of The Magic Word are hesitant to speak of metonymic displacement here, or even to trust themselves to a catalogue of rhetorical figures.* (Foreword xlii)

Derrida explains that the philosopher/psychoanalysts are reluctant to speak the names of rhetorical figures because they deal with non-semantic as well as semantic associations of words, associations Burke plays with freely, sometimes too freely to stand pragmatic tests. Rhetorical figures, Derrida says, "supposes that each lexical element, whether or not it is repressed (in the strict sense of the word) as (a) thing has an angular, if not crystalline, structure, like a cut gem, and maintains, with it allosemes or other words, contact—a contiguity sometimes semantic, sometimes formal—according to the most economical line or surface." Although he seems to be focusing on forms as structures rather than as actions, he modifies his earlier point: "One of the first consequences of this placement is the recognition of the cryptonymic character of certain meanings that had hitherto been interpreted un-circuitously and inflexibly: for example, the threat of castration. The terms in which that threat is evoked would themselves be but cryptonyms of repressed pleasure words" (Derrida, Foreword xlii). The analyst deconstructs and reconstructs, with little attention, it seems, to the reader's share.

However, as Derrida breaks into question-and-answer format, the writer and reader begin to emerge: "But with what name? No crypt without edification: an edifice, and edifying speech. Take a look at the one he signs, under the title Memoires, with the name the Wolf Man. It consolidates the crypt: to lead the reader astray with the stamp of the final seal. But if the edification of such a safe place implies more than one, always—who signs and with ciphered seal?" (Foreword xliv). The Wolf Man becomes active—

> He had edified a crypt within him: an artifact, an artificial unconscious in the Self, an interior enclave, partitions, hidden passages, zigzags, occult and difficult traffic, two closed doors, and internal labyrinth endlessly echoing, a singular discose crossing so many languages and yet somewhere inside all that noise, a deathly silence, a blackout. He will die with or through the crypt within him. As he saw it, first, as he lives it sell, for he is still alive at the very moment I write this without knowing. (xliv–xlv)

Derrida continues to ask, "But who, he?" and "For him, but who?" (Foreword xlv). He explores the Wolf-Man's naming:

> The Thing (tieret) would perhaps be the Wolf Man's name if there were any such thing here as a name or a proper name. He gave himself no name. *Beneath* the patronymic he received from civil society without being present to the certification of his birth, *beneath* the second name he pretended to adopt from the international psychoanalytic society and with which he signs his memoirs and his will, another cryptonym, he seems to call himself by the name of the Thing (xlv).

Derrida continues to questions, "He, but who?" (xlv).

Possible answers include not only the Wolf-Man but also the authors: "In rushing, at the risk of cutting off, the question 'Who signs here?' I am not asking, that goes without saying, which of the two, but how are they first-named, in their proper and common names(s): Nicolas Abraham and Maria Torok?" (Derrida, Foreword xlviii). The question becomes more complex: "Why try to say—what Nicolas Abraham lived, in his own name, what he saw in a name, in Marika Torok. And in others, among them his friends" (xlviii). The following sentence and the last in the Foreword extend the "who" finally to include the reader: "In you, anonymous reader in this much-sealed case" (xlviii).

My reading of Burke, Fish, Freud, the Wolf-Man, Abraham and Torok, and Anna acknowledges the long-lasting effects of Anna's teasing, nurturing, teaching, drawing, seducing, and killing herself, not only on her brother but also on me. My reading also acknowledges the long-lasting effects on me of her being seduced, incorporated, criticized, ignored, interpreted, and translated, as well as admired and loved by her brother, father, and psychoanalysts. As a rhetorician, I distinguish between sexual seduction and symbolic persuasion as different in kind, and I can understand them as different in degree. The challenge of rhetoric is not only to discover the available means of persuasion but to assess the probable gains and losses of persuasion through violence and persuasion through collaboration, knowing that all acts are uncertain and that all must stand "pragmatic tests."

My reading is not an argument that "Anna" performed any of the actions mentioned above nor that my reading is correct. I have created Anna from contradictory views of her provided by the Wolf-Man's written, reported, and interpreted words and by interpretations of her by Freud, Fish, Brooks, Abraham, Torok, and others. Like other daughters and sisters in fiction, Milly Bloom and Caddy Compson for example, Anna arises from various, often contradictory constructions with which I collaborate. My reading does not replace any scenic explanations but rather proposes a scene in which a woman is listened to and granted persuasive power, a topos to consider for "social reasons."

Reading to Identify: Motives, Acts, and Probable Consequences of Acts of Symbolic Persuasion

From a Burkean perspective, the scenes that Abraham and Torok construct, the father's seduction of his daughter, and her seduction of her brother, must be read alongside other proposed primal scenes to gauge their explanatory power not only as a "programmed consequence of a mechanical determination," as Fish discusses in connection with Roger Brown, not only as an act of forced entry and violent rupture, as Derrida suggests, not only as socially constructed by interpretive communities of readers, but also as collaborative acts of meaning-making by people who are divided and different from each other and therefore seek identification. From this array of interpretations, the rhetorician selects, not because one is true and the others not, since they are all rhetoric, but, rather, because one is judged most likely useful in a particular context for specific people and purposes. Instead of a linear replacement model of research, the rhetorician seeks "perspective by incongruity" and a range of rhetorical options to choose among. For Burke, identification is the motive, scene, and act of getting along to avoid war.

ANOTHER MISSING POTION AND A POETICS OF PERSUASION

Many questions remain. I want to turn to only one: What is the missing potion (to use Plato's term for rhetoric in the *Pharmakon*) in Fish's analysis? I want to focus here on form, rather than on information, as that which arouses and fulfills desires and appetites. When Fish revised his article from the linguistics conference for publication in *Doing What Comes Naturally*, he expanded part IV, his conclusion. What does he do here that he has not done before?

Fish says that both Freud and his patient are "caught up in the dialectic of independence and control" ("Psychoanalysis and Rhetoric" 548). The Wolf-Man remains forever "in the feminine position of submission," represented in Freud's and Fish's analyses and in the female Egyptian figure he gave to Freud (549). Is he ever able to do what he and Freud want him to do, to go his own way, independent of his fathers?

Fish explains that "it is the Wolf-Man who, by failing to go his own way, succeeds in becoming the perfect rhetorical artifact, a wholly made object" (Psychoanalysis and Rhetoric 549–50). For Fish, the Wolf-Man is a piece of language, a textually produced entity (550). And for Fish, rhetoric is the artifact not the act of creating the artifact. He approaches language from the perspective of poetics, as "thing-made," rather than from the perspective of rhetoric, "thing-making." He also implies that if the Wolf-Man could have walked away from his female submissiveness to Freud, he would not have been paralyzed by ambivalence, and that Freud, if he could have walked away from his feminine submissiveness, would not have been paralyzed by ambivalences. But in the final paragraph of his essay, Fish himself slips into a rhetoric of ambivalence and out of his rhetoric of control. He explains that he has spoken "as if that mastery (of Freud) was absolute," as if the often-repeated claims to be "the register of forces external to him were nothing more than feints, pieces of strategy" (553). He adds that "they are surely that, but they are more; they are expressions of ambivalence in Freud that mirrors the ambivalence he finds in his patient: he wants at the same time to be masculine and feminine and to be at once the generating source of truth and to have the truth impressed upon him by a power whose force he cannot resist" (553).

What is intriguing here is Fish's uncharacteristic ambivalence and his more explicit recognition of the persuasiveness of the uncertain and indeterminate. He concludes his essay by asking questions about Freud, opening up the conclusions he has already reached, and in so doing he invites readers to ask the same questions about him and about ourselves:

> Is this the face of confident masculine self-assertion beneath which lies the reality of a nature more retiring and female? Or is the feminine claim of inferiority a mask—a bold- faced pretense of being not bold—for the aggression it barely conceals? Which is the rhetorical posture and which the stance of "Freud" himself? Neither psychoanalysts nor rhetoric will permit an answer or even ask this question, and we are left, like the analyst and his patient, in the oxymoronic state of constant wavering. (Fish, Psychoanalysis and Rhetoric 554)

This is an example of Theory Despair, another version of Fish's Theory Hope and Theory Fear, both of which were named in his question (correction, comment, and answer) for Derrida after the linguistics conference and in the published proceedings where Fish also pronounces: *"One who has learned the lesson of rhetoricity does not thereby escape the condition it names"* ("Power, Meaning, and Persuasion" 171). Fish says that Freud "can only know what he knows within the rhetoric that possesses him and he cannot be criticized for clinging to knowledge even when he himself could demonstrate that it is without extra-discursive foundation" (171).

Burke teaches us that we are all limited by our terministic screens, our language, our bodies, and our hierachical, rotten-with-perfection tendencies. He also teaches us that we can, however, learn to see beyond the limitations of our words, attitudes, identities, and situations by revising our terms, adopting the comic corrective, and identifying with others. According to Burke, we live in a rhetorical world of uncertainty, incompleteness, imperfection, ambivalence, and ambiguity. This is a condition to cultivate, study, and exploit, in order to develop the resources of rhetoric to help us get along with each other:

> A perfectionist might seek to evolve terms free of ambiguity and inconsistency (as with the terministic ideals of symbolic logic and logical positivism). But we have a different purpose in view, one that probably retains traces of its "comic" origin. We take it for

granted that insofar as men cannot themselves create the universe, there must remain something essentially enigmatic about the problem of motives, and that this underlying enigma will manifest itself in inevitable ambiguities and inconsistencies among the terms for motives. Accordingly, what we want is *not terms that avoid ambiguity, but terms that clearly reveal the strategic spots at which ambiguities necessarily arise.* (Burke, *GM* xviii)

He continues to explain that ambiguity is the context for rhetoric and change:

> Hence, instead of considering it our task to "dispose of" any ambiguity by merely disclosing the fact that it is an ambiguity, we rather consider it our task to study and clarify the *resources* of ambiguity. For in the course of this work, we shall deal with many kinds of *transformation*—and it is in the areas of ambiguity that transformations take place; in fact, without such areas, transformation would be impossible. (*GM* xviii)

Burke's motive is practical, not utopic, although he recognizes the possibilities of connection and transformation in difference and division, if we are willing and able to accept limitations in us and in language. Reading enthymematically teaches us to act collaboratively with writers in response to what we find missing, silenced, implicit, incomplete, and ambiguous. Reading to identify educates us to live in uncertainty with others.

PART III
A LESSON IN WRITING: ATTITUDES AND ACTIONS FOR WRITING AND REWRITING

4 Burke's Writing Theories and Practices: "Human Life as a Project in 'Composition'"

"Action" by all means. But in a complex world, there are many kinds of action. Action requires programs—programs require vocabulary. *To act wisely, in concert, we must use many words.* If we use the wrong words, words that divide up the field inadequately, we obey false cues. *We must name the friendly or unfriendly functions and relationships in such a way that we are able to do something about them.* In naming them, we form our characters, since the names embody attitudes; and *implicit in the attitudes there are the cues of behavior.* If your naming is of such a sort, for instance, that you place your hope of salvation in a church, even a corrupt church, and if that church is on the side of great wealth in social issues, your very character is enlisted in the cause of wealth. You personally may never be called upon to "act," in the brute sense of the word. You may act, a generation later, in the names and attitudes you bequeath to your children. Hence, it is an act for you to attempt changing your attitudes, or the attitudes of others. (Burke, *ATH* 4; my emphasis)

One confronts contradictions. Insofar as they are resolvable contradictions, he acts to resolve them. Insofar as they are not resolvable, he symbolically erects "higher synthesis," in poetic and conceptual imagery, that helps him to "accept" them. Thus, Thomism defined certain important contradictions of ownership as unresolvable, and erected a series of transcendental bridges, poetic and critical fictions, for producing a synthesis atop the antithesis by the organizing of a unifying attitude (backed by logic, ritual, and economic patterns).... *Each frame enrolls for "action" in accordance with its particular way of drawing the lines.* (Burke, *ATH* 92; my emphasis)

If people persist longer than chickens in faulty orientation despite punishment, it is because the greater complexity of their problems, the vast network of mutually sustained values and judgments, makes it more difficult for them to perceive the nature of the reorientation required, and to select their means accordingly. They are the victims of a trained incapacity, since the very authority of their earlier ways interferes with the adoption of new ones. (Burke, *PC* 23)

A Motive for Writing: To Act Wisely, in Concert

In *Attitudes Toward History*, Burke says the Symbolic "should enable us to see our own lives as a kind of rough first draft that lends itself at least somewhat to revision (*GM* 442) announces the "basic view of life as an education: We learn by suffering" (*ATH* 415). Throughout his rhetoric, writing is the act of identification that can equip us for living with others. His definition of people as *animal symbolicum* and his definition of language as constructive, nonreferential, hierarchical, and incomplete both motivate us to learn to get along. We can learn to regard ourselves and each other "not as *vicious*, but as *mistaken*" (*ATH* 41) and to recognize that if "people persist longer than chickens in faulty orientation despite punishment," it is because they are "victims of trained incapacity (*PC* 23). We can learn to act as agents who make choices about how we use language, recognizing our choices as constrained and the consequences as uncertain. We can learn to read motives and situations critically, develop strategies that encourage identification, assess probable consequences of our symbolic actions, select wisely among available options, and act in the face of uncertainty, all for the purposes of identification with each other. If we define and desire writing as action, we need a program and a vocabulary; and if the action we seek is identification, we need to cultivate attitudes of acceptance, uncertainty, and the comic corrective.

We can also choose to do otherwise. In this chapter, I draw primarily on *Permanence and Change*, *Attitudes Toward History*, and *The Philosophy of Literary Form* to develop Burke's lesson on writing as identification and to demonstrate how he teaches through what he says and what he does in writing to engage his readers in symbolic action. I develop a program and vocabulary for teaching writing as identification, aware that programs become programmatic and vocabularies become rigid without ongoing revision and an attitude of the comic corrective. This is not the complete nor the only lesson in writing that Burke teaches; it is a lesson for life, not only for the classroom.²⁵ And it is also my construction, motivated by my desire to advocate a rhetoric of identification for today.

I first consider Burke's motives for writing and his attitudes toward writing and toward education in general and teaching writing in particular. I then examine the contexts for attitudes and motives that inform a lesson in writing as acts of identification. I focus next on agents of identification, writers and readers, who must be willing to undergo change in our identities and situations in order to come to terms with each other. Changes in identity entail loss to varying degrees and kinds; they also involve the possibility of a rebirth. I then turn to how Burke arouses expectations that encourage readers to participate through titles, opening lines, and other methods for setting the stage, adjusting identities, and cueing readers to play their parts. I explore his "Dictionary of Pivotal Terms" to argue how he selects, defines, and uses terms to teach us to revise our identities, our language, and our situations in order to identify with others and encourage them to identify with us.

Throughout, I consider how Burke writes to invite readers to collaborate with him and how he teaches us to assess the differences in motives and probable consequences of logical and enthymematic persuasion in the realm

---

25. My earliest lessons in Burke were taught by W. Ross Winterowd in person and in *The Contemporary Writer* and by Richard M. Coe in *Form and Substance: An Advanced Rhetoric*, both of whom related rhetoric and writing to living, in the classroom and beyond. Throughout this chapter and the next, I argue for teaching and practicing Burke's lessons in writing as identification and as equipment for living, not to the exclusion of other definitions of writing and not without critique. Within a school setting, I argue that teaching the academic essay, variously defined and widely taught in composition courses, can be taught more effectively by contrasting its various forms and by contrasting it with other modes of discourse that have recently been excluded from college writing courses, expressivist and current-traditional rhetorics, multi-genre and multi-voiced essays, and writing for public audiences. In short, I argue for teaching and practicing the (1) analysis of attitudes, motives, and purposes in ourselves and others; (2) the reading of situations; (3) the development, practice, and assessment of the probable consequences of many strategies and kinds of writing in specific contexts; (4) the development of critical judgment to make wise choices among the available options; and (5) acting in uncertainty about the consequences of symbolic actions.

See Sharon Crowley's *Composition in the University: Historical and Polemical Essays* for a critique of teaching writing in required composition courses. From my perspective, she associates rhetoric only with political rhetoric, so that when rhetoric is not political in the way she defines, rhetoric disappears. She also locates problems with teaching composition and the academic essay in particular in the "universal requirement."

of rhetoric. As we read Burke, we learn "to act wisely, in concert" with him and how to apply his lesson of identification in other contexts.

Motives and Attitudes for Writing to Identify and Create Meaning Collaboratively

Burke's analogies between writing and living and his life-long endeavor to develop the resources of rhetoric to avoid war threaten the very core of contemporary notions of the self, even postmodernist conceptions, and the foundations that define local and global relationships—power, domination, self-interest, and corporate interest. His interpretations also undermine certainty as the force of persuasion and cultivate uncertainty and collaboration as the heart of *animal symbolicum*. The analogies present writing as action consequential in the world that, like other actions, must be motivated and learned through practice, with guidance, response, and ongoing revision. Learning to write is a life-long process, as we learn to adapt what works in one context to new situations. Writing is always a gamble, a guessing game, a judgment call: we can never be sure that what we do will work to engage readers, but we can learn to make sound judgments.

Inconsistencies, contradictions, and limitations characterize Burke's rhetoric, as I interpret it, but he is consistent in practicing what he advocates, identification as his primary method of proof and revisions in language, identities, and situations in order to *do something* about life as endless violence, oppression, suicide, and war. Burke summarizes his rhetoric of identification in various ways but always with the following attitude:

> The progress of humane enlightenment can go no further than in picturing people, not as *vicious*, but as *mistaken*. When you add that people are *necessarily* mistaken, that *all* people are exposed to situations in which they must act as fools, that *every* insight contains its own special kind of blindness, you complete the comic circle, returning again to the lesson of humility that underlies great tragedy. (*ATH* 41)

Reading and writing educate us to identify with others by revising our identities and terms and to gain perspective by incongruity by seeing "from two angles at once." By doing so, we can learn to "see around the corners of our orientations." We also learn "the lesson of humility that underlies great tragedy." (*ATH* 41)

I add the last sentence above, taken from the first quotation above, on September 11, 2001. Having tried earlier today to continue work on chapter 5, an application of Burke's lesson in writing as identification to James A. Berlin's lesson in writing as ideological action, I now return to this chapter with the television still on across the room but with the sound turned off, so that I can hear the radio beside me. I had thought this chapter was as finished as I could make it, but as I reread Burke's case for enlightenment above, I knew I had to place my writing in the context of today's events, as far as I know them. I do so in part because Burke's lesson in writing as identification seems even more critical today, in a world that too often and too quickly rushes to judgment and relies on nonverbal violence. I do so more personally to cope with the destruction and responses to it mediated before me by acknowledging human life as a project in composition that no one controls completely but that we can attempt to revise. I want to remember that we can "act wisely, in concert." I watch firefighters, police, and emergency workers acting together to save the lives of others without distinguishing among them and without worrying first for their own safety. I see a city and a nation gathering together, although I fear scapegoating and the consequences that follow for both victims and victors. How will we as individuals, as countries, as cultures choose to act? What choices do we have? What choices can we imagine?

Later: I began revising this chapter without erasing the disjunctions between what I wrote before and what I wrote after the devastation in New York, Washington, D.C., and Pennsylvania. I have also inserted italicized sections throughout, written when I couldn't keep writing, overwhelmed by images, thoughts, and feelings. Through juxtaposition, I hope to create perspective by incongruity and dramatize the deep and wide complexities, simplicities, and possibilities of identification to life with ongoing revisions.

There is a loud cry today, to which identification in reading, writing, and living responds.

ACTION/MOTION: EDUCATION/TRAINING: BURKE'S RHETORICAL APPROACH TO EDUCATION

In his works of the 1930s and 1940s, Burke develops a rhetorical approach to education in general and to reading and writing in particular. He promotes an attitude of uncertainty as a firm basis for revisionary and collaborative actions.[26] Despite repeated warnings that what works in one context

---

26. In his introduction to John Dewey's *The Quest for Certainty*, Stephen Toulmin argues that the ten lectures "show how different John Dewey's philosophical methods and arguments were from those of William James or Charles Sanders Peirce, and so how misleading it can be to lump them all together, as the single school of

will not necessarily work in another, he articulates his ideal for education in 1937 in *Attitudes Toward History*: "How adapt man to the needs of worldwide empire progressively made necessary by the conditions of technology?" (Burke, *ATH* 356).

'pragmatists.'" His aim is to put "John Dewey's arguments alongside those of his younger contemporaries, Ludwig Wittgenstein and Martin Heidegger" to see "just how deeply his critique of traditional epistemology was capable of cutting" but how it "offered also, in outline, a positive view about 'the relation of knowledge and action'" (ix). For studies of Burke's and philosophy, see Timothy W. Crucius's *Kenneth Burke and the Conversation after Philosophy*; Samuel B. Southwell's *Kenneth Burke and Martin Heidegger: With a Note Against Deconstruction*; and Steven Mailloux's *Reception Histories: Rhetoric, Pragmatism, and American Cultural Politics*.

For a discussion of Burke, Dewey, Richard Rorty, and pragmatist philosophy, see Frank Lentricchia's *Criticism and Social Change*, pages 1–20. In his summary of Rorty, Lentricchia criticizes not only pragmatism but the "metaphor of conversation," with which Lentriccia explains he is also "in sympathy" because of the "effort to set the classical tradition in philosophy aside, to change the subject, as he puts it" (Lentricchia, *Criticism and Social* Change 15). If Lentricchia weren't using Burke as his model of an academic intellectual, we might read the following also as a critique of Burke's "liberal idea of society" in his anecdote about the unending conversation in the parlor:

> Despite the fact that he comes squarely down on the side of history, against all versions of a "beyond," the problem, here, as before, with the fathers of American pragmatism, is that there is only a rarefied, liberal idea of society or history at work in Rorty's position. The choices for him are stark: either his version of a multi-voiced, uncoordinated cultural conversation or a repressive "reality" that demands a single discourse and a single voice. The missing term in Rorty's analysis is "society," and I suspect that this very absence accounts more than a little for the warm reception his neo-pragmatism has won in post-structuralist circles.

If we put "society" back into Rorty's analysis, we will quickly see that the conversation is not and has never been as free as he might wish; that the conversation of culture has been involved as a moving force in the inauguration, maintenance, and perpetuation of society; that the conversation of culture, in other words, displays some stubbornly persistent patterns. Cultural action is a shaping power, but it is not original: it is underwritten by something else. You cannot jump into this conversation and do what you please. It is hard to get into; harder still to speak on your own once you do get in; tougher yet to move the conversation in any particular direction that you might desire. For this conversation has been propelled and constrained mainly by collective voices, sociohistorical subjects, not by private ones, not by "autonomous" intellectuals. (16)

For me, as I argued in chapter 1, the missing term in Lentricchia's ideological analysis and in his construction of Burke as an ideological critic is "rhetoric."

This ideal remains crucial today as technology and communication have expanded dramatically to create global rhetorics, economics, politics, and other ways of getting along and not getting along. The challenges of communication across different languages and cultures with traditional and innovative technologies require new and revised theories of education and methods of teaching reading and writing. Burke's rhetorical approach to education was a counterstatement to other educational methods and philosophies of the 1930s. During WWI and the depression, he argues against efficient and mechanistic education that "trains" people, and he argues against stimulus and response approaches that guarantee "trained incapacity" (Burke, *PC* 7).

Because all work results in "occupational psychoses," a phrase Burke borrows from Dewey, and in "trained incapacity," which he borrows from Veblen, Burke advocates that we adopt the comic corrective and other revision strategies to see beyond the limitations of our own perspectives and to counteract tendencies in ourselves and in language to end-of-the-line thinking and acting. Through his borrowings from Dewey, Veblen, and others, he demonstrates that writing and reading are usefully understood as acts of collaboration, revision, and translation.

As Burke says in one of the passages that opens this chapter, when there are conflicts, we try to resolve them; when we cannot, we try to transcend them, in order to deal with them effectively. Writing as identification assumes that because people, purposes, and places change, writing is best understood as rewriting. Through rewriting ourselves, situations, and texts we may identify with others and encourage them to identify with us. We may practice "good writing," incorporating conventions established by communities and cultural contexts, but we must also revise our practices in order to make our "writing good for" specific situations.

We too often limit the teaching of writing in universities to academic discourse defined in a certain way, even though we know that writing changes across the curriculum and changes more dramatically outside the university. We often teach students to compartmentalize and leave behind their personal lives and their fuller intellectual and writing lives. This is not necessarily the case in individual writing classrooms, where teachers and students must communicate in a give-and-take. We also often teach through repetition, by assigning the same kind of writing again and again, as if other forms or genres would be too much for students to handle. We know we don't learn words, sentences, or genres in isolation; we learn by doing, with guidance and response from others, evaluating and revising to communicate and create meaning with others. We also learn by contrasting rhetorics.

On 9/11, on our Comp/GAT Listserv, I read instructors asking for and giving help to each about what to do in class on and after September 11. World events and personal lives entered every classroom of twenty to twenty-five students. I hope some learned new possibilities for academic writing. Some used personal, creative, expressionist writing, and others combined any forms available to them. Life crashed into academic writing, and writing became life-giving—private, academic, public, and more. We can also teach writing to identify with others, those within universities and out, with public and familiar audiences, for any reason whatsoever.

How? We can appear more directly, professionally, and personally in our talking, teaching, and texts, acknowledging our attitudes, motives, terministic screens, and our calculations of probable consequences. We can engage directly with students and readers by recognizing our limitations and seeking help from others. We can develop attitudes of listening and learning rather than knowing for sure. We can use indirection and roundabout routes, narratives, anecdotes, and the comic corrective. And we can rely on the other's prior and immediate experiences in collaborative meaning-making, so that they are convinced by their mutual constructions, as we do in daily life. We can do all of this or some of this, or more. We just have to figure out what to do when, where, how, why, and for whom.

We learn today that life is a project in composition.

Burke argues that we must educate rather than train people to write to identify, because identification is an action, not a motion. Like all actions, identification requires choice and judgment in specific situations, and with action comes ethics. Rhetorical education teaches us to choose wisely; training indoctrinates and can be useful and efficient for various purposes and contexts. Training works efficiently for specific kinds of learning and contexts because it prevents "provisional hesitation," the characteristic Jameson found in all of Burke's criticism that disqualifies him as an ideological critic. It is, however, this *provisional* hesitation that distinguishes between action and motion and *equips* us for living. The advantage of training is efficiency, while the disadvantage is rigidity and automatic motion rather than action. The advantage of education is the ability to act in various contexts, based on assessments of purposes, audiences, and situations; the disadvantage of education is the risk of thinking too much before acting.

Burke's Barnyard Approach to Education: "Chickens Not So Well Educated Would Have Acted More Wisely"

In chapter 1 of *Permanence and Change*, Burke illustrates his broad claim that all living things are critics by resorting to one of our animal counterparts: A trout, "having snatched at a hook but having had the good luck to escape with a rip in his jaw, may even show by his wiliness thereafter that he can revise his critical appraisals" (5).

While all living things are critics, they have different critical capacities. Burke makes a point that he maintains throughout as a correction to our tendency to become rotten with perfection and rigid in our thoroughness. The advantage of the trout's interpretative system is that "he has a more educated way of reading the signs," because "it is not so complex and thorough that it interferes with revision." He adds, "I do not mean to imply that the sullen fish has thought all this out. I mean simply that in his altered response, for a greater or lesser period following the hook-episode, he manifests the changed behavior that goes with a new meaning" (*PC* 5).

We have interpretive advantages over trout that result in part from characteristics in language and in ourselves; we also have disadvantages that result from the same source:

> Our great advantage over this sophisticated trout would seem to be that we can greatly extend the scope of the critical process. Man can be methodical in his attempts to decide what the difference between bait and food might be. Unfortunately, as Thorstein Veblen has pointed out, invention is the mother of necessity: the very power of criticism has enabled man to build up cultural structures so complex that still greater powers of criticism are needed before he can distinguish between the food-processes and bait-processes concealed beneath his cultural tangles. His greater capacity has increased not only the range of his solutions, but also the range of his problems. Orientation can go wrong. (Burke, *PC* 5–6)

Although Burke had not written his "Definition of Man" in 1935, we can see retrospectively that he begins to develop his definition of *animal symbolicum*: Remembering our animal identity teaches humility and the recognition that our assets as bodies using language are modified by our being rotten with perfection. As he reminds himself and readers often, "No, we are here being too thorough" (Burke, *PLF* 157) and "an over-exactitude of schematization, maintained throughout, would have wearied writer and reader both." (Burke, *ATH* 294).

As part of his comic corrective to everyone's tendencies toward end-of-the-line thinking and action, Burke uses the trout as evidence that all organisms interpret signs and that some even revise themselves based on the circumstances. The "sophisticated trout" changes his response "for a greater or lesser period following the hook-episode," "he manifests the changed behavior that goes with a new meaning," and he has "a more educated way of reading the signs" (Burke, *PC* 5).

Having established his serious yet comic context for education, Burke develops his definition of people as the only animals who can criticize criticism. Criticism, according to Burke, includes reflection and re-interpretation:

> Though all organisms are critics in the sense that they interpret the signs about them, the experimental, speculative technique made available by speech would seem to single out the human species as the only one possessing an equipment for going beyond the criticism of experience to the criticism of criticism. We not only interpret the character of events (manifesting in our responses all the gradations of fear, apprehension, misgiving, expectation, assurance for which there are rough behavioristic counterparts in animals)—we may also interpret our interpretations. (*PC* 6).

We can hesitate, experiment, and speculate. Burke continues to lead us comically and circuitously through his barnyard approach.[27] He moves from trout to Pavlov's dog to illustrate how animals interpret the meaning of sounds and how this meaning, in turn, affects them biologically and behaviorally. Chickens, he later reports, have been educated to respond to a specific pitch as a "food-signal" and ignore other pitches (*PC* 6). But education is not as simple as that, even for chickens or for critics. Correct interpretations are not automatic, and training that teaches people to respond only one way to a stimulus limits future and effective response in different conditions:

> But people never tremble enough at the thought of how flimsy such interpreting of characters is. If one rings the bell next time, not to feed the chickens, but to assemble them for chopping off their

---

27. Twenty years later in the "Prologue," he explains:
> "From the standpoint of these considerations, the book's references to animal experiments and the like are to be interpreted not as 'scientific proof' of anything, but merely as a scientific-seeming kind of Aesop's fable, a metaphorical way of 'revealing character.' For an experiment with organisms that do not use language cannot tell us anything essential about the distinctive motives of a species that does use language." (Burke, *PC* l–li))

heads, they come faithfully running, on the strength of the character which a ringing bell possesses for them. (*PC* 6)

Burke completes this passage with a line I believe he never repeats but with an attitude toward education that informs his rhetoric as a whole: "Chickens not so well educated would have acted more wisely (*PC* 6). Because "the devices by which we arrive at a correct orientation may be quite the same as those involved in an incorrect one (*PC* 7), we must learn to make sound judgments for a specific context, since situations are not the same: "an objective event derives its character for us from past experiences having to do with like or related events," whether the event is the ringing of a bell or a word. We bring our "past experiences" and education to bear when we interpret, but we must learn to make sound critical judgments in reading, writing, and living through guidance, practice, and from assessments of probable consequences.

Burke leads us enthymematically—animal by animal—inviting us all along the way to cooperate with him. He extends his discussion beyond the barnyard to verbal means that "impart character to events," such as labels like "Poison" and Marxist explanations that attribute a man's unemployment to "financial crises inherent in the nature of capitalism" (Burke, *PC* 7). Such labels are handy but risky because they may be inadequate to the task at hand, and we may take them as truths and expect others to accept them on that basis. Meaning is experimental and contextual for Burke in that we interpret new events by relating our past experiences with "like or related events" (*PC* 7) to the present situation.

If our judgments are automatic rather than conscious and considered, we may, like chickens, run around with our heads chopped off, at least for the time before we die. He impresses the point that our linkages between past and present must be tentative and changeable with a representative anecdote that equates us with undereducated savages rather than over-educated chickens: Savages could make fires by considering dry wood and friction as appropriate linkages in the process of fire-making. The serviceability of their orientation is less apparent when, because their Christian missionary and doctor wore a raincoat during storms, they linked rain coats with rainy weather, and accordingly begged him to don the rain coat as a medicine against drought. Irrigation would have been a more effective means, yet their attempts to coerce the weather by homeopathic magic were not "escapist" in the restricted sense. They were a faulty selection of means due to a faulty theory of causal relationships (Burke, *PC* 9). Actions regarded as primitive, foolish, or illogical may be understood as the result of faulty means-selection, "trained incapacity," and "occupational psychosis": "People may be unfitted by being fit in an unfit fitness" (PC 10).

The comic becomes tragic as Burke introduces briefly "escape mechanisms," including the "scapegoat mechanism" with its "subsidiary term, 'rationalization'" (PC 11). We causally associate people and groups with events, and we often act precipitously and thoroughly on the fictions of our own makings. Burke here repeats with new understanding his claim that linkages constitute all orientations and all interpretations: "Orientation is thus a bundle of judgments as to how things were, how they are, and how they may be" (PC 14). We cannot live without making connections among aspects of ourselves (psychology), among past events (history), between ourselves and the unknown (religion), between ourselves and the world (science), between ourselves and others (sociology, art, literature, music). We cannot stay alive without recognizing that our links, "interested," tenuous, local, and temporary, will often be faulty and require revision.

In the "Prologue" Burke admits his preoccupation with "thoughts of a Joining, a Categorical Joining, a Joining 'in principle,' a joining-at-one-remove by joining with the sheer Idea of Joining" (PC liii). Joining, linking, bridging, filling in the gaps, and joycings are ways to address conflicts and contradictions and ways to identify with others. The missing link in Burke's barnyard rhetoric, as in all texts, is what motivates us to act as *animal symbolicum*.

Burke has thus shifted in his barnyard schooling from trout, dogs, chickens, and rats, to "scapegoats" and "our human victims," identifying "our" ways with "theirs," all along the way. He asks us to connect what has gone before with what comes and to anticipate what will come. He asks us to take seriously what he has been treating with humor as he moves from his barnyard approach to personal and public spaces where scapegoating, violence, and the kill are variations of faulty means selection and the results of training rather than education.[28]

Because we have gone along with Burke's educational program for trout, chickens, and dogs, laughing all the way, we go along with him when he turns to human "scapegoats." We are implicated as human beings in scapegoating and being scapegoated; we are doubly implicated in that we construct with Burke and thereby experience the position of the one who scapegoats and the one scapegoated.

Throughout his rhetoric, Burke explores, develops, contextualizes, and evaluates means of identification. He approaches identification in terms of

---

28. See C. Allen Carter's *Kenneth Burke and the Scapegoat Process* and Rene Girard's *Violence and the Sacred* for rich analyses of the scapegoat process

attitudes, motives, and situations, so that we learn to choose among our options to identify.

Who's Author Now? Writing as Change in Identity and in Symbols of Authority

In the three works following *Counter-Statement—Permanence and Change: An Anatomy of Purpose* (1935), *Attitudes Toward History* (1937), and *The Philosophy of Literary Form: Studies in Symbolic Action* (1941)—Burke develops rhetorics of literature, psychology, history, philosophy, economics, and religion, to determine to what extent they can be used to educate people to identify with each other in reading and writing, so that in life we don't resort to war, suicide, and "the kill." In *A Grammar of Motives* (1945), he develops his theory of Dramatism and the dialectical relationships between act, scene, agent, agency, and purpose as ways to analyze communications and miscommunications, in order to create attitudes, terms, and actions that help us identify and get along with each other. In *A Rhetoric of Motives* (1950), he articulates his theory of identification, associating it, as we saw in chapter 2, with Aristotle's enthymeme and with all the actions that figures and tropes, indeed all language, call for from writers and readers. In *The Rhetoric of Religion* (1961), he assumes identification as the body of proof in rhetoric and more fully develops the concepts of writing and reading as revision and rebirth rituals. Throughout, Burke teaches and enacts forms as acts of identification.[29]

---

29. For many today, Burke's contribution to the rhetorical tradition is his theory of identification and his contribution to literary and cultural traditions is his theory of language as symbolic action or language as constitutive. Criticism of Burke is nevertheless conflicted and contradictory. As we saw in chapter 1, literary and cultural critics often read Burke as an ideological critic, and, while they rely on identification of a certain kind, particularly the reader's identification with the writer's authority, they are not concerned with mutual meaning-making, though they are very focused on collective action. Rhetoric, defined as figures and tropes, became defined as ideological action. As we saw in chapter 2, rhetorical critics analyze and apply Burke's methods of persuasion, but without recognizing identification as enthymematic and the enthymeme or collaborative meaning-making as the subject and body of proof in his rhetoric. And some who read Burke's rhetoric as primarily agonistic do not recognize conflict as a form of cooperation and therefore as possible grounds for identification and getting along. Complexities in interpretations of Burke, all of which are similar in overlooking Burke's revision of Aristotle's enthymeme into identification, may be illustrated by the general and introductory comments for part six on modern and postmodern rhetoric in the twentieth century in *The Rhetorical Tradition: Readings from Classical Times to*

Our world today is divided up inadequately, and we obey false cues and exhibit faulty means selections. We can no longer consider "getting along" as naïve, easy, passive, or impossible. We can no longer dismiss "getting along" as an over-simplification. We cannot ignore "getting along" as a means of verbal war to avoid violence. Of course, people are drawn to power and profit for safety, security, and rewards of many kinds, and these are also ways to encourage identification.

the Present by Patricia Bizzell and Bruce Herzberg. In the general comments, they write that in Burke's analyses "rhetoric merges with political, psychological, sociological, religious, and aesthetic investigations of human behavior" (14). In the same paragraph they write that he defines language as "motivated, hence as rhetorical" but emphasize that he "searches discourse for its ideological function of promoting identification with communities and their beliefs (14). In their introduction to part six on modern and postmodern rhetorics, they again emphasize Burke's interest in motives as "distinctly linguistic products" (1193): "As he explains in *A Grammar of Motives* and *A Rhetoric of Motives*, no form of discourse is exempt from motivation. Scientific and philosophical discourses attempt to describe systems of human motivation, and social discourses attempt to motivate. Thus, it is the business of rhetoric to categorize and analyze these discourses" (1193).

They move beyond these views of Burke's rhetoric later when they explain how Booth drew on Burke for his argument in *The Rhetoric of Fiction* "that all literature is discourse addressed to a reader" (1194) and then turn to Walter J. Ong's argument in "The Writer's Audience Is Always a Fiction" in 1975 that "writers cannot address an actual audience, but rather project the kind of audience that will be receptive to their work" (1194). They conclude this discussion and begin the next on reader-response critics in the 1970s with the following, without linking identification with collaborative meaning-making:

Reading thus involves a kind of negotiation between the actual reader and the role that the author projects for the ideal reader. For this reason, the reader has an active role in producing the meaning of the work. (1194)

They turn to literary and reading theorists, Fish and Wolfgang Iser, who "took a similar position but emphasized readers must be 'informed' or 'educated' for their interpretation to be correct," and "[r]eader response critics generally regard their method as context-sensitive, though not as rhetorical" (1194). They conclude this discussion by distinguishing between formalist and other methods: "Still, this method and others that oppose strictly formalistic methods (notably Marxist criticism, which seeks to describe the historical and ideological context of literature) operate on the principle that literature is a form of rhetorical discourse whose interpretation depends on context and response as well as on the structure of the text" (1194).

I argue that Burke's rhetoric incorporates motives, readers, formalist criticism, those who oppose formalism "(notably Marxist criticism, which seeks to describe the historical and ideological context of literature)," anything else available to develop the resources of rhetoric for the purposes of identification as equipment for living and avoiding war.

But even the desire to communicate and identify is an attitude that some see as threatening, as a compromise, a loss of self and property that lead to destruction. We need to separate out the delicate threads in negotiation and accept that loss to some degree and kind is inevitable. We must speak the languages of those with whom we identify and want to identify with us, and we must speak the languages of those from whom we differentiate ourselves, our "others." We must work to find shared values, shared problems, and shared goals with those we have called enemies. We must always aim to identify across differences by respecting rather than denying them: Burke shows us how differences can motivate connections. And we must remember we already modify or change our identities and our current situations in order to identify with others, as others revise themselves and their lives to identify with us. Such collaborations are negotiations of power and hierarchy that don't necessarily make all people equal, but they can make us cooperate.

One of the most difficult aspects of Burke's rhetoric, one that he worries with throughout, is that it requires us individually and collectively to keep revising who we are. What's at stake in any communication understood as identification is loss with the possibility of gain for all involved. What's at stake in persuasion understood as violence is also loss but without gain for the victim. Writers who identify with readers experience change; readers who identify with writers do also.

Dennis A. Foster, in "Interpretation and Betrayal: Talking with Authority" in *Reclaiming Pedagogy: The Rhetoric of the Classroom*, provides a Lacanian analysis of writing and teaching writing that deals with issues of identity, symbols of authority, and identification, though in other terms. Foster does not refer to Burke, but his essay helps me develop the critical changes in individual and collective identities that are central in his rhetoric. Foster begins by acknowledging that most writing assignments for university students require them to respond to figures of authority. The paradox for most students is that they must respect and resist authority and be both "'good students' and independent thinkers, imitators and originals" (Foster 35). Although I question one of his first assumptions, that students' relationships with authorities are limited, I agree that their relationship with authorities at the university level, in person and in their readings, are limited. They must learn and resist, imitate and modify, act dependently and independently, and calculate the likely gains and losses of education. Foster is concerned primarily about authority's threats to individual identities and psychologies, while Burke works with authorities, symbols of authority, identities, psychologies, ideologies, and cultures.

Foster uses Shoshana Felman's argument that "thinking 'is always both motivated and obscured by love'" (qtd. in Foster 35) to support his claim that our desires for mastery and control lead us to select texts as sources of knowledge.[30] He explains that "the insights passionate reading leads to always occur at the cost of a certain blindness, a limitation that need not devalue the significance of the insights" because "[b]lindness is a necessary part of the process" (36). The inability to commit to new texts, he says, "may, in fact, mark the limits of people's ability to learn something new." He modifies this by explaining the inability as psychological: "We must abandon some point of certainty to accept new figures of truth" (36).

Particular aspects of Foster's argument are familiar to readers of Burke—the loss of certainty, communication as love, the claim that "feelings of trust and desire" are necessary in reading, the understanding that insights from a particular perspective occur at the "cost of a certain blindness," and that reading entails loss and a sense of death. Foster's discussion of transference in reading also shares some dimensions of identification. He associates the relationship Lacan describes between the analysand and analyst as the Subject Supposed to Know to the relationship between the interpreter and the text/author being read: Transference occurs whenever "the love that was learned in childhood is transferred only another figure" (Foster 36). More specifically: Interpretation is largely motivated by this faith in an authority based on the repetition of what was originally an illusion, a projection onto a parental figure. Believing in writers makes the pursuit of their knowledge seem worthwhile, a goal both meaningful and attainable. Interpretation, that is, is a kind of love. . . . This productive relationship is troubled, however, by the promise's being false. Someone may emerge to reassure us, to keep us from recognizing the pattern of repetition, but no one has the authority of final truths. Authority in the sense I have been using it is a manifestation

---

30. Foster uses Felman's 1982 essay, "Psychoanalysis and Education: Teaching Terminable and Interminable." My source for her psychoanalytic ways of reading and writing and for her understanding of her project is her 1987 book, *Jacques Lacan and the Adventure of Insight: Psychoanalysis in Contemporary Culture*, which she presents directly as a lesson in reading and indirectly as a lesson in writing:

> This book, in other words, is perhaps less about Lacan than it is about a contemporary way of reading that psychoanalysis has made possible: a way of reading I have learned from Lacan, and which my reading of him on one level constantly enacts (puts into effect, plays out) while, on another level, it attempts to analyze it and account for its difference. Lacan indeed embodies in my view, above all else, a revolutionized interpretative stance and (though he never formulates it systematically) a revolutionary theory of reading: a theory of reading that opens up into a rereading of the world as well as into a rereading of psychoanalysis itself. (9)

of the Lacanian Phallic: that is, it is a delusion, a consequence of *meconnaissance*, a misrecognition in childhood that leads us to perceive that which we need to survive (a parent) as a kind of god. (36–37)

For Burke, identification is two-way, and both writer and reader are authorities or people who know, as well as people who need others to know. The balance of power is not necessarily equal, though power is shared. People are not consubstantial, and communication does not make us so.

Transference in Foster's interpretation or rewriting is from one who doesn't know to one who does and whose authority remains intact. He explains that the problem for students in responding to authority, in using symbols of authority, and in asserting authority becomes even more complex, "by the fact that the speakers and writers they come in contact with have dedicated much of their lives to perfecting the impersonation of authority as a necessary prerequisite to being heard" (Foster 37). He adds that "writers are assisted in their disguise by teachers who encourage, even require, a kind of belief in the 'classics,' the masters, the originals (i.e., 'fine writing') as if fearing that a lack of respect for authority will leave students skeptical and scornful of their betters" (37). He asks, "how can one move beyond the initially motivating, but ultimately obscuring power of transference?" (37).

Foster answers himself with his interpretation of Jane Gallop's reading of Lacan:

> If transference involves the enamored reader in the attempt to speak in the language of the Subject Supposed to Know, to transfer, to carry across, knowledge to oneself, then translation (derived from the past participle of the root of transference) is the completed transference, the realization of that knowledge in the reader's own tongue (Gallop 52). That difficult knowledge that had been desired in another is made one's own, different certainly from its authoritative form, debased even, some would say, as they might say all translations are less than the original. Translations, insofar as they are literally misrepresentations, are a form of traducing. To make the matter more explicit, the love that inspires interpretation leads eventually to betrayal. (37).

Foster makes another claim, built on this notion of locating authority in oneself by taking and separating from the Subject Supposed to Know and from the view that translation is a resistance to and betrayal of authority: "This story of rhetoric has been the development and analysis of styles of authority that produce such readings," which he has identified as the reading that "adheres to the spirit of the text." In other words, the history of rhetoric has been the development of styles of authority writers use to get readers to identify with them: "If writers would be persuasive, would be believed, they need to create readers who are willing to have some faith in them" (Foster 38).

In Burke's terms, writers invite readers who are willing to have faith in them, and they must have faith in their readers. Writing and reading are acts of mutual meaning-making, they are courtship rituals, and they are acts of loss. They may be interpreted psychologically, culturally, ideologically, and/or rhetorically, but each of these readings will have different motives and consequences: they stand pragmatic tests of use.

Foster uses Lacan again to move past a writer-reader relationship that is "necessary at certain periods for learning to take place, but it is also a limiting, even ultimately stunting relation" (38). He explains Lacan's strategy of displacing the "letter" from the context of the "larger Word" to another context, "to produce powerful effects at variance with the spirit of the whole" (38). It is "the supposition of wholeness in a text," Foster says, that "constitutes the impenetrable face of authority" (38). And if the reading of the letter "is not seen simply as a betrayal of the spirit, but as an acknowledgment of what a writer has in fact produced, we can begin to respond to the 'literal' power of writing" (38). The "first-year nonreader and those who read for the spirit" are linked by "the faith they share in authority and a disregard for the letter, for the material details of life that must be read even to be seen" (38).[31]

It is possible to read identification into the writer-reader relationship described above as dependence of the reader on the authority of the writer and of the analysand on that of the analyst. Identification is not for Burke the total submission of one to another with greater authority but, rather, a shift in authority for a specific purpose. Texts, authorities, and interpretations are never whole. Acts of reading and writing are relationships with imbalances of power, but all writers do not hold greater power than their readers, for example student writers, and all writers and readers must assert their author-

---

31. First-year "non-readers," like passionate readers who "read for the spirit," may share some characteristics with Jameson's "virtuoso readers," critics whom he scapegoats and with whom he associates Burke. Such readers produce "peculiar and sometimes eccentric textual interpretations" that are "at one with the projection of a powerful, non-systematized theoretical resonance." ("Symbolic Inference" 508) This critic "misguidedly but compulsively submits his materials to a rage for patterns and symmetries and the mirage of a meta-system" (508). Reading for the spirit may be motivated by an attitude of acceptance and a desire to identify. It may suggest Burke's "hysteric" who reads for a cure, who needs a dose of recalcitrance and a little distance from the "connoisseur."

ity and their lack of authority if they are to identify. The challenge, Burke teaches us, is to understand authority, identification, and communication as incomplete, partial, and temporary and to use power wisely for "social reasons." Without denying authority, in fact only by recognizing authority and power, can we identify with others; at the same time, power shifts as people give a little or a lot in order to communicate.

The intricacies of identification and power are exposed dramatically today (2004 and still in 2024) as politicians and the media scapegoat other individuals, Osama Bin Laden specifically, in order to create unity by focusing anger and hatred elsewhere and forcing new alliances. US leaders warn us not to associate citizens with terrorists because of similar physical appearances and backgrounds. "We the people" includes enemies within and without. National security failed, some say, because we had changed from personal communication and involvement by individuals within terrorist groups to satellite surveillance. Identification might have prevented 9/11. Some leaders say we must deal with—identify with "unsavory characters," even those who have committed crimes, in order to know about terrorist actions in advance. Leaders announce plans to draw lines differently to create new identities and contexts.

Much is said and written about identifying with those victimized in New York City, but little about identifying with people attacked and oppressed around the world, all as victims of failures to act collaboratively in order to survive. In the search for a restoration of national identity, authority, and power, many seek and promise death for the evil ones. It's not as simple as that.

Foster outlines his writing lesson drawn from Lacan in a sequence of stages. First, he places students in situations where they recognize "the power that writing has always exerted in their world," so that they realize "writing itself exists as an area where they might resist authority, and that the effects of authority can be reproduced in their own writing" (Foster 38–39). Teaching the principles of formal logic is central in this pedagogy because of its "emotional weight in Western culture" but more so because "deduction is a sign of truth, even more than being its method" (39). The teacher's lesson on logic is in part a persuasive strategy because it comes for students "as a moment of amazing certainty"; it is also important because "in experiencing this fever of certainty, one can learn to recognize and hence become immune to (or at least skeptical of) the sign of truth in logic" (39). This lesson is taught not to "undervalue deductive logic" but "to avoid overvaluing it" and to recognize realms of doubt and truth (39).

Foster's lesson here, in valuing deductive logic without overvaluing it, is an aspect of Burke's lesson on writing as identification or enthymematic. Individuals and groups may create emotional connections as well as logical connections between contradictions, conflicts, individual and collective freedoms, and various kinds of war. Burke argues that we cannot let the rhetorics of science and certainty dominate and destroy the rhetorics of emotions and uncertainty, when we have just learned the limitations of science, logic, and certainty. We need to cultivate rather than diminish the resources of rhetoric to help us get along, and we need to use logic to decide among our options for acting in a given circumstance.

Having made a bold statement that although formal deductive logic is rhetorically effective today, its limitations are serious, Foster modifies his claim to say that deductive logic is inductive in part. He is concerned with "validity" in interpretation and the distinction between logical and absolute truth: "Its inability to deal with what it must see as paradox or ambiguity does not deny its utility in its proper fields. The fact that deductive logic is ultimately grounded in intuition, metaphor, "inductive experience," tautology, and so forth, does not invalidate it, but rightly separates it from the realm of absolute truth." (Foster 39)

Foster claims that "the teaching of logic is "curative" in offering "amazing certainty" and truth, in bringing "the high merriment of discovering fallacies, with the delicious sense that anyone can detect falsehood once he or she has seen the shape of truth," and in coming as "a sort of inoculation, as a virus that, at least temporarily, can transform the apparent chaos of thought into replications of its own form" and make students "immune to (or at least skeptical of) the sign of truth in logic" (39). He acknowledges that students "cannot themselves produce meaningful syllogisms as a part of their arguments" and "can seldom ferret out the fallacies or reconstruct the enthymemes in any professionally written essay" (39). It is not clear to me how he defines "enthymemes" here nor the values he attributes to the enthymeme as opposed to the syllogism. He does value the distinction between inductive and deductive reasoning and the distinction between "absolute truth" and deductive logic, "ultimately grounded in intuition, metaphor, 'inductive experience,' tautology, and so forth" (39).

Limitations of the Lacanian argument for rhetorical purposes are that it schematizes transference between those with greater authority and those with lesser authority, without recognizing the gradient series and the various kinds of authority at play in human interactions. As in the earlier discussion of Stanley Fish's reading of Freud's analysis of the Wolf Man's tale, the weight in Lacan is given to those with a certain kind of authority—the analyst, the scientist, the critic, and the teacher—rather than to those with another kind of authority—that which must be recognized and exercised if the "real" authority is to be heard, read, and realized. Without the client, the patient, and the student, traditional symbols of authority are undermined and made inoperative. Inductive and deductive define each other, as the syllogism and enthymeme define each other; where truth lies is another matter. In the realm of doubt and uncertainty, in the realm of Burke's rhetoric, writers must learn inductive and deductive logic and syllogistic and enthymematic proof, as well as develop their judgment about which to use in a given context. Burke's rhetorical lesson in writing includes a psychological dimension of writing, but it is also grounded in histories and cultures. He identifies himself as a Marxoid/Freudoid and locates his rhetoric in the space between.

BURKE'S LABYRINTHINE TERMINOLOGICAL CITY OR HIS MOTIVATIONAL JUNGLE BOOK

By demonstrating the uses of summaries, taxonomies, and charts, he illustrates their persuasiveness but also their misuses.[32] Although "Rituals of Rebirth" (Burke, *ATH* 317) and "Identification and Identity" (*ATH* 263) are only items in his alphabetical list of terms, Burke gives a slant that emphasizes the comic corrective and interprets all the terms as a vocabulary of revision necessary for identification. For a brief example of how single entries incorporate other terms and actions, Burke concludes his extended definition of Imagery, and his thesis that "a break in continuity is revealing" (*ATH* 284), with a comic story of Stalin issuing a signed statement confirming a rumor that he had died. Burke suggests that "a portion of his 'identity' really *had* died" when his old friends became enemies and were executed (*ATH* 284–85). He shifts abruptly to another method of persuasion: "Our basic principle is our contention that all symbolism can be treated as the ritualistic naming and changing of identity" (*ATH* 285).

---

32. The persuasiveness of taxonomies of writing are evident in the influence of the following works, some of which I discuss further in chapter 5, along with others that James A. Berlin draws from: M. H. Abrams's four kinds of literary theories, mimetic, pragmatic, expressive, and objective, in *The Mirror and the Lamp: Romantic Theories and the Critical Tradition*; Roman Jakobson's addresser, addressee, medium, and message James Britton's poetic/expressive/transactional sorting and assessment of texts in *The Development of Writing Abilities*; and Robert Scholes's types in *Textual Power*. The rhetorical orderings of taxonomies are persuasive because they are clear-cut. They are also useful, particularly when the lines that divide can be redrawn to connect what was separated through new configurations and classifications.

By reorganizing his dictionary from alphabetical listings to clusters or radiations of terms, I associate revision and identification as pivotal in a rhetoric of identification.

States, Attitudes, and Situations That Require Revision

The first two terms in his dictionary, "alienation" and "being driven into the corner," are states or conditions that require change. In this definition, Burke uses some of the strategies he defines elsewhere in the dictionary and some ideas about identification that he develops earlier in this and previous works. He explains, for example, that the alienated cannot make sense of the world that seems "basically unreasonable" (Burke, *ATH* 216); they cannot connect with the world as they understand it.

Given their attitudes and motives, the alienated cannot create links and thereby construct meaning. This condition, he says, can be changed "somewhat by forming the allegiance to a new rationale of purpose" (Burke, *ATH* 216). Burke's rhetoric of identification is his overall attempt to help us develop a "new rationale of purpose" that will help us purify war and stay alive.

He shows how new allegiances may be formed as he explains differences between "alienation" and "earning" are "not absolute opposites"; they are "aspects of a single graded series wherein one is more-or-less employed or more-or-less unemployed" (Burke, *ATH* 247). With this relief, he says, terms and conditions may change.

"Being driven into the corner," or driving others into the corner, leads people to feel that the only way out is by fighting, killing, or dying. This condition results in part from thoroughness in taking matters to the end-of-the-line and from failing to discount and recognize a "graded series" (*ATH* 221). Situations appear to be all-or-nothing, but through "casuistic stretching," amplifying, reducing, and other revisions, there is relief and the ability to see anew.

A later third term in the dictionary for a state or condition is the "Good Life." A "project for 'getting along with people'" necessarily subsumes definitions of a "Good Life." In his summary, he includes many aspects of identification discussed earlier but in other terms: (1) "maximum of physicality" (Burke, *ATH* 256–58); (2) "maximum opportunity for expression of sentiments" and "[d]istrust of the passions" because they are "ambitious" and "stimulated to the maximum" by the "'creative psychiatry' of capitalism" (*ATH* 258); (3) "[c]onstruction, to channelize the militaristic by 'transcendence' into the co-operative" (*ATH* 258); (4) "[p]atient study of the 'Documents of Error' (*ATH* 258)." "Above all, criticism should seek to clarify the ways in which any structure develops self-defeating emphases ('inner contradictions'). It should watch for 'unintended by-products' and should seek to avoid being driven into a corner in its attempts to signalize them (*ATH* 259); (5) "[s]tress always upon the knowledge of limitations" (*ATH* 259); and (6) "[d]istrust hypertrophy of art *on paper*: "More of the artistic should be expressed in vital social relationships. Otherwise, it becomes 'efficient' in the compensatory, antithetical sense" (*ATH* 259).[33]

Burke concludes this section with an admonition: "So completely do we now accept capitalist standards that we test everything as a *commodity for sale*. Hence, we feel that *'a mere artist at living'* has 'wasted his talents'" (Burke, *ATH* 259; emphasis mine). He again reminds us that, despite his view of life as a project of composition and symbolic action as consequential in the world, there is a critical difference between the worlds we construct and the world. He insists on reality throughout his rhetoric: "One need simply note an important distinction in quality between this act and the act of a man who gets art on paper at the sacrifice of art of living" (*ATH* 260).

Other states, situations or, more accurately, attitudes are "Heads I Win, Tails You Lose" (Burke, *ATH* 260–63), "Problem of Evil" (*ATH* 314), "Efficiency" (*ATH* 248–52), and "'Earning' One's World" (*ATH* 246–47). Burke defines the first as a "device whereby, if things turn out one way, your system accounts for them—and if they turn out the opposite way, your system also accounts for them" (*ATH* 260). He articulates the bias of a rhetorical perspective for enthymematic rather than syllogistic proof:

> If a philosopher outlined a system, and we were able to locate its variant of the 'heads I win, tails you lose" device, we thought we had exposed a fatal fallacy. But as we grew older, we began to ask ourselves whether there is any other possible way of thinking. And we now absolutely doubt that there is. Hence, we should propose to control the matter not by elimination, but by channelization. That is, we merely ask that the thinker *co-operate with us* in the attempt to track down his variant of the 'heads I win, tails you lose' strategy. It will necessarily be implicit in his work. And we merely ask him, as a philosopher whose proper game is Cards-face-up-on-the-table, to help us find it, that we may thereby be assisted in 'discounting' it properly. (*ATH* 260)

---

33. See two visions of the good life in Cornel West's *The Cornel West Reader*, particularly 316–32, and in Martha C. Nussbaum's *The Fragility of Goodness: Luck and Ethics in Greek Tragedy and Philosophy*, particularly chapter 8, 11, and 12, pages 240–258 and 318–54.

He adds that "perspective by incongruity is a heads I win, tails you lose' device—and we hereby lay our cards on the table by saying so" (*ATH* 261–62). He explains that philosophers, "in helping us to play Cards-face-up-one-the-table, should look for two others manifestations of the 'heads I win, tails you lose' formula in their work. . . . They should seek to discover the 'master metaphor' they are employing as the cue for the organizing of their work" (*ATH* 262).

Gaining Perspective by Incongruity: Juxtaposing to See Differently

Another cluster of terms in the dictionary may be titled "Perspectives by Incongruity" because they help us see two things at once (though not at the same time) or see something from two or more angles: "Casuistic Stretching" (*ATH* 229), a pun that "links by tonal association words hitherto unlinked" (*ATH* 309), "Bureaucratization of the Imaginative" (*ATH* 225), and "discounting" (*ATH* 244). Burke also defines "perspective by incongruity" as "a method for gauging situations by verbal 'atom cracking.' That is, a word belongs by custom to a certain category—and by rational planning you wrench it loose and metaphorically apply it to a different category." (*ATH* 308). In this sense, particular situations assist if not force change, such as the "Forensic" (the forum, the marketplace), as they give rise to attitudes, rituals, terms, and conflicts. Burke continues here to associate scenes, strategies, perspectives, and forms of the mind, world, and text. The discrete items in his dictionary and the dialectical relationships among these terms dramatize several principles that inform his writing lesson: divisions between people and terms make communication possible; terms define each other not a reality beyond them, although there is reality that affects language and that language affects; we can associate, dissociate, collapse, subsume, add to, deny, and revise our terms in many ways. Therefore, our choices are ethical choices.

Figures, Tropes, and Other Bridging and Transcending Devices

Several of the terms are strategies for connecting and integrating disparate parts: including "bridging devices," "casuistic stretching," the "stealing back and forth of symbols," "symbolic mergers," and "transcendence." He also defines strategies of connection, such as "Clusters" and "Communion." Other strategies alert us, so that we can make connections, such as "Cues."[34] He presents other strategies such as bridging devices that involve readers in co-creating meaning. He doubts "whether the analysis of imagery can attain scientific precision" and, as he says about his own work in general, imagery "serves better to point in the general direction of something than for acute microscopic divisions" (*ATH* 274). But this is an advantage rather than a handicap from a rhetorical perspective because imagery and patterns of images require readers to relate qualitatively different and disparate aspects of an image, various images to each other, and images to life situations.

Burke refers back to *Counter-Statement* where he develops a way to "chart the overall tones of the poet's imagery by looking for the quality common to all uses of a word" (*ATH* 274) and where he discusses emotional connections that link parts of a work and the work to patterns of experience. Again, the reader must connect the earlier discussion to the current one. Language that he uses in earlier discussions of qualitative progression helps us supply the missing links:

> The underlying pattern is observable when an apparently arbitrary or illogical association of ideas can be shown to possess an "emotional" connective. The logical laxity of imagism has enabled psychologists, for instance, to discover such emotional connectives in the work of Verhaeren, connectives distinctly arising from the pattern of experience underlying his work. (*CS* 159).

"Emotional" connectives, "logical laxity," and connections between texts and contexts are terms and ideas he uses earlier to define the symbolists' major alteration in method, "qualitative progression" and then "syllogistic progression" and other enthymematic functions of figures, tropes,

---

34. See chapter 4, "Attitudes toward History: Conflict in Human Association," in Ross Wolin's *The Rhetorical Imagination of Kenneth Burke*. Wolin argues that *Attitudes* "remains largely neglected" and those who do so "tend to use it piecemeal for their ends instead of his" (91). He discusses the dictionary and the reviews of *Attitudes*, concluding with the following assessment: "The same sort of rhetorical problems faced Burke with *Attitudes* as faced him with *Counter-Statement* and *Permanence and Change*. Critics, blinded by their own intellectual and political interests, were prone to misreadings and were unable to treat Burke on his own terms. My argument is that critics can't treat texts or critics on *their* terms completely because we are all limited if not blinded by our terministic screens, and we can't treat texts or critics on *our* terms because then we aren't reading. We can try to identify our ways with others and encourage them to identify with us in acts of cooperative meaning-making, when we understand identification as partial and temporary. On the other hand, we can tend one way or another, and we can claim we're doing one or the other.

and language in general. In the next section, I want to examine more closely how Burke enacts and demonstrates his definitions in order to reinforce his lesson presented in terms of terms.

Burke's Lesson in Writing as Implicature; Or, How Burke Rounds Up Readers

Throughout the dictionary, as throughout his rhetoric, Burke writes in ways to prevent us from accepting his definitions as correct or unchangeable. While he defines "pivotal" terms that make change possible, *how* he defines, discusses, and illustrates his terms is perhaps even more instructive than his definitions. How he writes teaches by example how he revises his texts and his own thinking in order to identify with readers and to encourage us to identify with him.

His revisionary practices in the dictionary are familiar. He defines terms by associating them with other terms that are both similar and different, and, when different, he shows how they are different in degree, not in kind. He dramatizes how his definitions of terms change across contexts and how his recontextualizations require readers to juxtapose what he said before with what he says now and to bridge the differences, with the understanding that he has not rejected his previous definitions and uses of terms nor revised them forever.

He also provides examples and anecdotes that give perspective by incongruity, and he includes throughout the comic corrective. One example illustrates the strategy he uses throughout the "Dictionary" of discrete terms but also throughout his rhetoric: "Perspective by incongruity" is a "method for gauging situations by verbal 'atom cracking.' That is, a word belongs by custom to a certain category, and by rational planning you wrench it loose and metaphorically apply it to a different category" (*ATH* 308). He links verbal atom cracking to the methodology of the pun and then connects all these terms or actions to "casuistic stretching" (*ATH* 309).

As he defines "perspective by incongruity," he requires readers to connect qualitatively the different actions. By blurring his own distinctions, he teaches us to revise with purposeful flexibility. He cuts across the bias of his distinctions, defining terms in relationship to other terms, modifying terms in different contexts. Burke also crosses the boundaries of definitions he establishes and uses one to illustrate another, as he crosses conventions of defining terms and transgresses conventional boundaries between writer and reader.

For example, he speaks directly to readers, often in a conversational give-and-take style, and he admits his limitations, to engage us in general agreement: "However, even readers who are willing to agree with us in general may resent it that we have nowhere, in this book, offered a complete schematization of symbolic ingredients" (Burke, *ATH* 285). He writes this within his dictionary, "a schematization of a sort of symbolic ingredients." His point here is not to apologize, though that's what he seems to do, but rather to make his point more forcefully: "Our basic principle is our contention that all symbolism can be treated as the ritualistic naming and changing of identity" (*ATH* 285).

Later he speaks directly to readers, again to apologize, but he retracts his apology once we've forgiven him because, he says, what is missing paradoxically helps both writer and reader:

> Frankly, we were not sufficiently aware of our procedure until we neared the end of the book (that is, we did not verbalize our implicit method into an explicit methodology). It is probably better so, since an over-exactitude of schematization, maintained throughout, would have wearied writer and reader both. (*ATH* 294)

In his apologies, Burke establishes a personal relationship with readers to do further work, as William Carlos Williams does in his poem about eating the plums. In Burke's frank aside here, he admits his fault—unawareness of his procedure—but then redefines his fault as a strength, and a considerate one at that. He justifies his method because it benefits writer and reader alike. He also repeats the distinction between implicit and explicit that he makes throughout his critical works and shows us how they can be understood as matters of degree not of kind. Again, he treats the explicit or thoroughly realized as tiring for both writer and reader and as an ineffective means of persuasion the "over-exactitude of schematization" prevents the reader from active participation.

Throughout, his attitude of humility and uncertainty continues to draw us to his cause by inviting us to help him out: "we concede" (*ATH* 227), "admittedly a vague term" (*ATH* 329), and "a qualification is needed here" (*ATH* 335n*).

More personal conversations with readers often occur in digressions within the text or in footnotes that spread across pages. His footnotes may extend his argument, provide a perspective by incongruity, "insert a comic corrective," readjust means of identification, contradict what he has said, or do almost anything to keep us interested. In his long discussion of imagery, after a discussion of how Shakespeare in *Cymbeline* integrates the feudal and the mercantile worlds as Henry Ford has done in his plans to "grow Ford cars on the farm" (Burke, *ATH* 281), Burke inserts a note in which he identifies explicitly with readers: "At this point, the reader may legitimately ask: How does this observation [agree] [*sic*] with the present writer's proposal to retain the commercialist vocabulary, for exegetic purposes, at this late date?" (*ATH* 281n*). He admits "frankly" he likes it for its "quaintness," considers "embalm[ing] it stylistically" (perhaps in a footnote), and then explains that a society built above industrialism "must necessarily carry over much from the commercial symbolism of exchange" (*ATH* 281n*).

Burke here delights in order to teach, keeps us on our toes and mentally active, plays with levels of diction and kinds of exegetic writing, treats us like colleagues or friends in conversation, and integrates the feudal, mercantile, agrarian, and commercial worlds, all into a common grave or economy. We become his partners in criticism, tracking cues and tics and tell-tale signs, using all we can to figure out how to get along.

He also engages us by including us along with the many characters who populate his texts and notes, characters who are alive, dead, imagined, historical, fictional, variations of himself, and more: including Richard McKeon, Plato, Paget, Benjamin Paul Blood, "(a picturesque writer quite sensitive to such matters)" (243n), the banished Duke in *As You Like It* (Burke, *ATH* 262n*), the man who "referred to his wife and himself as being, for the time, 'mummies,' 'dead to social life'" (*ATH* 269n), "One who experiences difficulty in remembering the names of close acquaintances when introducing them (*ATH* 271n*), and his ghost-writing self working on a book on drugs (*ATH* 251n*). His dictionary is a stage for comedy.

Readers, along with the author, join the Encyclopedists (Burke, *ATH* 216); the "French Encyclopedists" (*ATH* 330); "Children in their moral thoroughness" (*ATH* 220); Malinowski whose phatic communion designates "an easy way of establishing a bond" with others (*ATH* 235); philosophers "whose proper game is Cards-face-up-on-the-table" (*ATH* 260); a cluster of literary critics, including Blackmur, Spurgeon, and Krutch; Shakespeare and many of his characters; Marx and Engels; and "Your correspondent," Burke (*ATH* 255). He aligns himself with some and against some, filling the parlor of his dictionary with many voices in heated conversation, while reaching with words across the abyss also created by words.

Representative anecdotes, like larger narratives, put opposites together (Burke, *ATH* 230), making clear that "everything is its other" (*ATH* 231), if you're willing to do the work and stand pragmatic tests. They include the comic with the tragic and provide perspectives by incongruity: Every machine contains a cow-path" (*ATH* 228); Socrates who "converted the business of phatic communion into an extremely annoying occupation" (*ATH* 235); "the motivational jungle" that requires "a good basic proposition to have in mind when contemplating the study of motives would be: Anybody can do anything for any reason (*ATH* 353); and the Flea School of Art (*ATH* 250–51). Narratives convince because we accept the reality of own experiences in shared meaning-making and what we have in part constructed.

Despite the fluidity of terms, attitudes, and actions in his rhetoric, he often builds on a set of interrelated claims about uncertainties in life and in language: "In a sense, incongruity is the law of the universe; if not the mystic's universe, then the real and multiple universes of daily life (Burke, *ATH* 311). "Similarly, words are public properties, and the individual 'has a stake in' their public ownership. He cannot merely 'delegate' powers to them. It would be as true (or as over-simplifyingly false) to say that they delegate their powers to him. He uses them, and they use him" (*ATH* 333).

But even these claims are assertions of metaphors not truths. They are what he thinks might work in certain contexts to help us identify with each other. It is useful at times, he suggests, to understand all language as metaphorical, even this claim: "The mortmain of dead metaphors ("abstractions") that has gripped us since his time has rigidified this original liquidity" (*ATH* 230).

Through reading Burke, we develop the ability to construct meaning in uncertainty and to act with faith in others to help out by collaborating and testing for social reasons. Particularly telling comments in the dictionary are his writings about how others write and about how he writes, even though it is often difficult to distinguish between these two ways of writing about writing. In his definition of "cues," for example, he discusses the "moral weighting" of terms and how we may use "many words which seem neutral, but in actuality possess hidden weighting" (*ATH* 237).

Burke illustrates his point with an anecdote that in turn describes his own processes of writing and becomes a lesson for us on writing with identification as the body of proof:

> A man organizes an essay. He necessarily chooses certain pivotal verbalizations about which he hinges his discussion. He chooses these particular verbalizations because they *appeal* to him. Some other terms might be substituted in their place, so far as the pure logic of the case is concerned. But he makes a selection in accordance with subtle, personal tests of "propriety." Though the words are, on their surface, neutral, they fit together into an organic interdependent whole precisely because of their common stake in some unifying attitude of his. We may get cues prompting us to discern the underlying emotional connotations of words that even the user may consider merely "scientific" or "neutral." By locating these,

we get glimpses of an organization than is apparent when we take the words at their face value. In this book, for instance, we have said much about the "comic frame." We have advocated, under the name "comedy," a procedure that might just as well have been humanism." Presumably we selected comedy because, for one reason or another, the word 'sounded better' to us. (*ATH* 237)

We are by now familiar with Burke's tendency to rely more on qualitative than syllogistic progressions. This "subtler organization" gains adherence through action by readers with writers and by appeals to the reader's authority in collaborative meaning-making. The more direct, logical method depends more on the appeal to another's authority and on acceptance. In his definition of "discounting," Burke presents "a man, writing on the run, as we all do, cannot supply all the modifiers" (*ATH* 244). Without presenting the caricature as himself, we recognize Burke and his methods of writing:

> For instance, we have talked about the limitations of the caricature or polemic. If one knows how to discount such forms, making due allowance for the ways in which necessities of emphasis drive one into the corner, realizing that a sentence cannot be designed to say everything at once (recalling that a man, writing on the run, as we all do, cannot supply all the modifiers) one can properly discount, and so properly use. If a man says "yes," you cannot conclude that he is a "yea-sayer," until you know the question he is answering. Often you cannot take a sentence at face value (you do not "understand its meaning" until you know the biographical or historic context subsumed by the speaker when he spoke it). (*ATH* 244)

In Burke's discussion of "Symbols of Authority," he refers directly to himself and to how he, as a literary critic, writes:

> Our own program, as literary critic, is to integrate technical criticism with social criticism (propaganda, the didactic) by taking the allegiance to the symbol of authority as our subject. We take this as our starting point, and "radiate" from it. Since the symbols of authority are radically linked with property relationships, this point of departure automatically involves us in socio-economic criticism. Since works of art, as "equipment for living," are formed with authoritative structures as their basis of reference, we also move automatically into the field of technical criticism (the "tactics" of writers). (*ATH* 331)

Burke teaches the tactics of all writers who revise themselves and their words to persuade through mutual identification.

Burke's Appeals to Readers: Syllogistic and Qualitative Progressions, Logical and Temporal Priorities

In *Permanence and Change, Attitudes Toward History,* and *Philosophy of Literary Form,* Burke continues to progress as he says the symbolist did, "from the one thing to the other by ellipsis," (*CS* 68) and he teaches us how to progress qualitatively with him.

We learn as we read anecdotes, narratives, and arguments as stories, "not merely a linear progression, but a fruition" (Burke, *CS* 45). We follow his lead in his "systematic search for a dialectic of many voices" (*CS* xi). And we experience and examine how he writes essayistically, "songfully," and "clinically," not sure just when he is inquiring and when "pamphleteering" (*CS* vii, viii), leaving us to make connections and figure out the meanings in his "indeterminate wavering" (*CS* vii). As he makes claims and assertions, he also questions and undermines them: we must make sense. He continues to "return to inconclusiveness" (*ATH* 24), as an attitude that prepares us to listen, learn, and identify with others.

Burke's lesson in writing, as I construct it, does not replace other lessons: it's not as simple as that. Writers must figure out what will work for themselves and their intended readers in particular contexts and remember that traditional syllogistic argument is the dominant and persuasive form within the academy and often within the culture. What kinds and variations of appeals are we hearing now that we didn't hear before September 11?

As teachers of writing, we must draw from all of our available resources when we teach others to write, to read their own writing and writing by others critically, to understand writers' purposes, intended readers, and their contexts for writing, as well as to figure out what works for them, how, and why. We must also encourage students to read their own drafts and final copies aloud to themselves and to others and to read writing by others critically, to understand and assess other writers' intentions, ways of writing, and contexts for writing.

Writing as identification and collaborative meaning-making teaches writers to experience and understand writing and rewriting, as well as reading, speaking, and listening, as collaborative actions. We recognize that logical arguments, stories, poems, songs, and more are constructions we can make, re-make, and perform for various purposes and audiences. We learn to use language to construct ourselves in relationships with others, as we communicate with others, who in turn revise us.

We can also examine definitions of knowledge as power of one over another and contrast the motives and probable consequences of this simile with knowledge as the power of collaborative action for mutual benefit and identification as personal and cultural action and knowledge.

The Gist, the Gesture, the Gusto: A Summary of a Lesson in Writing as Identification

I am sure it is clear that I am not advocating we write or teach students to write like Burke. That would be comedy and not a comic corrective. I am sure it is clear that I have not learned to write like Burke, despite my respect for his lessons. But I am proposing that we write and teach students to write to identify with others, so that we keep learning "to act wisely, in concert."

As Burke explains how the "nature of our language" can lead "us to be shocked at the idea of putting opposites together," he demonstrates that, by using strategies such as discounting, casuistic stretching, perspective by incongruity, transcending and bridging devices, graded series, and cuts across the bias of our distinctions, we can gain a "truly liquid attitude towards speech." This attitude can be used when "lacunae are felt," with a result, he says, that will "be a firmer kind of certainty, though it lacks the deceptive comforts of ideological rigidity" (Burke, *ATH* 231). This "truly liquid attitude towards speech" doesn't guarantee that we will be effective, or even heard. It doesn't mean we are not always ideological. Nor does it mean that we ignore, accept, or reject traditional authority. It does mean that there are many kinds of knowledge, including know-how, and that there is space and time for contrasting rhetorics and gauging what might work to help us identify with others in given contexts.

The toughest lesson is learning what to do, when, where, how, why, and for whom—in writing, reading, and living. Developing sound judgment is a lesson never to be learned; rhetoric is the practice and action of decision-making; and identification is taking the chance that collaboration offers rebirth and relief from war.

"Humility," "uncertainty," and the consideration of alternatives seems like weakness, but, worse, like violence, because they may result in further violence. This is a primary danger of a rhetoric of identification, for there are times to act quickly and with force. The consideration of alternatives and probable consequences doesn't necessarily deny resolve: In fact, hesitancy can constitute and sus-

tain long-lasting resolve. "Humility," "uncertainty," and "resolve" are attitudes and actions that can help us communicate across a world of differences, if we are willing to risk loss for the sake of peace.

This is a purpose, idealistic yet pragmatic, something to strive for and keep us on course, even when actions fail, attitudes falter, and other actions are deemed necessary. With a clear motive, we can be flexible and strategic in our uses of various means to identify with others and to encourage them to identify with us, and we can calculate the probable gains and losses of identification. The "greater complexity of problems" cannot stop us from trying everything to get along, revising our texts, ourselves, our words and worlds, as we are always being revised by them.

5 Burke's Lesson in Writing to Identify Compared to Berlin's Call for Writing as Ideological Action

> The peril of complexity is diffusion. The peril of power is monotony. (Burke, *CS* 160)

> We prefer to be somewhat shrewd in our notion of the way in which collectivism must emerge. Primarily, we feel that it may enter "by the back door," as signalized in that highly ironic term of modern economists, the "socialization of losses." (Burke, *ATH* 160)

> Hugh Duncan asks in his introduction to Burke's *Permanence and Change*: "Why, in a world of many disparate perspectives, is the "poetic" perspective ("Man as Communicant") to be treated as foremost? Can the author make cogent claims that this particular perspective represents more than merely his special "occupational psychosis as a literary man? (*PC* xxviii–xxix). He answers his own question: "Burke argues that the author can make cogent claims because "whatever the race of human beings may be in their particularity, they are all members of the symbol-using species" (*PC* xxix).

In Burke's Prologue, he asks the question himself and then answers: "For whatever the race of human beings may be in their particularity, they are all members of a symbol-using species. Accordingly, the author dares hold that the 'Poetic' perspective is foremost 'in principle.'" He adds:

> To say so is not by any means to say that one expects such a perspective upon human motives to command authority. Political, military, and industrial powers are much more likely to 'set the tone,' so far as the "implementing" of perspectives is concerned. But the perspective that views man in terms of his symbolic involvements may enjoy at least a universally *corrective* function—or, if not that, then perhaps it may at least be found to go with the "brooding

dimension" as regards human motives. And so one will constantly be coming upon it, even in the midst of the great pyramidal structures of authority that, while their strength is a mockery of the 'poetic perspective's' weaknesses, are all prime examples of its claims, since they all bear witness to man's great reliance upon language, terminology, *symbolism*. (PC lvi–lvii)

Earlier, Burke wrote: "There is no reason why prose should continue to be judged good prose purely because it trails along somewhat like the line left by the passage of a caterpillar" (*TBL* xvi).

A REAFFIRMATION OF A RHETORIC OF IDENTIFICATION ON SEPTEMBER 11, 2001

I am writing as television and radio report on the devastation in New York, Washington, and Pittsburgh. I can't keep watching; I can't keep writing. Television images whirl in my peripheral vision then spiral deep inside.

We tried to call Jane before six our time, nine New York City time, even though we knew she'd probably already left for work. No dial tone. I hung up, complaining about the telephone. I tried again, still thinking something was wrong with our phone or with how I was dialing. But not on the third try. Why would the circuits be overloaded early on a Tuesday morning? September 11 wasn't a holiday, was it? Martha called. We called Walter in Wyoming as we turned on the television.

We don't know where Jane is in the city. We watch and wait. John leaves to teach his classes. It's 8:00 our time, 11:00 NYC time, but all time stops. I'm at the table where I work, trying to steady myself, but I turn to watch repeated images of slim pointed planes like ballet slippers glide into the towers of the World Trade Center, easy as you please. The towers collapse into themselves, and dark clouds balloon into the air like a nuclear blast. Like in the movies, people below run from and to the destruction, coated by dust and dirt into mummies.

Jane calls about 11:30 her time to say she's okay, crying softly, "All I can think about are the people we've bombed." When she left the International House this morning, she knew nothing. When she walked up from the subway, she saw and heard the second tower fall. She had to get off the phone because people were lined up behind her to call to say they were alive and to find out about friends and family. I forgot to ask her what she would do and where she would go.

I'll write to get a grip. I'll listen and record what I hear on the television across the room. I'm afraid of what I'll hear; I'm afraid of what happens that I don't even know has happened. Local news interrupts to say that certain schools are closed in Tucson. National news continues with images of preparations for disaster relief. The perpetual images of destruction return, interspersed with mediafaces talking and talking. The cover of control can't hide their fears. The stream of talk connects us throughout the country and beyond, to keep us from falling off the face of the earth. I move from my table to hover around the television, my computer in my lap.

A Post-Ideological Age: Now, Where Are We?

In September 2001, when I visited a graduate seminar in eighteenth and nineteenth century rhetoric, I head the term *post-ideological* for the first time. Then early the next morning in the *Arizona Daily Star*, an hour or so before learning about the attacks on the World Trade Center (WTC), I read "post-ideological" in an editorial by Richard Rodriguez, "Migrants, the New Rebels."[35] I read that there is not a more revolutionary figure in the world than the so-called "illegal immigrant": "You would think Fox, Mexico's president, who was once an executive for the Coca-Cola Co., would understand the irrelevance of government when it comes to the new economic forces at play in our post-ideological, global economy (B5)"

"Back to lower Manhattan," someone says, and I stop writing to see and hear what has happened. Hundreds of emergency workers and the press wait, ready to enter the warzone. Only a handful of ambulances have come out. Another bulletin: Bush says that US military are on alert worldwide.

---

35. On the Opinion page, B5, in the *Arizona Daily Star* for Tuesday, September 11, 2001, Maureen Dowd, William Safire, and Claudia Lewis joined Rodriguez to provide for me a context for the day's events. Dowd writes in "Film's 'Mad Prophet' Eerily Prescient," that "Paddy Chayefsky's ominous predictions from the Ford era about the damage to American democracy from the Pac-Man game of networks gobbled by companies gobbled by other companies gobbled by consortiums gobbled by foreign investors have come true." Safire writes, "In the fog of economic war, one incontrovertible truth is clear: The budget projections of Congress and the White House will continue to be horrendously out of whack." And Claudia Lewis in "N-Word Still Stings Civil-Rights Fighters" writes about Jennifer Lopez's "casual use of the n-word in a recent recording" and the "generational divide, between the hip-hop generation, for whom the word is 'no big deal,' and a generation now elderly, the members of which fought against the racism they saw in that word."

Worldwide war? This is a post-ideological world? I prefer the ideological one of yesterday?

Burke teaches us that we can imagine and name differently for social reasons and that our namings must stand pragmatic tests. What namings will be helpful now? What namings will be persuasive? For what purposes—an eye-for-an-eye, turning the other cheek, military aggression, dialogue, negotiations, conversation, identification? Of course, we don't have individual and free choice in our namings, interpretations, and actions. Whoever thought that? But that doesn't mean we can't try to use language to learn, teach, construct, and persuade. According to Burke, that's what we have, the motive and ability to communicate. To what end is up to us; to what end is also up to others. Language use must stand the test of the collective. That's our grounding.

Today we are victims not victors. How will we use this new national identity? How will others? How are we converting it already? I watch a city gathering, not fleeing, and I feel a nation rallying through television, backed by corporate America, its symbols of authority still crumbling before us. Have we in one fell swoop returned to an ideological age that moves quickly to end-of-the-line thinking and acting? We have been painted into the corner this morning, to say the least. Is war the only way out? Isn't there still a little time and space for hesitation, thinking, assessing, and choosing within the current constraints? Is rhetoric dead? Does the individual no longer matter? Why do we have to claim that what went before is dead in order to assert that some other understanding might be useful? It's not as simple as that.

As ideologies collide in horrible images before me, I don't think it's wise to assume we live in a post-ideological or an ideological world. Those are cuts in the cheese that is the universe, made for specific purposes and anticipated consequences. Where do such hyper-claims get us? In another pre- or post-something or other? In an imagined position with the authority of hindsight and retrospective arrangement that allows us to revise from a temporal priority, what happens, to a logical priority, to say what happened and why as if we know for sure? We need foresight and hindsight, temporal and logical priorities, logical and analogical persuasion, but we still have to figure out what to do when. We can't rush to judgment. We can't jump to conclusions before asking what's happening today, what happened earlier today, what will happen in a minute? Why and how?

We can't see the grounds we stand on, but we can try to see around the edges of our terms, around the edges of the soles of our shoes or bare feet to identify with others and see from two angles at once. That is, if we're willing to resist our tendencies and risk changes in who we are, in our language, and in situations in order to come to terms, not war. People can also jump, as I see before me on the screen, when they see no other way out.

Have we moved from this morning's post-ideological analysis and run smack into the face, heart, and guts of violence and death; the consequences of certainty, perfection, and absolutism; the acts of people who believe they're right and know the truth better than anyone else and don't mind dying for it, letting others die for it, or forcing others to die? Who doesn't think they're right and have the right to prove it, maybe not die for it or have the force to get others to? Destroy others before they destroy us, more than they already have this Tuesday morning. Where do we draw the lines? When do we redraw the lines?

What if we've finally hit a wall that holds firm or gives and falls to bury us dead or alive? What number will do now, and do for what? Will declaring we're in an ideological world or a post-ideological world change anything? Will "post-philosophical" do? What have postmodernism and poststructuralism done? What about rhetorical, a-rhetorical, post-rhetorical, or rhetoricality? What will we do to stop what happened today from happening again? Nothing for sure is for sure.

Why not ad bellum purificandum *for a start? It's a slow start, a gamble, not on language but on people acting together through language for the purpose of getting along. But who wants to purify war that people are dying from at this very moment, with promises of more attacks coming from the sky or from somewhere else? The purification of war is the only purity Burke seeks; otherwise, he prefers the muddle, the barnyard, the give-and-take, the wars of nerves, the haggling, the conversing, and the contradictions and conflicts of life. That's where he thought he might make a difference, make a name, make a home. He did, and he stayed right there on Amity Road, not far from the city, getting along as best he could with himself and others, reading.*

What else is beyond the imagination? Beyond words, but certainly not for long? How long did it take for news broadcasts to begin? Who told whom to say what? say it how? say it when? Who made those decisions? What is the source or origin of today's events? Journalists are writing around the world. Networks of power and persuasion—technological, economic, medical, governmental, political, religious, educational—rapidly fire back and forth. Trade of all kinds and commodities continues, with migrants, terrorists, business people, and others encircling the world and re-mapping nations, races, religions, classes, genders.

A rhetoric of identification is idealistic, yet urgent, too complex yet too simple, pie-in-the-sky yet grounded in global give-and-take. Who's willing to give a little for the sake of others? Am I willing to lose what I've got? Just how much of what I've got? Injustice divides, defeats, and deadens us to each other. The "peril of power is monotony." What's the current cost of war fought in the name of justice? What's the face of justice today? Who gets the profits? And just how many refrigerators does it take for us, not to keep our butter hard, but to show that we belong and prove that others don't? Belong to what and to whom? Will animal symbolicum ever feel adequate or adequate enough? More cars, more houses, more viagra, more surgery, more whatever promises change that seems upward and onward to perfection but will inevitably one day convert downward. You can bet your bottom dollar on that reversal, along with many more, in the story of life here on earth. This is the way of the world, like it or not, so what're we going to do about it? That's Burke's question, and his answer was to develop the resources of rhetoric to help us identify with each other. He said that's what we want to do, despite overwhelming evidence to the contrary, because we are divided, incomplete, inadequate. We have to build equipment for living together and then revise it and begin again and again. That didn't stop Burke; he just kept trying everything, revising, and trying again.

Terrorism unites a nation divided by class, race, gender, sexual orientation, and much more. Elsewhere, people are united for and against the United States. The center did not hold, and neither will the borders, no matter how armed. We can't live isolated within countries, governments, classes, genders, religions, economies, philosophies, or rhetorics: Categories and bodies bleed.

As Rodriguez writes so simply, workers are transgressing all borders, laws, rules, and regulations, remaking the map of the world, not in search of citizenship or domination over others but in search of work in order to survive. Why can't we stress the human desire to work to survive and connect with others rather than the human desire to climb the ladder and look down on others or on us? Hot air rises. So does cream, and it sours. The Upward Way leads Downward and Upward again, in the recycling of life.

We forget (or can't forget) we're animal symbolicum; we can't remember the comic corrective that lets us forgive ourselves and others for being who we are here on earth.

When I read Rodriguez' article early, at sunrise, I imagined immigrants and refugees entering across the US/Mexico border in Nogales, about an hour south of Tucson. I remembered the written and visual portraits of many workers who died during the past summer, and every summer before, in heat over one hundred degrees as they attempted to cross the border and move towards what they believed to be a better life, a place to work and survive. I couldn't have imag-

ined this morning that those seeking death for themselves and others, not work and not life, would have landed in New York today. Sure, some day, we've been taught to expect and defend against that, but not today. Why? Life means little without the prospect of a future; life means little with only the prospect of a future beyond life. We live in a contact zone, a war zone, a state of babble. The sky is falling. Can attitudes, terms, and actions do anything? If so, what words? How do we hold on? What do we hold on to? Do we have to hold on? If we let go, will we find new ways to live?

I'll stop and call John.

Out of 184 patients—ten are critical, two have passed away. The hospital is completely mobilized. Bellevue and St. Vincent's are where the most critically injured will be sent. Cardinal Edward Egan assures people the medical and religious communities will do their best for their loved ones. Triage centers are in place. Everyone is covered in gray matter.

Voices are confident, kind, and calm. Dr. Ackerman says St. Vincent's is well-staffed now, but he is worried about later. I don't know him but worry too, about now and later.

A fourth plane crashed about forty miles outside of Pittsburgh in Somerset County. Only blurred shots are available now. Will someone doctor the photographs? Why and how? Flight numbers of planes hijacked and crashed are posted: American Airlines Flight 11 and Flight 77; United 175 and 93. Numbers. 266 people have lost their lives; thousands killed and injured in NY and DC, Bush's words, as best I can hear and record them: "Freedom attacked by a faceless coward." That freedom will do something, but I couldn't catch what.

Tom Brokaw reports that the two icons of American capitalism have been destroyed. He said it, but he continues. No time to stop and think about that, not now at least, not with so many icons still reaching upward and the US in a national state of emergency. Borders with Canada and Mexico are closed. Local news interrupts to report that people can go into Mexico, for business reasons, I think the reporter said? Can Mexicans enter the US?

"Return to life as normal," someone advises. Someone says, "dealing with the carnage in lower Manhattan." Norm, normal, abnormal, pre-normal, post-normal, hyper-normal, normalized, normalization. Everyone's trying to make sense of scraps, bits and pieces, reports, speculations, fragments, direct statements, photographs, movement, looks, silences, and disparate parts. Making sense through relating with others.

Somebody reports on a telephone interview with Senator John McCain, linking NYC and Arizona, or is our representative in Washington or somewhere else? We're all everywhere, scattered around, like it or not. McCain says satellite surveillance is fine, but we have to "divine" (his word) people's motives, and we need to do more work there. He means wherever our enemies are, but where's that? I like the magic touch, the verbal alchemy, the religious quality; more, I like rhetorical consideration of motives, even of spies collaborating with the enemy to find out their motives and actions and sometime becoming one with another. Terms define each other and are inextricably related: us/them. War as collaboration? But who wants personal contact rather than the safer distance of technology, especially for the sake of others? That's what we've witnessed today, or was it for the sake of self or God? Time to stop and think before we act and react, but that's risky too.

"*. . . effect on the business of this country.*" *(Forget the quotes I'd already forgotten. I'm recording what I hear, probably want to hear, all I can hear, not what was said.)—Pearl Harbor different—attach (case in point: I heard "attach," but it must have been "attack." If we understand war as cooperation, perhaps we can transform a disease into wellness?). The gains and losses of distinctions and differences; the advantages and disadvantages of understanding differences as differences in degree or in kind; and the results of making cuts across or along the biases of differences—races, genders, classes, religions, theories, disciplines, nations, ages, and traditions. In a world of differences, we privilege some and not others; the work is to figure out which ones to privilege in particular circumstances for social reasons, for justice, for the good of all.*

Nothing's "pure" on earth, so let's live with it, not die fighting for what want (won't) ever be and what's not ours to begin with. We won't fall to pieces, at least no more than people already do, than some already do. And some die. We'll still have to figure out what to do when, where, how, why, and for whom, with careful attention to motives and probable consequences, risking loss for the sake of a common good.

Undermining or Transcending of Claims and Counterclaims

How can I possibly keep this chapter as it was, as if nothing's happened to cross the borders of my text? I don't want to. I want to mark the revisions that the events of 9/11 made on me, on writing, and on teaching writing. I want to persuade others to write and teach writing and reading as a means of getting along collaboratively and as preparation for further collective actions. This curriculum includes an attitude of uncertainty that leads us to cooperate with others; the desire to get along with people rather than dominate and kill; the willingness to risk change and loss, with the possibility of gain for oneself and others; and the ability to read motives and situations, learn and practice strategies for creating identification, select among available options, assessing probable consequences, and acting in uncertainty. This is a lot to ask and to give. There's nothing "right" about it: it's rhetoric. Given what happened, who wants this solution? Given what happened, who wants anything but this?

BEFORE 9/11: BUT NOW, WHERE WERE WE?

Here's the beginning of the draft that was:

James A. Berlin in both *Rhetoric and Reality: Writing Instruction in American Colleges, 1900–1985* (1987) and *Rhetorics, Poetics, and Cultures: Refiguring College English Studies* (1996) acknowledges his debt to Kenneth Burke, particularly for his theory of language as socially and dialectically constructed and consequential in the world. In *Rhetoric and Reality*, he uses Burke to revise rhetoric into political action. Although he relies less on Burke in *Rhetorics, Poetics, and Cultures*, he assumes in the second book the arguments he makes in the first and attributes to Burke. Across the two books and many articles, Berlin builds his conception of the right relationship between rhetoric and reality, as he (1) revises political rhetoric into ideological action aimed to subvert dominant discursive formations and hegemonic powers in search of social justice, (2) revises the teaching of rhetoric and composition in universities into global ideological action, (3) transforms teachers and students into social epistemic workers, and (4) refigures power within English departments by aligning those in rhetoric and composition with those in cultural studies to gain control from literature.

Berlin's own rhetoric, traditionally academic in his reliance on logical arguments based on historical, archival, and textual research, radically changed the individual and collective identities of many teachers of rhetoric and composition in community colleges, colleges, and universities. In *Rhetoric and Reality*, he does so through a familiar rhetorical strategy, divide and conquer, to develop his theory of epistemic rhetoric and persuade readers to join him in a new and improved identity, theory, and practice. He contextualizes the older rhetorics of science or pseudo-science, including psychology, and he situates epistemic rhetoric in both philosophy and politics to give epistemic rhetoric and the teachers of epistemic rhetoric greater authority within English departments and stronger connections to transformative work worldwide.

More specifically, he creates a taxonomy or chart to incorporate a dream and a prayer; he tells a linear, progressive, narrative history that moves toward what's best by replacing what's been. The objectively presented taxonomy of rhetorics and their related epistemologies—objectivist, subjectivist, and epistemic—and their related politics—conservative, liberal, and ideological—rewrites the history of writing instruction. It discards what was, to present what's new and best, epistemic rhetoric. His history, of course, leads in part to a denial of history, as we all rewrite history for specific motives and probable consequences.

Berlin's comprehensive yet specific analysis in *Rhetoric and Reality* is convincing because of how he argues and the kinds of evidence he gives. He knew how to encourage readers to identify with him to change our identities and our situations within English departments. His arguments, counter-statements to 1980s politics, economics, and education, appealed to us as we sought change in our collective and individual identities.

As we had learned to interact more closely with students throughout the processes of writing, we faced *with* them ways of constructing personal and public identities and their individual and collective selves in writing, as we recognized our positions as evaluators and faculty within school hierarchies. Approaches to writing as processes for different kinds and scenes for writing, did not necessarily replace textual and current-traditional methods but, rather, broadened the scope and circumferences, as psychoanalytic, historical, and reader response criticism extended the boundaries of analysis beyond the text itself, the object of formalist and new critical perspectives.

Berlin provided another counter-statement to what was flourishing. He convinced us by example to use and teach argument, analysis, critical research methods, and conventions of academic discourse that were also more persuasive in English departments and in higher education where they were already practiced. He also demonstrated how these practices could be used for the more broadly social and political purposes that teachers of writing sought. At the same time, he demonstrated the apparently contradictory desire for disciplinary status as well as the workloads, positions, ranks, and merits of traditional academics, specifically literary scholars.

Based on his taxonomy and other methods of engaging readers to identify with him in *Rhetoric and Reality*, Berlin writes *Rhetoric, Poetics, and Cultures* as a direct call to action. He argues forthrightly for a change of identity in teachers and students into a collective of social epistemic workers, and he argues for a refiguring of power within English departments and a redefinition of them as sites for global social justice. As he expands the goals of teaching writing, rhetoric, and cultural studies as specific ideological actions, he revises the role of community colleges and universities, particularly land grant universities, to serve the needs of the citizens of the state by subverting the status quo and oppression within the state and world.

My purposes in this chapter are to use the lesson in writing that I attribute to Burke in chapter 4 to discuss Berlin's lesson. I also draw from chapter 1, particularly on the distinctions I make between rhetoric and ideology and on my claim that Burke privileges rhetoric and subordinates history, psychology, ideology, religion, economics, and more, all to the status of means of persuasion. He realigns other disciplines to create another hierarchy with rhetoric as key, to address the problems in communication that lead to war. His interdisciplinary rhetorical work also spans all areas within English, including creative writing, literature, linguistics, film, folklore, and cultural studies. He works with all institutions at the national and international level, rather than with institutions of higher education or a particular institution. He *focuses on* a rhetoric of identification and *focuses off* other rhetorics, not as a substitution or replacement of the "sound traditional approach" but as "an accessory to the standard lore" (Burke, *RM* xiv).

I begin with the specific references to Burke that Berlin makes in *Rhetoric and Reality* to demonstrate how he selects from and uses Burke for his purposes. I contrast his selections and purposes with my own. I examine Edward Corbett's early reading of Burke's method of rhetorical analysis to contrast his reading with Berlin's later interpretation. I contrast Berlin's uses of a taxonomy and of oppositions to Burke's understanding and uses of charts and oppositions. I also contrast Burke's enthymematic, collaborative method of proof to Berlin's use of logical appeals and the consequent writer-reader relationship. Berlin unites teachers and students in composition with him as social epistemic workers, but he continues to position himself as the model who transforms students. His relationship with his readers is similar, in that he identifies with readers and encourages us to identify with him, with weight on his authority.

Berlin's rhetoric continues to be persuasive, as ideological purposes subordinate a rhetoric of collaboration. Throughout, I evaluate the gains and losses of Burke's overinvestment in rhetoric and Berlin's overinvestment in politics and ideology.

What's missing for me from *Rhetoric and Reality* are not subjectivist and objectivist rhetorics, because Berlin himself uses them effectively along with epistemic rhetoric in his writing. What's missing is the explicit recognition of the values of such rhetorics and methods of teaching in specific contexts with particular students, and the importance of attitude in the uses of any methods, philosophies, and theories. What's missing from *Rhetorics, Poet-*

ics, and Cultures is not students, because they are central as the objects who will benefit from his theories and practices, but rather what students bring to the interaction between students and teachers. This recognition of students and what they bring does not have to be interpreted as some essential self, complete unto itself. Social epistemic rhetoric does not need to exclude expressivist and current-traditional rhetorics nor the dialectical relationship between self and other and self and social. It's not as simple as that, as Burke teaches us. What's also missing for me is another lesson Burke teaches: we can read literature as rhetoric and use the resources of poetics for formal and stylistic identification in order to learn to get along. The aim is to expand the resources of rhetoric and develop our abilities to use and select from the resources in given contexts in order to war with words.

Berlin's Final Plea for Collaboration: A Broader Invitation to Teachers of English

Berlin's texts demonstrate the persuasiveness of his authoritative stance, his logical arguments, his convincing uses of various kinds of research, his certain conclusions, and his attitude toward his readers. He invites readers to identify with him as a revolutionary scholar/teacher dedicated to acting, in classes, in writing, and in the world, for changes to improve the lives of others. Although he seems to write with little doubt, his works demonstrate how he collaborates with others in his research, reading carefully and critically and aligning himself with or against other scholars in an ongoing academic conversation. He also presents himself as professionally collaborative by using traditional academic conventions. Ironically, perhaps, he supports rather than threatens academic standards by his use of the traditional method of proof and means of persuasion. Despite what he advocates, he also extends the traditional goals of education in America through his ways of writing and his conceptions of power and hierarchy within English and in the world.

In his conclusion, he includes English teachers at all levels in his effort to transform their traditionally accepted identities as gate-keepers, teachers of literature, social workers, therapists, and public servants. College composition teachers become professionals, as well as professors, public intellectuals, and agents of social change. Justice begins at home in English departments and in colleges and schools as teachers of English, teachers of reading *and* writing, collaborate across school/university boundaries:

> I thus want to make my last word a plea for collaborative effort. No group of English teachers ought to see themselves as operating in

isolation from their fellows in working for change. Dialogue among college teachers and teachers in the high schools and elementary schools is crucial for any effort at seeking improvement to succeed. For too long, college English teachers have ignored their colleagues in the schools, assuming a hierarchical division of labor in which information and ideas flow exclusively from top to bottom. It is time all reading and writing teachers situate their activities within the contexts of the larger profession as well as the contexts of economic and political concerns. We have much to gain working together, much to lose working alone. (Berlin, *Rhetorics, Poetics, and Culture* 180)[36]

Berlin's final words are a plea for collaboration and for what he deems is good if not best for all. Although he creates identification with his readers and listeners in order to persuade, he advocates teaching writing as a conversion of students into social epistemic workers and advocates the transformation of teachers into professional epistemic workers. He recommends that we widen the scope to include teachers of epistemic rhetoric at all levels.

As he attempts to unify teachers with his ideological persuasion, he ignores students who in fact connect and transgress the various levels of education, elementary, secondary, community colleges, and universities. They also need to be included, not only as ones who need to know but also as ones whose knowledge and experiences are needed so that teachers know more. A rhetoric of identification transforms all participants, all of whom are teachers and learners for each other, rather than converting some for their own good.

---

36. In the Afterword, Berlin's colleague and friend Janice M. Lauer explains how Berlin on the morning of his death had been making "final revisions based on extensive reader reviews from NCTE and eighteenth-century scholars at Purdue" (*Rhetorics, Poetics, and Culture* 181). She writes that his "re-visioning of the field of English" was "dear to Jim" and explains the driving motives of his work:

> He had a passion for the profession, seeing its potential for empowering students to critique and revise the cultural conditions shaping their lives. A fighter for social justice, he considered the current material and political arrangements in the Western world as marginalizing and disempowering them. Opposing these conditions, he maintained, was an important mission of the field of English, with composition in the forefront. Despite his two earlier books on the history of composition instruction in changing economic and political conditions, histories of the field of English were still overlooking the composition and its central role. This book strives to retell the history of English studies in the United States, analyzing the complex relationship between rhetoric and poetic, between composition and literature. (181).

Neither Burke's rhetoric nor Berlin's rhetoric is adequate for all kinds of teaching and learning, nor is it useful for all teachers, students, and contexts. We still have to figure out when, where, how, why, and for whom to use the act of identification as a means of changing identities, cultures, and contexts and promoting collaboration.

That's the beginning of the draft of this chapter before 9/11 when attacks on the US blasted national boundaries and penetrated the icons of capitalism and government and the people within them to refigure individual lives, nations, and the future. The attacks exploded my thinking and writing and tore my academic discourse, designed in part to exclude what the writer doesn't know and can't control in a linear and logical order, including aspects of herself that aren't professional. Although ideology as a subject and method of critique is current in academic writing today, the personal, the roundabout, and enthymematic proof are, for the most part, absent from academic discourse.

Questioning My Motives and Understanding: Why Write about Berlin?

Even before 9/11, I had my doubts. Berlin's work has always been charged for many reasons: it marks the major shifts in rhetoric and composition studies in the decades since the 1960s, since I became a teacher and scholar. As he makes clear, the changes he documents are ones that many others made happen, and his arguments for social epistemic rhetoric grew out of the work of his predecessors and current colleagues and friends. But Berlin was able to analyze and synthesize a wealth of material and to speak and write persuasively to readers as colleagues in ways that continue to ripple throughout the profession: He taught us how to become professionals by what he wrote and how he theorized, researched, and wrote. At the same time, he restricted what counts as professional to the standards established by literary scholars and the university as a whole. He emphasized logical arguments and restricted the teaching of writing and rhetoric to social epistemic rhetoric that negates how expressivist and current traditional rhetorics can persuade students to write and rewrite when teaches choose wisely for specific students and contexts. He criticized notions of the individual, and he restricted writing to the ideological and to a specific ideology.

More specifically, he revised the field of rhetoric and composition (1) from process and politics to an explicit ideological orientation and specified social actions to fight hegemonic powers; (2) from teaching students to write to think, learn, and negotiate, to teaching to transform students into ideological workers; and (3) from a professional organization of teachers, to teachers as professionals, authorized by research, history, theory, and practice. He expanded globally how we in rhetoric and composition can fight injustice, but this emphasis turned us away from the local, the individuals in our classes and departments, and institutions. His correction has become an over-correction and has lost the dialectical.

At the time, though, Berlin was our spokesperson, in part because he connected our past to the present in the late 1980s, gathering together the political origins of rhetoric, the battles for civil rights in the 1960s, the protests against Vietnam, and the oppression of global economies, with enough looseness so that we were invited to join him in the political formation of the history of the field, the intellectual work of teaching writing and rhetoric, and the reformation of English Studies. He rallied us by offering an interpretation to justify our desires to teach writing to students, and he gave us a set of distinctions to realign power relationships in traditional English departments in the 1980s. He showed a way to transform liberal politics and activism of the 1960s into 1980s action with "epistemic rhetoric," a redundancy required to reinforce the legitimacy, authority, and status of rhetoric not only in rhetoric and composition but also in English and in the humanities.

Later, in *Rhetorics, Poetics, and Cultures* he established us, at least symbolically and imaginatively, as dominant within English through an alliance with cultural studies.[37]

He was a leader with whom we identified. But who was this "we," what were our motives and identities, what have been the consequences of our actions, and what can we learn from these actions that will equip us for living now?

The Reality of a Rhetoric of Exclusion and Hierarchy in Composition and Rhetorical Studies

I first read *Rhetoric and Reality: Writing Instruction in American Colleges, 1900–1985* in 1988, after having read his articles that led to the book. I think I realized even then that Berlin's history and classifications realigned teachers of composition and rhetoric by distinguishing us from each other. His analysis provided a mirror in which teachers of writing could see ourselves in a new way, sorted and ranked, as current or out-of-date; as teachers

---

37. For more on this alliance, see Victor Vitanza's *James A. Berlin and Social-Epistemic Rhetorics: A Seminar* (Parlor Press, 2021).

or researchers; as subjectivists, objectivists, or social epistemic workers; as romantics, realists, or political activists.

Further divisions followed, with research, for example, branching into historical, cognitivist, empirical, quantitative, qualitative, ethnographic, and archival.

A hierarchy grew among methods of research to privilege some and reject others. For example, cognitivist researchers, most notably Linda Flower and John Hayes, drew on psychology and learning theory to define writing as problem-solving. Through protocol analysis they studied individuals making choices in writing. Berlin and others were critical of their focus on cognition and focus off contexts of situations, cultures, and ideologies. Problem-solving was associated with science and business, although Freire's problem-solving pedagogy was highly acclaimed for its focus on critical cultural consciousness. The trajectory of Flower's work, however, has led to a powerful integration of the self and social, cognitive and the cultural, and current-traditional, expressionist, and social epistemic in her literacy teaching and research.

As scholars in rhetoric and composition have been dominated by the ranks and hierarchy of the academy, we have continued to scapegoat each other, as well as others in English studies.

September 12, 2001: I turn off the radio and turn on the television and sit down to write, but I check email. I turn on the radio and turn off the sound on the television. I'll return to chapter five and work on the bits and pieces.

I return to the Spring 1995 issue of *Rhetoric Review* that includes articles I reread often. As a group, they help me criticize my ongoing construction of Burke's identification, how my reading of Burke differs from Berlin's, and my understanding of the persuasiveness of Berlin's ideological lesson on writing on scholars in rhetoric and composition. Although several authors refer to Berlin, I am particularly interested in this issue as an early site of conflicts and contradictions about the conflation of rhetoric and ideology in the field and, more specifically, in Berlin's social epistemic rhetoric.

The spring 1995 issue of *Rhetoric Review* begins with a symposium on peer reviewing in scholarly journals. Susan Hunter concludes the symposium with "The Case for Reviewing as Collaboration and Response," in which she stresses listening and learning as constitutive of collaboration in writing and publishing. In the second article, "The Feminization of Rhetoric and Composition Studies?" Janice M. Lauer presents her stories of the disciplinary formation of rhetoric and composition as a "web of friendship" (280). In the next article, "Remapping Rhetorical Territory," Cheryl Glenn challenges the "Western Paternal Narrative of rhetoric" (292) and provides new maps and directions to include women in the histories, theories, and practices of rhetoric. Frank Farmer's emphasis is clear in his title, "Voice Reprised: Three Etudes for a Dialogic Understanding." Ellen Gardiner, in "Peter Elbow's Rhetoric of Reading," argues that the "taxonomic critiques [of Elbow] oversimplify his theoretical and pedagogical position within the field of composition studies" (321).

I will return later to the next article by Marshall W. Alcorn Jr., "Changing the Subject of Postmodernist Theory: Discourse, Ideology, and Therapy in the Classroom," and to his email exchange with Victor J. Vitanza. In the article, Alcorn explains that "Berlin's account of a liberating postmodernist pedagogy depends upon two contradictory and highly suspect models that purport to describe changes in political identity" (339). The first, which he says Berlin appeals to in his description of classroom practice, "is an "awkward synthesis of humanist and postmodernist beliefs. Berlin assumes that because the subject is a structure of ideological conflict, this conflict can lead naturally to a kind of resolution through knowledge and political action," but that the "postmodernist subject, unlike the humanist subject, is *essentially* a structure of discourse conflict" with "no mechanism or motivation for being anything *other* than such a structure of conflict" (339–40). Because a "teacher could never hope to change the structure of, or resolve the conflict in, a subject by merely adding more discourse or conflict to the subject" (340), his purpose is to propose a psychoanalytic model for change. I will return later to the ideological/psychological issues here that Burke wrestles with throughout his rhetoric. For now, my purpose is to indicate the conflicts and contradictions in each of the essays between rhetoric and ideology and rhetorics of collaboration and rhetorics of conflict in teaching.

Dennis A. Lynch in "Teaching Rhetorical Values and the Question of Student Autonomy" also examines the relationship between rhetoric and politics and possibilities for social change. His analysis of *The New Rhetoric* has helped me over time understand further my reading of Burke's identification.

For my purposes, Lynch provides a useful summary of pages 13–62 of *The New Rhetoric*, beginning with its claim that argumentation requires "an effective community of minds" and specific conditions, including the following that are also integral to Burke's rhetoric of identification: (1) a "common language"; (2) "rules or norms that permit a conversation to begin"; (3) a "circumscribed set of people to be addressed"; (4) "a sincere interest in 'gaining the adherence' of one's interlocutor"; "a certain modesty on the part of the initiator of the argument (captured in the fact that one does not put one's beliefs beyond question"; (5) "a certain modesty on the part of the initiator of the argument (captured in the fact that one does not put one's beliefs beyond question)"; (6) "a concern for one's interlocutor, and an interest in his or her 'state of mind'"; (7) "a willingness not only to listen but to try to understand"; (8) the "'practical commitment of those who take part in the argument'"; (9) a "recognition of the enabling and inhibiting effects of institutional constraints on discourse"; (10) "a desire 'to be regarded as a member of a more-or-less egalitarian society'"; (11) a "'willingness to eventually accept another's point of view'"; and (12) "the recognition and acceptance of the fact that participants may emerge from the discussion no longer exactly the same at the end as they were at the beginning—a willingness to change with the ongoing argument and an acceptance of change" (361).

Lynch's description of "a strange mix of conservative and at the same time potentially transformative impulses" (361) also informs my understanding of the gains and losses of Burke's identification today and classifications of it as liberal, conservative, humanist, and more:

> On the one hand, the authors [Perelman and Olbrechts-Tyteca] assume the possibility of relatively stable communities of interlocutors; they do not address the question of ideology; and they do not examine the possible, insidious forms of pseudo-consensus that may and do disturb contemporary readers. On the other hand, the authors do maintain that the relationship between speakers and audiences are historically bound and contingent affairs (even the much debated "universal audience"); and however much they may rely on notions of "individuality" and "intention," the authors need not be read as simple-minded humanists: for instance, they privilege practice over theory, and, in the conditions that make serious argumentation possible (see nos. 7, 11, and 12 in the list above), they describe what amounts to a rhetoric of action and self-overcoming. (362)

Lynch continues to explain that "[w]hat is missing from *The New Rhetoric*, among other things, is a more sophisticated discussion of the connections between thought and action, among rhetoric, myth, and ideology, and *between 'symbolic action' and the increasing institutionalization [of] our practices*—which is to say, finally, a more complicated discussion of the relations between rhetoric and power" (362; my emphasis). He adds that his aim "is not to argue that *The New Rhetoric* itself may survive the postmodern attack on humanism" but "that even a relatively conservative reading of *The New Rhetoric* argues for a commitment to some of the specific social and political values that less-conservative rhetoricians and compositionists have recently sought to bring into their classrooms and teaching practices (Berlin, Bizzell, Crowley, Jarratt, Trimbur)" (362–63).

My question now, as in 1995, is why do we academic *animal symbolicum* tend to use terms, for example, *postmodernism, attacks on humanism, liberal*, and *conservative*, as clear-cut distinctions and referential truths rather than as symbolic actions, motivated and consequential? As Lynch concludes this section with a recognition of the limitations and the values of *The New Rhetoric* and his advice that we not dismiss it, he also recommends an inclusive rhetoric rather than one that replaces what has gone:

> To understand someone within a serious rhetorical situation, according to Perelman and Olbrechts-Tyteca, is to establish a real relationship that develops over time, one that engages the whole person (within an institutional setting), requires a willingness on our part to accept a change in our circumstances, and, possibly, to "become what we are not" (Foucault; Gadamer; Rorty). (363)

In his final section, "Teaching Rhetorical Values and the Question of Student-Autonomy," he explains that the "value of autonomy is not in question for the rhetoricians discussed above" (Lynch 364). He then asks,

> The question, in other words, is not, should we teach students the values that make rhetoric possible *or* should we teach students in a manner that respects their autonomy. The question might be better asked in this way: How can we encourage in students the values that condition the successful practice of rhetoric without undermining the independence of thought they will need in order to participate maturely in public forums?" (365).

What is missing from the arguments offered by Marius and Phelps regarding "autonomy" and "student-autonomy," is

> an explanation of the relation among independence and dependence as it affects our efforts to understand what needs to be done or affects our efforts to be autonomous in our decision- making- as well as an articulation of the differences between, for example, ethical, intellectual, and political autonomy. (365)

Michael Hassett's "Sophisticated Burke: Kenneth Burke as a Neosophistic Rhetorician" provides for me an implicit response to Lynch's statement that what's missing from *The New Rhetoric* is "a more sophisticated discussion of the connections between thought and action, among rhetoric, myth and ideology, and between 'symbolic action' and the increasing institutionalization [of] our practices—which is to say, finally, a more complicated discussion of the relations between rhetoric and power" (362). Hassett interprets Burke as a "Neosophistic Rhetorician." In removing him from the company of those who, as Lynch says, "rely on the notions of 'individuality' and 'intention'" and who are "simple-minded humanists" (362), Hassett makes Burke useful for postmodern theories and "keep[s] him in the conversation as an important voice" (338).

Finally, Brenda Jo Brueggemann in "The Coming Out of Deaf Culture and American Sign Language: An Exploration into Visual Rhetoric and Literacy," teaches us about an embodied language and helps me explore the dimensions of Burke's conception of people as bodies that learn languages.

Burke's "Philosophy of the Bin" and Berlin's Classifications: The Blurring of Lines

In his final chapter of *Rhetoric and Reality*, "Conclusion and Postscript on the Present," Berlin revises his taxonomy of major rhetorical theories from 1960–1975 to present them as more fluid than he did earlier and to note the progress some scholars and teachers have made, as he moves them from his former classification to let them join those who practice and teach epistemic rhetoric. In sum, as he defines the major theories, he sorts and ranks teachers of composition and rhetoric into the three categories, with the understanding that the last is best and should replace the other two. He draws lines to organize and align the troops with him and his position, solidly based in history, research, and theory.

Until his conclusion, he treats his taxonomy as accurate and inflexible, but in conclusion he converts it into a heuristic designed to motivate teachers to change their ways and become stronger teachers. And his evidence demonstrates that his strategy worked because the categories no longer work:

> I should at the start mention that the taxonomy I have used in discussing rhetoric and writing up to 1975 does not prove as descriptive after this date. The most important reason for this has been the tendency of certain rhetorics within the subjective and transactional categories to move in the direction of the epistemic, regarding rhetoric as principally a method of discovering and even creating knowledge, frequently within socially defined discourse communities (Berlin, *Rhetoric and Reality* 183).

Instead of taking the credit for this tendency, he gives the credit to Fredric Jameson and, roundabout, returns it to himself, with the approval of "the major American Marxist critic of the time," the same one who assessed

Burke, as we saw in chapter 1, as deficient in the article to which Berlin refers. He also associates his theory of epistemic rhetoric with major ideological and philosophical critics and includes all as rhetorical:

> Behind this has been what Fredric Jameson has characterized as "the discovery of the primacy of Language or the Symbolic" (186). Rhetoricians of all stripes have become involved in the discussions encouraged by poststructuralist literary and cultural criticism, by Marxist and other sociologistic speculations on culture, and, especially, by the reawakening of philosophical pragmatism as led by Richard Rorty. All share to some extent an emphasis on the social nature of language, locating language at the center of the formation of discourse communities which in turn define the self, the other, the material world, and the possible relations among these. As I have suggested elsewhere, thinkers as diverse as Alfred North Whitehead, Susanne Langer, Michael Polanyi, Thomas Kuhn, Hayden White, Michel Foucault, and Rorty, have put forth the notion that the elements traditionally considered the central concerns of rhetoric—reality, interlocutor, audience, and language—are the very elements that are involved in the formation of knowledge (Berlin, "Contemporary Composition"). To these theorists I would add the names of Jameson, Roland Barthes, Raymond Williams, Terry Eagleton, Edward Said, and Frank Lentricchia. Rhetoricians operating from a variety of perspectives have appropriately turned to these figures and others like them in discussing their enterprise, and in so doing have underscored the epistemic nature of rhetoric. (Berlin, *Rhetoric and Reality* 183–84)

Berlin corrects what he meant to say earlier:

> I should emphasize that I am not suggesting that these new developments have led to an inevitable collapse of all schools into epistemic rhetoric camp. I am simply saying that certain rhetorics, in the way they have begun to consider the symbolic and social context of discourse, have introduced elements ordinarily associated with epistemic rhetoric. (*Rhetoric and Reality* 184)

As he discusses "Expressionistic rhetoric," the "more extreme manifestations" of which "have vanished," he says that the work of Elbow, Macrorie, Murray, Coles, and Gibson "still attracts a wide hearing"; nevertheless, "there have been efforts to characterize certain branches of this rhetoric as epistemic" (Berlin, *Rhetoric and Reality* 184). His criticism of Kenneth Dowst, who now "looks upon certain uses of language as epistemic, forming as well as expressing knowledge," is that "these uses are still primarily involved in shaping private rather than social versions of knowledge, and are distinct from a rhetoric that serves non-epistemic functions—in persuasive or expository writing" (184–85).

Here Berlin redraws lines he drew earlier, but he continues to use terms like *private* and *social* as discrete and referential rather than dialectical and rhetorical. He has thrown out non-epistemic functions, private versions of knowledge, and individual scholars and teachers.

The clarity and certainty of Berlin's terms and classifications make his work persuasive as teachers and scholars in rhetoric and composition continue to professionalize and restore the discipline of rhetoric to its rightful place within English and the academy.[38]

The disciplining that motivates his taxonomy and the problems with any grouping emerge as he disciplines and then reassigns David Bartholomae. Berlin says Bartholomae's earlier work on error analysis, for example, associated him with cognitivist approaches, but he can now be moved firmly (by Berlin) into the ranks of the epistemic category, calling on the discussions of discourse communities in Foucault and on the cultural analysis of Said, as well as on "the rhetorical speculations of Kenneth Burke and Patricia Bizzell" (185).

It is ironic that Berlin draws here on Burke. Error analysis may be treated as cognitivist and may be treated as epistemic, depending as Burke says, "on the basis of some strategic element common to the items grouped" (*PLF* 302). Burke defends himself against reviewers who have found "'intuitive' leaps that are dubious as 'science'" in his approaches to literary works, by saying that they "are not 'leaps' at all": "They are classifications, groupings,

---

38. See Thomas P. Miller's *The Formation of College English: Rhetoric and Belles Lettres in the British Cultural Provinces* as an excellent example of a history that in stressing rhetoric counters histories that emphasize literature in college English, such as Gerald Graff's *Professing English Literature: An Institutional History*. Other recent works that attempt to redefine English from the perspective of rhetoric and composition include *What Is English?* edited by Peter Elbow; *The English Coalition Conference: Democracy Through Language*, edited by Richard Lloyd-Jones and Andrea A. Lunsford; and W. Ross Winterowd's *The English Department: A Personal and Institutional History*. Two books that include essays by scholars in rhetoric and composition, cultural studies, and literature are *Redrawing the Boundaries: The Transformation of English and American Literacy Studies*, edited by Stephen Greenblatt and Giles Gunn, and *English as a Discipline; or, Is There a Plot in This Play?*, edited by James C. Raymond. In the last collection, see my essay "Making Do, Making Believe, and Making Sense: Burkean Magic and the Essence of English Departments," 143-59. See also issues of the *ADE Bulletin* as an ongoing definition of the attitudes, terms, and actions of English departments.

made on the basis of some strategic element common to the items grouped" (*PLF* 302). He later admits: "It would, I admit, violate current pieties, break down current categories, and thereby 'outrage good taste,'" but "'good taste' has become *inert*'" (*PLF* 303). He explains further: The "classifications I am proposing would be active. I think that what we need is active categories," that "will lie on the bias across the categories of modern specialization" (*PLF* 303). He concludes that the "Philosophy of the Bin" in "contemporary specialization" can be added to the "Philosophy of the Being" and the "Philosophy of the Becoming" (*PLF* 303). A "sociological approach should attempt to provide a reintegrative point of view, a broader empire of investigation encompassing the lot" (*PLF* 304–04)." His classifications are strategic and rhetorical rather than scientific and true.

WHERE HAVE ALL THE EXPRESSIVISTS GONE WHO NEVER LEFT BUT ARE NOW RETURNING?

Today, I'm just trying to stay afloat by writing, with words in my head, on my computer, and on television. William Stafford says in *Writing the Australian Crawl* that we have to have faith that writing, like water, will keep us afloat. We have to reach way out, put our heads down, pull, and kick, accepting the support, not fighting it.

Stafford and Burke came to the Wyoming Conference the same summer. They didn't know each other but knew of each other. They seemed to hit it off. One night a group of us went with them to the Cowboy Bar, on Ivinson near the train tracks, where a bullet hole is still in the wall above the bar. Burke sat in a chair to watch people play pool as he listened and talked with others. We went upstairs and sat in a large semi-circular booth. Stafford told us about how he begins his classes, by waiting for students to ask about the course, waiting for them to ask if they should get books from the bookstore, waiting for them to ask about assignments? Through silence, he lets students take the initiative and gain authority.

In *Writing the Australian Crawl* he wrote about sitting down every morning, with pen and paper in hand, waiting for the nibble. On any given day he might not get a catch, but he surely wouldn't if he weren't waiting, ready to accept what comes on the page.

In rhetoric and composition, we don't study or write much about Stafford, Corder, Murray, Macrorie, and other professional and creative writers to learn about writing and teaching writing. Have we set ourselves so at odds with literature and with the "creative" that we only understand writing as academic and ourselves as academic professionals? Have we narrowed the scope and circumference of what counts as writing and teaching writing so that we exclude writing that doesn't fit a formula? I don't think so.

Donald Murray's writing, that of a journalist, poet, fiction writer, and essayist, continues to inform the teaching of writing across the country, particularly in schools, even though it has been dismissed for focusing on individual students, their personal, academic, public, and political experiences, and their revisions. Liberal politics perpetuate the status quo. Certain ideologies erase the past, the history of writing and teaching writing. It's as if those of us who learned from and taught from Murray, Coles, Shaughnessey, Corder, and Macrorie should circumscribe the past in order to gain access to what's current, instead of taking responsibility for selecting among and combining various means of teaching students in given contexts. We can incorporate current ideological critique of expressivist discourse, current-traditional rhetoric, creativity, subject position, subjectivity, and more, without rejecting past theories, practices, and histories to show that we belong. We can realize that situations change, that what worked won't necessarily work in new contexts, and that we have to discover and adapt means of persuasion and use all that is there to use.

Many, including Wendy Bishop, Mike Rose, Jacqueline Jones Royster, Sondra Perl, Nancy Sommers, Martha Marinara, Keith Gilyard, Julie Jung, Richard Miller, Jane E. Hindman, Ellen Cushman, Victor Villanueva, Kathleen Blake Yancey, and others, combine academic, expressive, and creative writing. Teaching of writing through contrasting and combining forms, genres, voices, and more continues with more added force and current understanding. It's difficult to describe Burke as an academic writer because the term seems too restrictive. Critics like Paul Jay, Greig Henderson, D. Diane Davis, Ross Wolin, and others are exploring how he writes as creative, poststructuralist, and contingent. Is he a current-traditionalist, an expressivist, and/or a social epistemic worker, or a rhetorician? We choose, taking our chances, knowing our selections are temporary and partial, and accepting that our choices are constrained.

CORBETT'S CONSTRUCTION OF BURKE'S RHETORICAL ANALYSIS IN THE LATE 1960S

In the draft written before 9/11, I analyzed Edward P. J. Corbett's introduction to his 1969 *Rhetorical Analyses of Literary Works* to figure out Burke's earlier place in the academic world, before scholars in English, Communication, and Speech identified him as a rhetorician. I also wanted to create a

Burke through Corbett to contrast with Berlin's Burke and my construction of Burke.

Corbett uses M. H. Abrams's classification of the four kinds of literary criticism in *The Mirror and the Lamp*, a taxonomy used also by Warnock, Fulkerson, Berlin, and others.[39] He uses Abrams's schema but also his authority to legitimize rhetorical analysis by including it under Pragmatic Criticism and then revising that label into Rhetorical Criticism. In this and other ways, the introduction suggests that the relationship between rhetoric and literature in the 1960s was not unlike the relationship Berlin later presents.

Corbett distinguishes between rhetorical analysis and other literary critical methods by defining the term *rhetoric*, providing a history of the discipline of rhetoric, and using Abrams's taxonomy for literary criticism in the Western tradition: "the Work itself is set up in relationship to three external elements—the Universe, the Author, and the Audience" (xv). Objective Criticism focuses on the work itself and attends to "formal integrity and structure," the "constituent elements of matter and form which make it an aesthetic whole" (xv). Mimetic Criticism studies the work in relationship to the world or reality that the work represents. It focuses on "the truth, verisimilitude, the plausibility, of the representation or *mimesis* embodied in the literary work" (svi). Expressive Criticism "regards the work in relation to its author" and is "interested primarily in the psychology of the creative act" (xvi).

Pragmatic Criticism, or Rhetorical Criticism, considers, according to Abrams, the work of art as "a means to an end, an instrument for getting something done, and tends to judge its value according to its success in achieving that aim" (qtd. in Corbett xvi). Corbett explains that "[s]ome students of rhetoric are wary of any rhetorical criticism that studies the literary work in relation to the external author and audience. Robert M. Browne, for example, "prefers a rhetorical criticism that remains inside the work for its study of the interrelationships" (xx). Corbett quotes from Browne's 1967 "Rhetorical Analysis and Poetic Structure":

> The rhetoric which derives from the poet's extra-poetic intention [somewhat the same thing that Wimsatt means by "intentional fallacy"] may be called *external* rhetoric, external because both poet

---

39. See John Warnock's 1973 *College English* article, "The Relation of Critical Perspectives to Teaching Methods in Composition," Richard Fulkerson's 1979 "Four Philosophies of Composition" in *College Composition and Communication*, and James A. Berlin's 1982 *College English* article, "Contemporary Composition: The Major Pedagogical Theories," from which he builds *Rhetoric and Reality*.

and readers are outside the poem. But rhetoric enters the poem in a third and more intrinsic way: inside the poem there are speakers and hearers and processes of persuasion. We sometimes use the term *rhetoric* to apply to this *internal* rhetoric of the poem, and consider its speakers as rhetoricians. (qtd. in Corbett xx)

The intentional and pathetic fallacies have excluded authorial intention and audience responses, but Corbett, treading lightly on the grounds of literary criticism, responds to Browne's distinction between intrinsic and extrinsic to reinforce rhetoric and extend the limits of rhetorical analysis through Burke and Booth:[40]

> One can gain some valuable insights into the workings of a literary piece by concentrating on the rhetorical strategies operating within the work—and some of the critiques in this collection do just that—*but those critics, like Kenneth Burke and Wayne Booth, who have examined what Browne calls "external rhetoric" of a literary work, obviously do not feel that they are engaging in a bastardized form of rhetorical criticism.* (xx; my emphasis)

Corbett turns quickly to less risky but still related issues of *ethos* and the implied author. He quotes Thomas O. Sloan from "Restoration of Rhetoric to Literary Study": "Rhetorical criticism intensifies our sense of the dynamic relationship between the author as a real person and the more or less fictive person implied by the work" (qtd. in Corbett xxi). He also quotes Booth from *The Rhetoric of Fiction* to emphasize the reader:

> Though some characters and events may speak by themselves their artistic message to the reader, and thus carry in a weak form their own rhetoric, none will do so with proper clarity and force until the author brings all his powers to bear on the problem of making the reader see what they really are. The author cannot choose whether to use rhetorical heightening. His only choice is the kind of rhetoric he will use" (qtd. in Corbett xxi).

Corbett's introduction dramatizes retrospectively the extent to which Burke's counter-statement to literary criticism in 1931 was oppositional and

---

40. See chapter 1, "The Intrinsic/Extrinsic Merger," 7–42, in Greig E. Henderson's *Kenneth Burke: Literature and Language as Symbolic Action*, for a rich discussion of the intrinsic and extrinsic in Burke's rhetoric.

suggests why Burke initially contextualizes his rhetoric in poetics, aesthetics, and literature.[41]

BERLIN'S USES OF BURKE IN *RHETORIC AND REALITY*

From my draft before 9/11, I include the following examination of how Berlin uses Burke for his purposes, dissociating him from poetics and aesthetics and aligning him with rhetoric and politics, to contrast with my reading. Berlin uses Burke from the first page to the last to authorize epistemic rhetoric in *Rhetoric and Reality*, even though, as we have seen, Burke advocates that critics use all there is to use rather than classify methods as discrete and inherently better than others. Berlin acknowledges his debt to Kenneth Burke on the first and last pages of "An Overview" and refers to Burke throughout.

He begins by asserting that "[l]iteracy has always and everywhere been the center of the educational enterprise" and by distinguishing between rhetoric, "the production of spoken and written texts," and poetic, "the interpretation of text" (Berlin, *Rhetoric and Reality* 1). He unites the two by claiming that they have both been "the indispensable foundation of schooling, regardless of the age or intellectual level of the student" (1). Although he will "examine the forms that rhetorical instruction in writing has taken in the twentieth-century college classroom," he will be "glancing at the corresponding developments in poetics" because "from the start" writing and reading have "been lodged in the same department in the modern university" (1). "More important," he writes, "as Tzvetan Todorov, Kenneth Burke, and Charles Sears Baldwin have demonstrated, rhetoric and poetic historically have enjoyed a dialectical relationship, the one's functions being defined and determined by the other's" (1).

Berlin here uses Burke, along with Todorov and Sears, to justify his arguments about how writing instruction "has been shaped by instruction in literature" and how "approaches to literary interpretation have been affected by methods of teaching the production of rhetorical texts" (1). Although he uses Burke because he demonstrates the dialectical relationships between rhetoric and poetic and between reading and writing, Berlin clearly weights

---

41. See Ross Wolin's discussions throughout *The Rhetorical Imagination of Kenneth Burke* about how Burke tried and failed again and again to make his work persuasive to literary critics and other New York intellectuals. See his work, and Jack Selzer's *Kenneth Burke in Greenwich Village: Conversing with the Moderns*, for cultural, historical, and biographical work on Burke.

rhetoric over poetics as he progresses. He concludes the overview with another reference to Burke:

> Furthermore, there are the lessons learned from Kenneth Burke's work—especially his discussion in *Language as Symbolic Action* of the ineluctability of 'terministic screens'—the lessons of recent Marxist theory and of French and American poststructuralist cultural critics, the lessons from the contributions of American Neo-Pragmatists—particularly Richard Rorty—and, most important here, the lessons garnered from the poststructuralist historiography of Hayden White and Michel Foucault—all strongly arguing that it is impossible to perceive any object *except* through a terministic screen" (17).

He explains that a purpose of the introduction has been "to be candid about" the nature of *his* point of view and "its interpretative strategies" (17).

Berlin first links himself with Burke, White, and Foucault, but then dissociates himself from them:

> I might also add—although by now it is probably not necessary—that I have been especially influenced by Burke in my understanding of rhetoric. In my historical method I have found suggestive the work of White, most notably his discussion of the relationship between modes of emplotment, modes of explanation, and modes of ideological implication. Also valuable to me has been Foucault's discussion of the relationship between knowledge and power in discourse communities, and the role of discursive and nondiscursive practices in shaping consciousness within these communities. I should add, however, that I cannot claim to be a disciple of any one of the three. (18)

His other references to Burke build on these. For example, in "Rhetoric and Poetics in the English Department," he discusses the dialectical relationship between rhetoric and poetic, "the two serving as binary opposites, each giving the other significance by contrast" (25). He relies on Burke's "Rhetoric, Poetics, and Philosophy" and on Todorov for the distinguishing features of the two: "rhetoric is concerned with symbolic action in the material world, with practical consequences as an end, while poetic is concerned with symbolic action for itself, with contemplation of the text for its own sake" ("Rhetoric and Poetics" 26). He later refers to Burke's *Counter-Statement* and *Attitudes Toward History*, which "provided a model for a social and dialectical approach to both rhetoric and poetic" (*Rhetorics, Poetics, and*

Cultures 90), and he discusses Winterowd's *Rhetoric: A Synthesis* and Burke's influence on rhetoric (*Rhetorics, Poetics, and Cultures* 134).

In Berlin's reference to Michael Leff's "In Search of Ariadne's Thread: A Review of the Recent Literature on Rhetorical Theory" as the "best overview" of the subject, Burke reappears as an authoritative influence:

> Leff outlines four different senses in which rhetoric may be regarded as epistemic, but the most extreme is the one at issue here. In this point of view, rhetoric is epistemic because knowledge itself is a rhetorical construct. *Having historical precedents in Vico and Marx and a brilliant modern articulation in Kenneth Burke, this stance argues that epistemology is rhetorical,* it is the antithesis of the positivist contention that reality is empirical, with language simply reporting what is determined outside its domain. (Berlin 165; my emphasis)

The argument that all knowledge is a rhetorical construct is familiar today, but what is interesting is that "rhetoric" needed to be bolstered by "epistemic," a term from philosophy, with an emphasis on knowing and inventing, rather than on arrangement, style, or delivery.[42] As Berlin contextualizes epistemic rhetoric in even more recent works, he incorporates Richard Ohmann who in his 1964 "In Lieu of a New Rhetoric" does "some of the spadework for an epistemic rhetoric" (*Rhetorics, Poetics, and Cultures* 168). He says that Ohmann draws on Burke but that "the spirit of Burke is present throughout" (169), and he notes that in Ohmann's pedagogy the "text-audience relationship considers the appeal from ethos in the search for a Burkeian identification" (171). Berlin also recognizes that Young, Becker, and Pike in *Rhetoric, Discovery, and Change* "look upon rhetoric from a Burkeian point of view, seeing it as the effort of a writer to establish identification with an audience by understanding that audience's perspective and attempting to get it to understand the world through the writer's perspective" (*Rhetorics, Poetics, and Cultures* 171). He undercuts immediately this collaborative definition of identification: "This is a 'discussion rhetoric' rather than a rhetoric of persuasion; it is based on mutual respect and is dedicated to discovering shared interpretations of experience" (171). Here Berlin reveals his distinction between discussion, collaboration, and identification and a rhetoric of persuasion; his privileging of persuasion over identification; and his linking of persuasion with politics and ideologies and identification with discussion between and among individuals.

---

42. See Robert L. Scott's "On Viewing Rhetoric as Epistemic," "Rhetoric as Epistemic: Ten Years Later," "On Not Defining 'Rhetoric,'" and "Rhetoric Is Epistemic: What Difference Does That Make?" Also see Michael Leff's "In Search of Ariadne's Thread: A Review of the Recent Literature on Rhetorical Theory."

In his conclusion, Berlin turns again to Burke after he has said his taxonomy is not as "descriptive" after 1975 because "certain rhetorics" have "begun to consider the symbolic and social context of discourse" and "introduced elements ordinarily associated with epistemic rhetoric" (*Rhetorics, Poetics, and Cultures* 184). As mentioned earlier, he now relates Bartholomae to epistemic associated with Burke, Foucault, and Said. He then considers new directions in classical rhetoric that he also identifies as epistemic, but he does not consider the enthymeme, perhaps because of his concern with epistemology, drawn from philosophical discourse, and his interest in invention. His categories separate style from invention and perhaps the enthymeme as a figure from the enthymeme as action.

S. Michael Halloran, for example, calls "for a rhetoric of public discourse" and responds to William Grimaldi's *Studies in the Philosophy of Aristotle's Rhetoric* in *Essays on Classical Rhetoric and Modern Rhetoric*, edited by Connors, Ede, and Lunsford.[43] Berlin links the essays by Ede and Lunsford, James Kinneavy, and John Gage as "avowedly concerned with epistemological issues": "each in its own way argues for the centrality of invention in Aristotle—taking positions which move in the direction of considering his rhetoric to be, in a certain limited sense, epistemic" (*Rhetorics, Poetics, and Cultures* 185). He acknowledges that Aristotle's rhetoric is not primarily rational but doesn't explain what it is:

> From these points of view, Aristotelian rhetoric is not primarily rational and deductive—as it had been interpreted in the fifties, for example—but is a system that provides heuristics encouraging the discovery of knowledge in the probabilistic realm of law, politics, and public occasions, discoveries that include the emotional, the ethical, and the aesthetic as well as the rational. In this scheme, while knowledge may not be a social construct, it is discoverable through social behavior. (*Rhetorics, Poetics, and Cultures* 185–85)

This passage further differentiates Burke's lesson in writing as identification from Berlin's lesson in writing as epistemic in *Rhetoric and Reality*. First, Berlin seems to assume that Aristotle's *Rhetoric* exists apart from uses and abuses of it. He also suggests that invention is limited in Aristotle, per-

---

43. See chapter 2 for discussions of Grimaldi's work on the enthymeme and essays influenced by his scholarship in *Essays on Classical Rhetoric and Modern Discourse*. Berlin does not include James Raymond's essay on the enthymeme nor Grimaldi's and Raymond's linkages of the enthymeme and collaborative meaning-making. Paradoxically, Berlin's focus on the distinction between private and social versions of knowledge and his privileging of the social seems to result in a focus off of identification and the collective creation of meaning.

haps because the *Rhetoric* also includes discussions of situations, motives, arrangement, and style, perhaps because these are more obviously related to expressionistic and current-traditional rhetorics, as he has defined them, and perhaps because of the privileged culture to whom Aristotle's *Rhetoric* was addressed.

Grimaldi draws a finer, more subtle line, as we saw earlier in chapter 2. He demonstrates that the *Rhetoric* presents the enthymeme as the "body of proof" in rhetoric that appeals to the whole person, through appeals to *ethos, pathos, and logos*, depending on the particular context. The rhetor's task is to discover and invent means of persuasion and to choose logically among them; the rhetor appeals to the whole person, not only to logical reasoning.

I haven't worked on this chapter of disparate bits and pieces for several weeks: I don't want to make the chapter appear coherent and sustain a line of argument like a clothesline. I prefer the chordal approach, a narrative with plots within plots, and anything that allows us to stop and think rather than follow through to the end of the line. I seek "provisional hesitancy" to consider possibilities and preparations for further acts. There's too much going on in classrooms, listservs, and on television and radio. What are the social responsibilities of a critic?

Burke's Rhetorical Imagination and Song: A Cure for What Ails Us All

I picked up Ross Wolin's *The Rhetorical Imagination* (2001), which arrived from Amazon.com the week before September 11, 2021. I found myself agreeing, disagreeing, and writing all over the book. I turned down the tips of pages and then whole pages and finally groups of pages (Wolin 53–61, 71–90, and 205–21). On the inside pages of the front and back cover, I began clustering his statements and page numbers where he wrote about cuts across the bias of traditional categories and disciplinary lines (73), poetry as the means to achieve collective ends (89), identification and ideology (186), style as identification (186), and proof by identification (188). I noted page numbers that discuss identification, such as pages 75, 82, 92, 178, 103, and more. I starred passages that demonstrate where Burke extends and rearticulates connected terms and ideas without explicitly mentioning identification. Wolin's point is that these practices make reading Burke difficult, but it also reveals how Burke thinks.

Yes. He shows us his mind at work. As we experience how he creates, we join in, identifying with his false starts, confusions, and roundabout ways. We get tangled in the loose threads, respond to his requests for help, and grab on when he twists, turns, and contradicts himself. He doesn't want to control or dominate readers, but he does want to stretch us into making leaps we're not trained to take and turns that our inflexibilities resist.

I'm particularly interested in Wolin's discussions of the development of Burke's rhetoric, which he explains in part by the early negative reactions to his work and his ongoing attempts to find ways to be read and accepted. Throughout, he incorporates reviews of Burke and the correspondence collected by Paul Jay between Burke and Cowley to support his claims about Burke's developing thoughts.

When he writes that Burke "makes his case in new ways," I knew the book would be particularly valuable for me. And when he describes Burke's treatment in *Counter-Statement* of "form as a psychological relationship between the audience, the artist, and the artwork" and then develops this point more fully later (*CS* 219), I began to fear what I would find—that which I was trying to construct myself, arguments for identification as collaborative meaning-making and demonstrations of identification as the body of proof in Burke's rhetoric.

When I read recent books like Wolin's, Selzer's, Wess's, Kastely's, and others, I can't read for wanting to write. Having written all over his book, I stopped and decided to rein myself in by writing a review no one asked for.[44] *I was ready though to return to this chapter, still hanging loose like that portion of the tower we watched for weeks, filled with holes like a piece of sculpture or lace, like an enthymeme inviting us to act. But I hesitated and again charted some of Wolin's references that I read as references to identification but not necessarily supportive of my interpretation (75, 82, 92, 100, 103, 178). For example:*

> Yet literature also works by leading an audience to a conclusion, the effect gained by the final comprehension of the message after being taken through some "course" of apprehension. This amounts to a leading to a conclusion. Burke found this second sense of inducement so important that he devoted much of the discussion of symbolic appeal in "Lexicon Rhetoricae" to the theory and practice of leading the audience (in particular, "progressive form" and "qualitative form," which involve natural progressions of thought and feeling). Inducement as leading is so important to Burke that throughout his career he paid great attention to how logical progressions, telos, and entelechy feed into symbolic appeal. (Wolin 75)

---

44. I have since read Ann George's review of *The Rhetorical Imagination* in *Rhetoric Review* 21 (2002): 190-93.

"Perspective by incongruity," like orientation and motives, is a re-articulation of another idea from Counter-Statement, *eloquence. . . . As Burke points out in* Counter-Statement, *for example, qualitative progressive forms may work through opposition, contradiction, negation, and other such juxtapositions. . . . Eloquence, then, is a specifically literary means for achieving the more general kinds of perspective by incongruity developed in* Permanence. *But the differences run deeper. In the section on the function of metaphor (PC 94–96), for instance, Burke asserts that abstract thinking in general is metaphorical and that "schools of thought" (science in particular) arise out of metaphors writ large. (Wolin 82)*

Because acceptance frames are profoundly symbolic, Burke believed that literature is an especially appropriate starting place for understanding their nature, characteristics, and function in human affairs. In a description of his first intentions for "Acceptance and Rejection," Burke told Cowley that he intended to explore "how thinkers, of either the imaginative or conceptual sort, build vast symbolic bridges to get them across the gaps of conflict," including how "frames of acceptance become irrelevant, and even obstructive.". (Wolin 100; quoting Jay, 212–13)

The idea that identification and style are part of proof offers Burke's characteristic challenge to be wary of any explanatory system. Style has been part of rhetorical theory for two thousand years. Yet much of what we have learned about it amounts to competing taxonomies. Style is the least satisfactorily explained of the five canons because it is ineffable. We really do not have a clear idea of how style works other than saying of a particular stylistic choice that "it works." Burke has the most sophisticated explanation of style (in "Psychology and Form" and "Lexicon Rhetoricae" in Counter-Statement*), but he still relies much on the unsubstantiated assertion that there is some kind of psychological disposition to respond to certain forms of language in certain ways. For instance, regarding "qualitative form," he says: "We are prepared less to demand a certain qualitative progression than to recognize its rightness after the event. We are put into a state of mind which another state of mind can appropriately follow" (Wolin 190; quoting Burke, CS, 125).*

WOLIN'S PORTRAIT OF BURKE: TEACHING "SONGFULLY" RATHER THAN IN A "CLINICAL FASHION"

Wolin explains that in "Order," the third and last section of the main text of *A Rhetoric of Motives*, Burke "is not simply being repetitive; he focuses on the concept of hierarchy, exploring the extent to which we can push this principle as a central element of rhetoric" (201–02). In his "Preface to the First Edition" of *Counter-Statement*, Burke describes how in two chapters he treats issues "somewhat songfully" but later discusses them "in a more clinical fashion" (viii). In the following representative anecdote, Wolin presents Burke through a story, image, and song, instead of through the analysis and argument—the "more clinical fashion"—that characterizes most of his work; he also acknowledges here how Burke teaches through explicit instruction but also through action that invites readers to participate with him:

> Reading this part of the book, we are students in a master class observing the virtuoso. I recall a film of Pablo Casals teaching at a university. Casals critiqued student performances and played the cello. One student played her piece repeatedly, for after each performance Casals said it was not quite right and that she should do it again. He told her that she was playing the cello as if were merely a cello. Try to make it sing, he urged. It worked. In this final part of the *Rhetoric*, I wonder if Burke is asking of us, as observers of this hierarchy in literature and the rhetoric of human motives, to watch him sing. (Wolin 202)

I want to add that Burke asks us to "watch him sing" in order to encourage us to sing along with him. In the preceding part II, Burke teaches us how identification works and has named the action and associated his term with Aristotle's enthymeme.[45]

Victor J. Vitanza's "Dear Jim" and His Wasteland Warning

Victor J. Vitanza writes *Negation, Subjectivity, and the History of Rhetoric* to, for, and with Jim Berlin, whom he addresses directly and indirectly. His book, like many articles and books by others in rhetoric and composition, are living dialogues with Berlin. Vitanza continues a discussion and

---

45. See John Clifford's "Burke and the Tradition of Democratic Schooling" for a discussion of "what some Marxists call disidentification": "Burke is not a messenger of despair or cynical resignation. On the contrary, his political insights allow for, even call for, oppositional thinking, or what some Marxists call disidentification. Burke, who believes with Dewey that the function of education is to reform a limiting, unjust society, is also sanguine about the ability of teachers to intervene in the dominant discourse to alter its direction for the better." (34)

collaboration with Berlin in "The Wasteland Grows." The history of this article illustrates the collaborative nature of the research associated with Berlin's work. The online article, given as a plenary address to the Research Network Forum but not published before, "supplements and complements" his "Response" *JAC* to Julie Drew's "(Teaching) Writing: Composition, Cultural Studies, Production" in the same issue that includes criticism of Vitanza's "polemical address" ("The Wasteland Grows" 411).

My purpose in this and in the final section is to discuss several articles that approach Berlin's work from cultural studies, ideological, and psychoanalytic perspectives, all of which address issues of identity and teaching writing from these perspectives, aim to transform students ideologically, and assume rhetoric and ideology as synonymous. Reading these 1990s articles from different journals dialogically and retrospectively at times also demonstrates how priority is given to ideology or psychology and consequences follow from the selection of terms, in contrast to Burke's exploration of identity, persuasion, and proof with rhetoric as his key term. I will indicate the strengths and limitations of Burke's lesson in writing as identification through this discussion.

After Vitanza provides the context for his online article, he adds: "Make of this what you will" (1). As usual, he implies far more than his words say, as he explains what he understands as "an important problem—if not, the problem—in rhetoric and composition theory and pedagogy" (1). He repeats that he will "toss the problem out for your consideration," inviting readers into the symbolic action, to experience the problem not only to critique it. Without doing so explicitly, he shifts from rhetoric and theory to "cultural studies, cultural critique, or cultural criticism or whatever you wish to call it," acknowledging these three as different but conflating them in "the reliance on bringing Reason to bear on ethical-political problems. On Social Change" (1). He questions the value of "thought-thinking-thought that would teach students to identify the contradictions in the social fabric and to set about correcting those contradictions." He asks directly: "in the name of 'making' knowledge (doing research), whether or not teaching students cultural studies and other similar studies makes them seek for a better world that is obtainable" (1). He answers with similar directness: "I want to suggest to you, on the contrary, that cultural studies may lead only to cynicism" (1).

Vitanza explains that he writes for the good of his colleagues in rhetoric and composition, more specifically for those in the social-epistemic schools, all of whom he realizes he may "infuriate":

> I say "for their own good[s]" with a pun on the word goods. Yes, I refer to my colleagues' commodities, not just to the economics of their thinking about liberating students in writing classrooms so as to bring about social change, but to the new generation of cynics that they may very well be producing. This is my concern: not the Mods, not the Postmods, but the commodities. The Objects being produced who believe. (*James Berlin and Social Epistemic Rhetorics* 132)

He adds that "for many who see and strip away false consciousness, there is no liberation or cure, but only an ever-growing cynicism, an ever-growing wasteland within them, or what Peter Sloterdijk calls in *The Critique of Cynical Reason* an "enlightened false consciousness (qtd. in Vitanza 133).

Vitanza next quotes Slavoj Žižek who, in *The Sublime Object of Ideology*, quotes Sloterdijk and defines the term I had overlooked in my earlier readings, *post-ideoleogical*:

> We can account for the formula of cynical reason proposed by Sloterdijk: "they know very well what they are doing, but still, they are doing it." If the illusion were on the side of knowledge, then the cynical position would really be a post-ideological position, simply a position without illusions: "they know what they are doing, and they are doing it." But if the place of the illusion is in the reality of doing itself, then this formula can be read in quite another way: "they know that, in their activity, they are following an illusion, but still, they are doing it." For example, they know that their idea of Freedom is masking a particular form of exploitation, but they still continue to follow this idea of Freedom. (qtd. in Vitanza 133)

Vitanza translates the "combinations and permutations" of Sloterdijk's sentence into the following:

> A de-territorialization followed by reterritorialization, in the scene(s) of cultural critique, does not bring the expected liberation. . . . Reason/rationality, when used to expose what it foresees as superstition, magic, etc., is a banal strategy. (By "banal strategy" I mean the militaristic use of Reason to win over what is called superstition, magic, etc.). (133–34)

Vitanza turns to a memory of Berlin's "honesty—the brute and raw honesty" (135). At the Marxist Literary Group at CMU, Berlin presented a paper "questioning his success as a teacher of social liberation" which included an anecdote of a student who knew he was "being manipulated by the media machine" and "had become an object in the mediascape, but nonetheless continued cynically to purchase the products that were the object of his media-driven desire" (135). Berlin asked: "How might we take this and other similar students to the other side of what we might deem social liberation?" (135). There was silence to Berlin's question and to Vitanza's question that followed: "Whether or not we who taught cultural studies, etc., were producing a generation of cynics, as I have once again attempted to ask here today" (135). He adds that silence to both has continued but that "[w]e can no longer be complicit with this y/our silence" (135).

Both Berlin and Vitanza are questioning the persuasiveness of reason/rationality or logical proof as the effective means of persuading students to "social liberation." He imagines his academic audience's response: "Really, Really, Victor, how could anyone who is concerned with developing a discipline or any disciplinary thinking be with the idea of forsaking Reason/rationality!! And what's this stuff about Enlightenment thinking leading to fascism?!" (134).

A Burkean response might be: Why forsake reason? Enthymematic proof does not deny logical proof. It's not as simple as that. Use all that there is to use to persuade ourselves and others to purify war, but, first, figure out what to do, based on a reading of motives and situations and an assessment of probable consequences. Further, don't confuse such rhetorical action with illusions, unless the association is useful. And what about the comic corrective and the attitude of uncertainty that cultivates listening, learning, and collaborating with others to act collectively? Burke's message might be similar to his recommendation at the 1935 American Writer's Congress: the traditional rhetoric of ideology won't work to persuade others today to join in. Americans don't want to be identified as *workers*: use *people* instead. Changing from *worker* to *people* will certainly require a change in attitude, terms, and actions, and there will be a loss of your identity and situation, but there might be a gain, if persuading others is what you're after more than maintaining the status quo. Identification may be a better bet than logical proof.

The Difficult Task of Changing the Subject of Postmodernist Theory from Ideology and Psychology to Rhetoric: Collaboration among Berlin, Alcorn, and Vitanza on Student Resistance

In his 1995 article, "Changing the Subject of Postmodernist Theory," Alcorn analyzes Berlin's weighting of ideology over psychology and equating rhetoric and cultural studies in "Poststructuralism, Cultural Studies, and the Composition Classroom." He also explores some of the ideas about educating students for ideological change that Vitanza later considers in his 1999 online version of his address to the Research Network Forum that I discussed above. Berlin's 1992 article and his 1996 *Rhetorics, Poetics, and Cultures*, with its focus on the transformation of students into epistemic workers and on disciplinary refiguration, provide context and motive for the articles. Burke provides me with the angle of analysis.

In 1995, Alcorn explains that he supports "the postmodernist composition program Berlin advocates," but, because he largely agrees with Berlin, he feels "it important to argue that the human subject is more complex than Berlin and others theorize" (331). Berlin's "Poststructuralism, Cultural Studies and the Composition Classroom" he says, "suffers from an unproductive tension between the human subject described by postmodernist theory and the human subject appearing in his actual description of classroom practices (Alcorn 331–32). He argues that a Lacanian approach to the subject would offer "more useful ideas both for negotiating the ideological conflicts generated in the classroom and for achieving the cognitive power that Berlin seeks," because Lacan's subject is "more structured" and "structured by libidinal signification that it cannot easily bring into responsible self-awareness in the manner Berlin describes" (332). He claims, "Berlin's pedagogy is essentially another version of liberal humanist ideology in which freedom, rationality, and knowledge become the means for personal and social change" (333). Berlin's term *penetration*, "though hinting at more complicated psychological processes, in fact, becomes a pedagogy dependent upon free choice and rational speech" (334). He asks: "Why does Berlin describe a *constructed* subject in theory, but a *free* subject in classroom practice?" (334).

From my Burkean angle, Berlin's emphasis on culture and ideology minimizes choice, a central act in Burke's rhetoric and in the rhetorical tradition, but one that is never "free." In rhetoric, people are constructed as agents who make choices and are able to do so in language, even though choices are constrained by situations and by others. People may also be analyzed as agencies, scenes, acts, purposes, and more, but all actions must stand pragmatic tests. People are also constructed as individuals and groups, but individuals exist in that bodies are separate, but we are bodies that learn language, according to Burke, and we can connect through language and act collectively through identification. All constructions are incomplete and temporary; all constructions are contradictory and uncertain; and all constructions are rhetorical actions.

For Alcorn, however, "Berlin makes clearly visible the contradictions in the various modules of postmodernist theory he has spliced together to fashion a persuasive pedagogy" (334). Alcorn seems to understand the contradictions and "splicing together" as problems rather than possibilities for revision and change, and he suggests that there are ways to construct without splicing bits and pieces into a temporary whole. Postmodernist theory, in its integration of ideology, psychology, rhetoric, and more, seems to represent the most progressive theory, but all theories are partial and temporarily and contextually persuasive. From Burke's perspective, the ongoing work of critics, teachers, and all *animal symbolicum* is to act wisely in concert *for social reasons,* recognizing that people must be persuaded to act, to act in concert, to agree on what's wise because we fear change, loss, and death. We resist uncertainty.

At this point in his article, Alcorn turns to Diane Macdonell's 1986 *Theories of Discourse* for her analysis of the contradictions, which he says have been "extensively debated" (334). She criticizes Foucault "for not adequately accounting for the possibilities of political resistance": "If subjects are always an effect of the ideological power of discourse, she asks, how can subjects ever resist that power?" (334). She, therefore, "labors to account for the source of resistance to ideology," and, like Berlin according to Alcorn, "the subject is always composed of antagonistic ideologies" (334). He says Macdonell "implies that another ideology is always already comprising the subject" and "[t]he reformation of subjectivity, then, is not a matter of replacing one ideological structure with another but of giving greater strength to an ideological structure that is already present, though thwarted, in the structure of subjectivity" (334).

In Burke's terms, ideologies, like all discourse, are incomplete and contradictory, which means they invite participation—interpretation, translation, extension, modification, and more—from others. While people resist change, we are always changing. We can also learn to see around the limitations of our screens through weightings and revisions of terms, identities, and situations; these revisions are necessary for us to identify with others, and we do indeed want to get along. Resistance to identification with others is resistance to change. Resistance is also an act to maintain collective and individual identities and situations, constructions known as realities and truths, which are sacred altars of our pieties. Burke's focuses on creating identification through the use of ideologies, politics, economics, psychologies, and any other means available. Persuading us to consider the possibilities of identification and developing those possibilities are Burke's primary tasks. They are the order of his priorities, an order he maintains to keep him focused on *and* focused off.

Into his discussion of student resistance, Alcorn includes "disidentification," the term Macdonell introduces from Michel Pecheux from "Language, Semantics and Ideology: Stating the Obvious":

> "Disidentification," she says, "can be brought about by political and ideological practices which work on and against what prevails" (40). Macdonell, however, is vague about how these political and ideological practices actually operate. If subjects are structures of ideological conflict and disidentification is the key to the reformation of subjectivity, according to what principle do minority exercises in disidentification gain power over majority exercises in standard ideological identification? Do minority forms of identification gain power by simply talking more, or is there some logic of persuasion involved in effective forms of disidentification? Macdonell does not answer these questions, but she ends her book by calling for more study of "reformism in discourse." (qtd. in Alcorn 334–35)

Burke focuses on identification as loss with the possibility of gain rather than on disidentification as loss with the possibility of gain. By subordinating ideology to the status of means of persuading people to identify, he can deal with language by using, not dismissing or denying, psychology, ideology, identities, and situations. To study "reformism in discourse," we can cast the issue as Burke does in terms of rhetoric: If subjects are constructions of rhetorical conflicts and identification is the key to reformation of subjectivity, according to what principle do minority exercises of identification gain power over majority exercises in standard rhetorical identification? Burke's explorations of acts of identification and misidentification, as well as his development of the resources of a rhetoric of identification, make clear that there is no final answer to these questions, certain for all situations, but the questions do motivate, create attitudes, influence selections of terms and strategies, and encourage collaboration. The appropriate response to the questions, in the realm of rhetoric, is action based on the study of motives and situations, the assessment of available means of persuasion, and the calculation of probable consequences.

Burke incorporates and revises Freud's psychological use of the term *identification* and Marx's ideological use into his rhetorical definition of *identification*. As we have seen, he explicitly locates *identification* in the rhetorical tradition and associates it with Aristotle's enthymeme in *A Rhetoric of Motives*. His angle prevents him from being one of many for whom, according to Alcorn, "the power of post-structuralist theory lay precisely in its ability to explain the subject's inability to be anything other than an ideological effect" (335). His approach prevents him from being too closely aligned with those who explain the subject's inability to be anything other than a psychological effect. Burke's lines do fall at or about the same places as Althusser's claim that individuals don't freely choose or change ideologies. But Burke's definition of people—as symbol-using animals, who have agency in using language but who are also agencies used by language—contrasts with Althusser's understanding of ideology as the condition of people. (336). We have seen earlier in chapters 2 and 3 how rhetoric plays into Freud's psychology and how psychology informs Burke's rhetoric.

Alcorn turns later to Paul Smith's criticism in *Discerning the Subject* of "the tendency in Marxist theory to see ideology as always negative" and of the "passive nature of the post-structuralist subject" (336). He says that Smith, whom Berlin also refers to, "sought to theorize greater powers of agency for the subject and free the post-structuralist subject for political action" by using Lacanian theory "to complicate Althusser's ideological subject" (336). Smith's subject, constructed through Lacan, is not a "unified structure of ideology but a conflicted and heterogeneous collection of ideological discourse" (336). In Burke's terms, people act within the interstices, the fissures, the contradictions.[46]

Having presented a revision in poststructuralism from the subject as victim to the subject as agent, from "one limited theory of the subject to another limited theory of the subject," Alcorn presents both as an "easy theoretical flip from a theory that explains the subject's capacity for po-

---

46. See Lentricchia's discussion in *Criticism and Social Change* of Burke and Gramsci, particularly their similar views of "hegemony;" although, Burke "gave it no name" (76), as "fundamentally a process of education carried on through various institutions of civil society in order to make normative, inevitable, even 'natural' the ruling ideas of ruling interests" and as "a way of gaining 'free' assent" (76). This educative process, according to Lentricchia, is a process of "identity-formation" of the individual and the collective (77–78). He explains that "Burke's lesson, easily missed with his stress on the marathon character of historical repression, is not de Man's: the lesson is that radical rupture, not progressive change, is impossible" (79). More specifically, "One of Burke's ways of pinpointing structural instability in the tradition. . . is to declare that every so-called historical period is transitional; no period is there, in full presence—historical texture is ineluctably heterogeneous because every social formation is marked by a temporal fissure constituted by the simultaneous 'presence' of traces of older, residual modes of production with anticipation of an emergent critical mode working to establish authority" (79).

Lentricchia, however, excludes Burke's theory of identification as revision of identity and situations and as the method of proof in rhetoric. He is most interested in fissures in hegemony as sites of ideological changes, rather than fissures as grounds for identification and change.

litical insight to a theory that facilitates the subject's capacity for political resistance" (337). He challenges readers: "Let us be more realistic about ourselves and our profession. Let us more carefully consider the transformation in which we are encouraged to put our faith" (337).

He next addresses how teachers "desire to change other subjects by means of careful explanation and argumentative repetition of political desire" and how subjects, "while they do show multiple and conflicting identities, also reveal defensive resistances to discourse manipulations" (Alcorn 338). He proposes a third psychoanalytic model for change to replace Berlin's two inadequate models. This model constructs language as "in itself, a highly heterogeneous substance" that can "operate as coded information, able to influence political identity largely in terms of the old liberal categories of knowledge and truth" and can "act as a highly libidinal substance" (341). Libidinal language is the "material embodiment of human emotion, of emotionally charged thinking, and emotionally intense identification" (341). It is "the material instrument of subjective penetration": "seductive" rhetoric, invasive fantasy, and hostile assertion" (341). It is the "libidinal power of ideological language," with "its potential for attachments, attractions, organizations, repulsions, and bindings that create relatively stable sites of identification and disidentification wherein particular subjects locate themselves in a particularized language," that "a cogent postmodernist and cultural pedagogy requires" (341). He admits the limitations of psychoanalytic language "to describe ideological structures" but insists that it must influence postmodernist theory because it "has been most careful in describing the rational and irrational roles in terms of which subjectivity responds to linguistic inducements to change" (342).

Berlin, he says, describes ideological conflict as "a linguistic code a subject could logically read and rewrite," and "he wants to be rational and to appeal to the subject's ability to recognize conflictual codings and be free from bad conflict" (Alcorn 342). He refers to Mark Bracher who, in *Lacan, Discourse, and Social Change*, states: "I would go so far as to say that without reducing the unconscious conflict—whether by individual psychoanalysis, by cultural criticism, or by various other means—the changes of reducing injustice and intolerance are virtually nonexistent" (qtd. in Alcorn 342). He adds that "[r]hetorical scholars, especially, oversimplify the repressed tensions and desperate libidinal attachments that maintain conscious conflict" (343).

We have seen how Burke, for his rhetorical purposes, weights conscious action and unconscious motion, the individual and the collective, language and reality, and people's acts of choosing among symbols and the influences of language on people and the world. We have also seen why, how, and to what ends he draws lines and defines terms. Sharp-cut distinctions, however, may be essential at times, but they are not completely or permanently. They also obscure how terms shade off into each other or become the other. We therefore have to make do for specific people, purposes, and places, recognizing that others act differently for other reasons. We can work to identify and get along with others, or we can hold our own. From a rhetorical perspective, not from psychological or ideological screens, we can accept the muddle, drawing the line only for the purification of war.

Libidinal and Rational Language: The Means and Ends of Rhetorical Proof

Alcorn begins part 3 of his article by explaining that in an earlier draft he "ended by emphasizing the differences between libidinal and rational language," but he ends on "a more personal note (following one reviewer's suggestion)—with more generalized reflections upon the issues I have raised" (342). His current opening to the essay, he explains, was a response to an anonymous reader's suggestion "for sharpening the focus of my argument"; that reviewer turns out to be Berlin who "had reached many of the same conclusions that [he] was arguing for in the essay" (344). Alcorn says his "original draft had argued with him pointedly and even harshly on various issues," but Berlin wrote the following to Theresa Enos, editor of *Rhetoric Review*: "I have been reading in the very Lacanian materials the author mentions in the essay in preparation for a book titled *A Teacher's Guide to Cultural Studies*. Here I had planned to include a more detailed discussion of the subject in the postmodern epistemic rhetoric class" (qtd. in Alcorn 344). Berlin was to respond to Alcorn's essay but died a month after he wrote to Enos (Alcorn 344).

Alcorn says Berlin was "uneasy with the emphasis he was giving to personal experience" (344), and he was "uneasy with Berlin's refusal to see differences between ideological structure and libidinal structure": "Too often, logical and informative arguments have no effect on the commitments students have to ideology." This is because "the *real* binding effects between subjectivity and discourse are not made in relation to linguistic representations but to [sic] in relation to structural patterns of identity that are mapped out libidinally in the body" (345). He explains that Berlin and others helped him "see that libidinal structure *is* always ideological" because "all meanings operate as meanings in an ideological context" (345). He adds that "[w]hile this is true, it should not, however, imply that ideology and libidinal structure are essentially the same mechanism" and "[i]t is not the case, for example, that all conscious thought is equally ideological and libidinal" (345).

In these comments, as Alcorn argues against logical arguments, he claims the "*real* binding effects" between subjectivity and discourse are "not made in relation to linguistic representations" but "in relation to structural patterns of identity that are mapped out libidinally in the body" (345). The contrasts between Alcorn's psychological/rhetorical approach and Burke's rhetorical approach are evident, as Burke argues that binding effects result from identification between people who are creating meaning together using language. As Alcorn put it, ideology and psychology are not "essentially the same mechanism" and "all conscious thought is not equally ideological and libidinal" (345).

In November, 1998, Victor Vitanza asked Alcorn to respond to graduate students' questions about his 1995 article and to let him publish "the original-but-changed conclusion (124) to the *Rhetoric Review* article" as an "alternative 'original' ending" (*James A. Berlin and Social-Epistemic Rhetorics* 124). Alcorn agreed but explained that, although he had "not compared this carefully with the original, he knew the following was what he cut when he shortened and deleted the conclusion that most readers found "highly unclear" (*James A. Berlin and Social-Epistemic Rhetorics* 125).

The online ending seems more explicit in claiming that the "work of giving up attachments is not a simple rational decision" and that "it can be counter-productive to seek to change political identity by simply talking more clearly about politics" (*James A. Berlin and Social-Epistemic Rhetorics* 129). Students come to class "thoroughly knitted together by the libidinal forces of family relations, politics, and personal encounters with significant others" (*James A. Berlin and Social-Epistemic Rhetorics* 129). For many, he says "a discussion of politics, in the common sense of the word, can be largely diversionary from the complex and adventitious patterns of discourse interactions that need to occur in order for the subject to divest itself of that knotted complex of conflicted libidinal organizations that in each concrete case define the subject and the political attachments of the community" (*James A. Berlin and Social-Epistemic Rhetorics* 129). He concludes the original ending with the following plea:

> If we cannot be rational, intelligent, and libidinally penetrating about what makes us suffer and how we can cure it, we can produce neither politics nor analysis; we will merely repeat the discourse of powerful ideologies without any hope of change. Our libidinal experience of sufferance and our rational plans to avoid it are at the center of our need for politics, and our need as well for

self-consciously libidinal and libidinally rational expression (*James A. Berlin and Social-Epistemic Rhetorics* 130).

Alcorn concludes the 1995 essay by addressing the problem that subjects "would often rather suffer from a bad ideology than suffer from changing their ideology" (348). He asks how can "teachers work with this situation, this inability of subjects to be rational about libidinal attachments" (348). He answers his own question:

> If we can teach the fact that rational judgments about conflicting libidinal attachments are painful, elusive, but immensely important, then we will perhaps be in a better position to actually achieve some of the political goals that Berlin advocates. This teaching will be political, but it will also be personal. I do not think this dimension of the personal will be the kind of indulgent exploration advocated by Elbow and other expressivists. It will be experiential and especially conflictual, as Berlin himself advocated. But it will not emphasize liberation in terms of collective identity as idealized by Ira Shor and other social progressives. Recognition of a collective political identity is important and crucial for political action, but before we can *act* the values of a new political identity, we must first *adopt* a new political identity. And this change is not easy. Deep changes in our *awareness of* and *choices for* suffering—the kind of awareness often required for the formulation of a new politically [sic] identity—require mourning, and mourning is an isolating experience. It requires a space for personal reflection. No one else can do the work of mourning for us. It is not some kind of information that we can memorize and employ. Our most common response to those who try to push us toward mourning is anger and hatred, the gestures of the countertransference. And yet this change we resist may be what we most need. (348)

The limitations and strengths of ideological explanations of change are that they are ideological, and the limitations and strengths of psychological explanations are that they are psychological. The same is true for rhetorical explanations. From a rhetorician's perspective, all such explanations are motivated and consequential; they are matters of doubt and uncertainty, situated, partial, and changing. Like all rhetorics, they are persuasive at times. The advantages for me of a rhetoric of identification, rather than a psychology or ideology of identification, is that the focus is on people and how we use language for various motives in specific contexts in order to get along with each and act collectively to purify war. In addition, the method of proof credits participants' experiences in creating meaning together, and it credits appeals to many aspects of a person, if not to the "whole" person.

The advantages for teaching writing and reading as acts of identification is that it educates students to build on what language always requires to some extent, collaboration, and it teaches us to hesitate, so that we act wisely, in concert, in life.

In time, the agent and scene shifted. Osama Bin Laden if he can't be scapegoated if he can't be found, dead or alive. We can't fight the War on Terrorism against a celluloid or digital enemy leader: we can't war symbolically. We need Saddam Hussein to test our symbols of authority and to prove global hierarchy and individual and collective identities. It also seems we can't continue without a war and murders that were promised, murders that were the rallying cry to unite Americans.

But the cry fades as economic, political, and religious symbols of authority crumble, not louder than the Twin Towers but with continuing reverberations and repetitions. And people rise to resist corporate corruption, human violations within churches, deception and prejudice in politics, and unreliability and dishonesty in media accounts in this war on terrorism, a continuation of previous wars and alliances.

We need the rhetorics of the "comic corrective" and the "poetic perspective" to see ourselves and others as "mistaken" not "vicious," so that we recognize the possibilities, as well as the losses, in identification with others because we are different and therefore can help each other out. We probably need to accept, along with Burke, that a rhetoric of identification will not command authority: "Political, military, and industrial powers are much more likely to 'set the tone,' so far as the 'implementing' of perspectives is concerned." But while the strength of the "great pyramidal structures of authority" mock the "'poetic perspective's' weaknesses," they "are all prime examples of its claims, since they all bear witness to man's great reliance upon language, terminology, symbolism" (PC lvii; Burke's emphasis). At the same time, we need to keep trying everything to get along.

PART IV
A LESSON IN LIVING AS REBIRTH RITUAL: GETTING ALONG BY GOING ALONG UNTIL THE NEGATIVE SETS IN

6 Burke's Epilogue on Earth: A "Return to Inconclusiveness" as Equipment for Living Today

TL. First comes their use of language as a means of getting along in their everyday affairs. (Burke, *RR* 286)

S. They will be able to keep this distinction clear?

TL. By no means! Again and again, just because they have a word for something, and a feeling for the contexts in which the use of that word seems proper, they'll assume that there really is something to which the word is referring. Elaborate systems will be erected atop this error, doctrinal structures that are quite ingenious. But there will be enough rudimentary correspondence between words and things, with enough rudimentary awareness of the difference between the symbol and the symbolized, for them to find their way around, and multiply. (Burke, *RR* 283–84)

But there *is* a question, a question of language. Let's transpose it within the historical scheme which you bring up: *the notion of the definition of man by his language. Man is the animal that speaks, is the speaking animal.* There is that historical topos which comes back, and one thinks of Hamann, one thinks of some others, and it says—and that is to some extent Benjamin's concern here—"At the beginning was the word." Language is not human, it is God-given: it is the logos, as that which God gives to man. Not specifically to man, but God gives, as such. That's not at all the same as to say man is man to the extent that he has language. That it is divine or not makes little difference, and the more you take the sacred out of this picture, the better. But it indicates a constant problem about the nature of language as being either human or nonhuman. That there is a nonhuman aspect of language is a perennial awareness from which we cannot escape, because language does things which are so radically out of our control that they cannot be assimilated to the human at all, against which one fights constantly.... Things happen in the world which cannot be accounted for in terms of the human conception of language. And they always happen in linguistic terms, or the relation [to] language is always involved when they have [happened]. And good or bad things, not only catastrophes, but felicities also. And they happen. In a sense, to account for them, to account for them historically, to account for them in any sense, a certain initial discrepancy in language has to be examined. You can't—it cannot be avoided. (de Man, *The Resistance to Theory*, 100–01)

The essays gathered in the present volume were meant to reexamine the work of other theorists, in a manner somewhat analogous to that found in *Blindness and Insight*, in order to determine what about the theoretical enterprise itself blinds it to the radicalness of reading and in order to disengage the principle of this blindness, which de Man came to conceive us as "resistance" for reasons I shall attempt to explore later. This volume too is unfinished. From the outset it was meant to include three essays of which two appear here in preparatory form and one not at all: essays on Bakhtin and on Benjamin, for which the papers included here were early versions still to be revised, and an essay on Kenneth Burke, which Paul de Man wanted very much to write for quite some time and which he considered the "social" counterpart to the more "formalist" essay on Riffaterre included here, though equally meant to arrive at a notion of inscription that would wreak havoc with the attempt to deal with history and the social only through its representational forms (Godzich xi). As discussed earlier, Burke, in his "Dictionary of Pivotal Terms," explains the concept of "Good Life," beginning with which a "project for 'getting along with people'" that "necessarily subsumes a concept of "the good life" (*ATH* 256). In his summary, he includes many aspects of identification he discusses earlier: "maximum of physicality" because there is "an over-emphasis upon 'things of the mind,' due partly to snobbism (the insignia of mental work ranking higher than the insignia of physical work)" (*ATH* 256–58); "Maximum opportunity for expression of the sentiments" and "[d]istrust of the passions" because they are "ambitious" and "stimulated to the maximum by the 'creative psychiatry' of capitalism" (*ATH* 258); "[c]onstruction, to channelize the militaristic by 'transcendence' into the co-operative" (*ATH* 258); "[p]atient study of the "Documents of Error" (*ATH* 258–59); "[s]tress always upon the knowledge of limitations" (*ATH* 259); "[d]istrust hypertrophy of art *on paper*. He adds: "More of the artistic should be expressed in vital social relationships" (*ATH* 259).

He extends this last point about "vital social relationships" by adding the following:

> Otherwise, it becomes "efficient" in the compensatory, antithetical sense. So completely do we now accept capitalist standards that we test everything as a *commodity for sale. Hence, we feel that a "mere artist at living" has "wasted his talents." Rather let him "release" his artistry through a total social texture. Let it take more "ecological" forms, though its "use value" as a commodity is thereby lessened.* (259; my emphasis)

Here Burke heeds his own warning about limitations, efficiency, and commodification by admitting: "To be sure, we do not thereby dispose of the whole issue" (*ATH* 259). He undercuts his own claims in order to maintain uncertainty because this is the position from which he as a rhetorician acts and because this is the position that promotes, as we have seen, "vital social relationships" or acts of identification. The act and attitude of uncertainty allows for the consideration of alternatives and prevents acting without thinking, rushing to judgment, and end-of-the-line thinking and acting. This hesitation is indeed "provisional," as Jameson noted, although for him as an ideological critic, provisionality is a problem. Within rhetoric, assessing motives, situations, means of persuasion, and probable consequences provides equipment for living through identification with others. Identification is collaborative action that also prepares us for further collective acts.

Burke concludes the section on "Good Life" by saluting "the pious tendency [of artists] to immortalize the transitory" (*ATH* 259–60), but his pieties include the transitory, the uncertain, the inconclusive. As usual, he doesn't stop here with art but with life: "One need simply note an important distinction in quality between this act and the act of a man who gets art on paper at the sacrifice of art in living" (*ATH* 260). As early as the preface to the first edition of *Counter-Statement*, he reminds us of this distinction between art and life that is critical to his rhetoric:

> And our "Lexicon" would not for the world make literature and life synonymous since, by comparison in such terms, the meanest life is so overwhelmingly superior to the noblest poem that illiteracy becomes almost a moral obligation. Rather, our "Lexicon" would look upon literature as the thing added—the little white houses in a valley that was once a wilderness" (Burke, *CS* x).

It is not as simple as that, however, for Burke. For him, language *is* symbolic action in the world that both affects people and situations and is affected by them. In his world, we are separate from each other and therefore desire to connect with each other, and we can associate and dissociate terms and realities, recognizing that our actions must stand collective, pragmatic tests. We can choose how to act, within scenic and language constraints, but we must act symbolically if we are to stay alive. This is the world according to Burke; this is the construction of the world that he figures will equip us for identifying with others and avoiding war and "the kill."

In *A Rhetoric of Religion* and *Language as Symbolic Action*, Burke continues to maintain both distinctions and connections between art and life, and he continues to teach us how to make sound critical judgments about associating and dissociating and other ways of using language—if and when our goal is to keep ourselves and others alive. He develops his theory of logology in order to continue his life's work with words, to round out this work, and to take his roundabout route through language and life. We might at this point reconsider Burke's overall purpose, *ad bellum purificandum*, as it is transformed once again into different terms in *The Rhetoric of Religion*: the "release" of "artistry through a total social texture," so that it takes "more ecological" forms, though its "use value" as a commodity is thereby lessened (*RR* 259).

Emphasizing dialectical relationships among forms of the mind, world, and text creates an ecological as well as a logological rhetoric and, perhaps more accurately, an ecological rhetoric. We must identify with each other as a way to purify war and stay alive and to keep our beautiful planet alive.

In the introduction to the third edition of *Attitudes Toward History*, Burke writes about "the invention of technical devices that would make the rapid obliteration of all human life an easily available possibility":

But now presumably a truly New Situation is with us, making it all the more imperative that we learn to cherish the mildly charitable ways of the comic discount. For by nothing less than such humanistic allowances can we hope to forestall (if it can be forestalled!) the most idiotic tragedy conceivable: the willful ultimate poisoning of this lovely planet, in conformity with a mistaken heroics of war—and each day, as the sun still rises anew upon the still surviving plenitude, let us piously give thanks to Something or Other not of man's own making. Basically, this book would accept the Aristophanic assumptions, which equate tragedy with war and comedy with peace. (*ATH* "Introduction" n.p.)

Here Burke invites us to join him in a prayer of thankfulness to "Something or Other not of man's own making," and he suggests what I will argue he demonstrates most explicitly in *The Rhetoric of Religion*, the need for us to learn to identify with "this lovely planet," as we have in part constructed it through language, as that collective construction has affected us and the world, and as the world continues to recreate us. Identification extends therefore to include identification with all people, with the world not of our own making and the world not wholly of our own remaking, and with our symbolic creations, conceived of and realized through language.

Again, matters aren't this simple, for we must always consider how our identifications, allegiances, and pieties affect others as well as ourselves. In a note in chapter 4, "Naïve Capitalism," in *Attitudes Toward History*, Burke presents "one little fellow named Ecology" among the sciences and predicts or warns in 1937 that "in time we shall pay him more attention" (150n*). He introduces "Ecology" into his discussion of the paradox of mercantilism with its "essentially *anti-patriotic* nature," a paradox he understands "to be at the very center of capitalist difficulties":

> For them, a nation had a favorable balance of trade when more goods were going out of it than came into it. And they "transcended" this confusion by recourse to a matter of symbolism; namely: "bullion." The preponderance of exports became "profit" rather than "loss" because it was matched by a preponderance of *symbolic imports*. For the symbol by which exchange was carried on was bullion, money—and the nation most successful in tossing real goods beyond its borders got back, in payment for its superiority, the inflationary symbolic equivalent, money." (*ATH* 149)

The "little fellow named Ecology" is a personification with which we are encouraged to identify, in part because he's certainly one of Burke's many identities but also because of our collective and individual overinvestment in the symbols of capitalism and the resulting imbalances. This figure is also a touch of the comic corrective who, Burke says, offers a lesson:

He teaches us that the *total* economy of this planet cannot be guided by an efficient rationale of exploitation alone, but that the exploiting part must itself eventually suffer if it too greatly disturbs the *balance* of the whole (as big beasts would starve, if they succeeded in catching *all* the little beasts that are their prey—*their very lack of efficiency in the exploitation of their ability as hunters thus acting as efficiency on a higher level, where considerations of balance count for more than considerations of one-tracked purposiveness*. (*ATH* 150n*).

> So far, the laws of ecology have begun avenging themselves against restricted human concepts of profit by countering deforestation and deep plowing with floods, droughts, dust storms, and aggravated soil erosion. And in a capitalist economy, these trends will be arrested only insofar as *collectivistic* ingredients of control are introduced, as with the comparatively insignificant efforts that

have already been organized by our state and federal governments. (ATH 150n*)

Here, as throughout his rhetoric, Burke examines how the tendencies in us and in our language toward hierarchy, perfection, thoroughness, and end-of-the-line thinking and action, all lead to an Upward Way but inevitably to a Downward Way because we are humans not gods. We must accept our limitations, counter our "one-tracked purposiveness," and act collectively through identifying with others. We must accept changes and loss in efficiency, identity, and situations in order to "get along." And we must find balance between our animality and our symbolicity, our individual and collective selves, and between us and the symbolic and non-symbolic worlds we inhabit. Burke asks us to seek perfection but only so far as this desire does not do us and others in. He asks us to exercise control of our appetites, our avarice, our greed, instead of seeking more to compensate for what we lack or lose. Just how many refrigerators do we animal symbolicum need, not to keep our butter hard, but to show that we belong?

Through logology, he teaches us to extend identification beyond human interaction. In his footnote, he attributes human qualities to symbols, in this case to "Ecology," so that we identify with the natural world and our constructions of that world, recognizing how both affect us and are affected by us. Throughout his rhetoric he searches for ways we can learn to accept our limitations as human beings here on earth and exploit them in order to identify with others, including others such as "Ecology," but also others, such as god terms of our own making.

It is useful at this point to remember again his definition of the critic's task as teacher of reading, writing, and living as he rounds out his discussion in *Attitudes* of the "patient study of 'Documents of Error'":

> Above all, criticism should seek to clarify the ways in which any structure develops self-defeating emphases ("inner contradictions"). It should watch for "unintended by-products"—and should seek to avoid being driven into a corner in its attempt to signalize them. Stress always upon the knowledge of limitations. (*ATH* 259)

As we have seen, Burke emphasizes the limitations of all attitudes, terms, theories, and actions, including his own. He also acknowledges directly and indirectly that his focus on rhetoric and identification is a focus off other motives, actions, and consequences. His claims are assertions of metaphors not truths, reinforced by his providing perspective by incongruity on his own conclusions. His methods are roundabout because his aim is education rather than the efficiencies of training and because the long way round is long, allowing for more times and places for others to join in the dancing of attitudes. Given his definitions of people and of language as incomplete and tending toward hierarchy, he avoids end-of-the-line thinking and acting that forces the issue of who's right and who's wrong, so that the only way out is war. He repeatedly reminds us that a "mere artist in living" is not a waste: it is a life most difficult and most essential for human beings to achieve, one focused on cooperation with others throughout the social and symbolic texture, so that we and the planet live on.

Before turning to his last two works and his lessons in how identifying with our symbolic creations metaphorically extend us, so that we see beyond ourselves and our lifetimes, I want to reinforce Burke's "Stress always upon the knowledge of limitations" (*ATH* 259), by contrasting his uses and misuses of rhetoric with Paul de Man's uses and misuses of rhetoric. "Wreaking Havoc" or Admitting We Don't Know and Therefore Must Try Everything to Learn to Get Along and Identify with Others: What's Radical about Being Human?

In the introduction to *The Resistance to Theory*, Wlad Godzich tracks the stages in de Man's criticism from the critical to matters of methodology and to "a stance that was properly theoretical" (x). He says that de Man, in writing the essays gathered together in the revised edition of *Blindness and Insight*, "had come to delimit a problematic that was fundamental to him, but which until then had been mediated through categories of consciousness and temporality inherited from the Hegelian substratum of phenomenology: the *matter of reading*" (*The Culture of Literacy* 160) as de Man began to conceive of it, is far more radical than any theoretical enterprise can admit. As we shall see later, reading disrupts the continuity between the theoretical and the phenomenal and thus forces a recognition of the incompatibility of language and intuition. Since the latter constitutes the foundational basis of cognition upon which perception, consciousness, experience, and the logic and the understanding, not to mention the aesthetics that are attendant to them, are constructed, *there results a wholesale shakeout in the organization and conceptualization of knowledge, from which language, conceived as a double system of tropes and persuasion, that is as a rhetorical entity, emerges as the unavoidable dimensionality of all cognition.* This was the view first adumbrated in "The Rhetoric of Temporality" and developed in *Allegories of Reading*. There followed a number of essays, now collected in *The Rhetoric of Romanticism*, in which implications of this conception of reading were explored over a historically circumscribed corpus. (*The Culture of Literacy* 160, my emphasis)

Burke accepts the "shakeout in the organization and conceptualization of knowledge" as a condition of his definition of "rhetoric," and he adds to the instability of knowledge the instabilities in identities and situations. While the organization and conceptualization of knowledge and how it changes in rhetoric are different from organization, conceptualization, and change in grammar and logic, rhetorical knowledge also differs from poetic knowledge, unless literature is broadly reconceived as rhetoric, as Burke does. The overlap between Aristotle's *Rhetoric* and *Poetics*, in plot, style, and figures and tropes, are treated differently from the two perspectives, with rhetoric focusing on action or thing-making and poetics focusing on a thing-made. In addition, the "shakeout" in Burke's rhetoric is, however, neither wholesale nor total because all angles are partial and contingent, including his own. There is no "wreaking havoc," because there is always uncertainty.

What's radical in his rhetoric is not reading and writing, rhetorically (enthymematically, qualitatively, identifying with others). What's radical is not accepting the conditions of being human, as he defines us finally and explicitly in *Language as Symbolic Action*:

> Man is the symbol-using (symbol-making, symbol-misusing) animal inventor of the negative (or moralized by the negative) separated from his natural condition by instruments of his own making goaded by the spirit of hierarchy (or moved by the sense of order and rotten with perfection. (Burke, *LASA* 16)

In his rhetoric *there is no* continuity between the theoretical and phenomenon, unless we create it temporarily and purposefully in language for rhetorical reasons. Because of "the incompatibility of language and intuition," we seek compatibility. He expects people who are divided to desire connection and disconnection. He expects us to disagree with his definition of *animal symbolicum*, and he expects that, if we do agree with it, we deny other definitions, such as *homo ludens* and *homo loquax*. By his definition, we tend to dramatize change as cataclysmic and as progressively upward. We seek perfection and certainty and defend against having to decide among available options in given contexts. We also forget to remember, even in the realm of rhetoric, that our assertions are rhetorical rather than right, although he reminds us and himself of this throughout his rhetoric: "It is not part of our contract here to make final decisions on these many matters" (GM 117). And it's not surprising that again and again we don't want to accept the strengths and limitations in ourselves and in language that make us human.

Burke's Pedagogy of Identification and de Man's Lesson in Resistance

Two entries in de Man's collection, the first and the last, concern teaching: "The Resistance to Theory" and Stefano Rosso's "An Interview with Paul de Man." They make clear the differences in Burke's and de Man's attitudes toward education, rhetoric, the sacred, communication among people, and living. These two essays, along with *The Rhetoric of Religion* and *Language as Symbolic Action*, provide additional ways into Burke's overall lesson in living, which we have already learned in part through his lessons in reading and writing as identification. What is missing in *The Resistance to Theory*, the essay on Burke that Godzich says de Man wanted to write, also invites action and encourages me again to claim that it is a good proposition to keep in mind that no one can ever get it right and therefore all of us need others to help us get along.

In addition, de Man's literary approach to rhetoric, juxtaposed to Burke's rhetorical approach to literature, returns us to literature defined broadly by Burke as early as *Counter-Statement* and to the rhetoric of religion as enacted as early as *Permanence and Change* and *Attitudes Toward History*. We are thus able to examine the distinctions de Man raises in the second passage above between the human and nonhuman and between the nonhuman and the sacred, without attributing the *logos* to the sacred but realizing the desire, attitude, and action of doing so, whether to God or to the God-term, as enthymematic, in that, first, we conspire (or not) in a creation of perfection to which we also aspire (or not) and, second, in that we collaborate with language mutually constructed to transcend where we are and to where we might be but are not.

de Man begins the first essay in the collection, "The Resistance to Theory," with the following strategy: "This essay was not originally intended to address the question of teaching directly, although it was supposed to have a didactic and an educational function—which it failed to achieve" (3). He presents himself as a failure, because we know he's not; we identify with him because of the authority that allows him to admit failure, and we identify with him also as a failure. A reversal, his association with the Modern Language Association that invited him to write on literary theory, efficiently authorizes him and corrects any misconceptions. But matters are not as simple as that:

> Such essays are expected to follow a clearly determined program: they are supposed to provide the reader with a select but comprehensive list of the main trends and publications in the field,

to synthesize and classify the main problematic areas, and to lay out a critical and programmatic projection of the solutions which can be expected in the foreseeable future. All this with a keen awareness that, ten years later, someone will be asked to repeat the same exercise.

I found it difficult to live up, in minimal good faith, to the requirements of this program and could only try to explain, as concisely as possible, why the main theoretical interest of literary theory consists in the impossibility of its definition. (3)

The "Committee," he says, "rightly judged that this was an inauspicious way to achieve the pedagogical objectives of the volume and commissioned another article" (3).

He gives this account, he writes, to explain the "traces in the article of the original assignment" and to raise "the question of general interest: that of the relationship between the scholarship (the key word in the title of the MLA volume), the theory, and the teaching of literature" (3–4). He efficiently draws lines that clearly distinguish his attitudes and actions about teaching and literature from Burke's, even though de Man credits rhetoric as the de-stabilizer of grammar, logic, and the *trivium* and as his excuse for not being able to "live up, in minimal good faith" to the MLA invitation. What he can do, he says, is "explain, as concisely as possible, why the main theoretical interest of literary theory consists in the impossibility of its definition" (3). The trouble, from a Burkean perspective, is that de Man seems to want to discuss language without dealing with the people who do things with words.

Even though the resistance to theory is a resistance to the rhetoric of language, he dissociates rhetoric from relationships among people to focus on language. He defines teaching as a "cognitive process" and subordinates the teacher and the learner: "Over-facile opinion notwithstanding, teaching is not primarily an intersubjective relationship between people but a cognitive process in which self and other are only tangentially and contiguously involved" (de Man 4). For him, the "only teaching worthy of the name is scholarly, not personal" (4). Further, "analogies between teaching and various aspects of show business or guidance counseling are more often than not excuses for having abdicated the task" (4). He juxtaposes the personal to the scholarly: "Scholarship has, in principle, to be eminently teachable," by which he means that literary scholarship "involves at least two complementary areas: historical and philological facts as the preparatory condition for understanding, and methods of reading or interpretation" (4). Having made his cuts, associations, and dissociations, he concludes his introduction, drawing deeper the divide between literature and rhetoric and between scholarship and scholars as people:

> Various developments, not only in the contemporary scene but in the long and complicated history of literary and linguistic instruction, reveal symptoms that suggest that such a difficulty is an inherent focus of the discourse about literature. These uncertainties are manifest in the hostility directed at theory in the name of ethical and aesthetic values, as well as in the recuperative attempts of theoreticians to reassert their own subservience to these values. The most effective of these attacks will denounce theory as an obstacle to scholarship and, consequently, to teaching. It is worth examining whether, and why, this is the case. For if this is indeed so, then it is better to fail in teaching what should not be taught than to succeed in teaching what is not true. (4)

DE MAN'S LOCATION OF BURKE AND POSSIBILITIES OF THE UNWRITTEN ESSAY

In 1986, de Man says the "wave of interest [in literary theory] seems to be receding as some satiation or disappointment sets in after the initial enthusiasm" (5). Before the 1960s, literary criticism was "not averse to theory, if by theory one understands the rooting of literary exegesis and of critical evaluation in a system of conceptual generality (5). He associates Burke with the "broadly shared methodology, more or less overtly proclaimed," informing *Understanding Poetry (*Brooks and Warren*), Theory of Literature* (Welleck and Warren) and *The Fields of Light* (Reuben Brower) or such theoretically oriented works as *The Mirror and the Lamp, Language as Gesture* and *The Verbal Icon*" (6). But he also dissociates Burke from them: "Yet, with the possible exception of Kenneth Burke, and, in some respect, Northrop Frye, none of these authors would have considered themselves theoreticians in the post-1960 sense of the term, nor did their work provoke as strong reactions, positive or negative, as that of later theoreticians" (6). These New Critical approaches "experienced no difficulty fitting into the academic establishments without their practitioners having to betray their literary sensibilities in any way (6).

In contrast, the approaches during the 1960s and into the 1980s, including structuralism, semiotics, the Frankfurt School, other Marxists criticism, phenomenology, and others, became, according to de Man, theoretical and threatened the academic establishment because their approach to literary texts was no longer based on non-linguistic, that is to say historical and aesthetic, considerations or, to put it somewhat less crudely, when the object of discussion is no longer the meaning or the value but the modalities of production and of reception of meaning and of value prior to their establishment—the implication being that this establishment is problematic enough to require an autonomous discipline of critical investigation to consider its possibility and its status. (7)

The "advent of theory, the break that is now so often being deplored and that sets it aside from literary history and from literary criticism, occurs with the introduction of linguistic terminology in the metalanguage about literature"; "linguistic terminology" means "a terminology that designates reference prior to designating the referent and takes into account, in the consideration of the world, the referential function of language or, to be somewhat more specific, that considers reference as a function of language and not necessarily as an intuition" (de Man 8).

He revises his question from why literary theory is threatening to "why it has such difficulty going about its business and why it lapses so readily either into the language of self-justification and self-defense or else into the overcompensation of programmatically euphoric utopianism what makes literary" (de Man 12). His answer is that the "resistance to theory is a resistance to the use of language about language" or to "language itself" or "to the possibility that language contains factors or functions that cannot be reduced to intuition" (12–13). It is here de Man names the "radical," defined, as I interpret it, as the verb or action of extracting the root rather than as adjective or noun:

> The difficulties extend to the internal articulations between the constituent parts as well as the articulation of the field of language with the knowledge of the world in general, the link between the *trivium* ["which considers the sciences of language as consisting of grammar, rhetoric, and logic (or dialectics)"] and the quadrivium, which covers the non-verbal sciences of number (arithmetic), of space (geometry), of motion (astronomy), and of time (music). *In the history of philosophy, this link is traditionally, as well as substantially, accomplished by way of logic, the area where the rigor of the linguistic discourse about itself matches up with the rigor of the mathematical discourse about the world.* (13; my emphasis)

Although de Man links poetics and philosophy elsewhere, he is building here to a different term or relationship among terms. Instead of linking logically or enthymematically, he subsumes rhetoric under literature and thereby converts rhetorical theory into literary theory, so that what is threatening in contemporary literary theory is rhetoric renamed "literariness":

> What matters for our present argument is that this articulation of the sciences of language with the mathematical sciences represents a particularly compelling vision of a continuity between a theory of language, as logic, and the knowledge of the phenomenal world to which mathematics gives access. In such a system, the place of aesthetics is preordained and by no means alien, provided the priority of logic, in the model of the *trivium,* is not being questioned. For even if one assumes, for the sake of argument and against a great deal of historical evidence, that the link between logic and the natural sciences is secure, this leaves open the question, within the confines of the *trivium* itself, of the relationship between grammar, rhetoric, and logic. And this is the point at which literariness, the use of language that foregrounds the rhetorical over the grammatical and the logical function, intervenes as a decisive but unsettling element which, in a variety of modes and aspects, disrupts the inner balance of the model, and consequently, its outward extension to the nonverbal world as well. (13–14)

Rhetoric, traditionally and for Burke, challenges the priority of logic, not by denying or replacing it, but by defining the enthymeme or identification as the heartfelt proof of rhetoric, and therefore making appeals to *logos, ethos,* and *pathos* enthymematic, in that writers must try to collaborate with readers and readers must agree to act with writers on shared though uncertain grounds. Rhetoric is the act of enthymeme-making, of figuring out what might persuade in given contexts in matters of doubt and uncertainty, including matters of mathematics and science.

For de Man, however, the question concerns the "relationship between grammar, rhetoric, and logic," for this "is the point at which literariness, the use of language that foregrounds the rhetorical over the grammatical and the logical function, intervenes as a decisive but unsettling element which, in a variety of modes and aspects, disrupts the inner balance of the model and, consequently, its outward extension to the nonverbal world as well" (14). He extracts "rhetoric" from its context of action, choice, enthymematic proof, and uncertainty and thus converts action into scholarship, something complete and completed. At the same time, he extracts "literariness" from literature, equates literariness with rhetoric, and replaces rhetoric of the *trivium* with his new term, "literariness."

Burke, as we have seen, defines logic and grammar as rhetorical and finds them useful means of persuasion in the realm of rhetoric. He also moves in a different direction from de Man when he revises poetics into rhetoric, demonstrating that all literature can be read as action. He uses rhetoric, rather than literariness, literature, poetics, rhetoricity, or rhetoricality, as his key term for contingency and change and for his action. He weights rhetoric; de Man weights literariness by linking it to rhetoric. He associates literariness with the "the uncertain status of figures of speech or tropes, a component of language that straddles the disputed borderline between the two areas," grammar and rhetoric (14), with stress on "status" rather than on "uncertain."

Figures and tropes, catharsis, and plot fall in the "margin of overlap" between Aristotle's *Rhetoric* and *Poetics*. They may be viewed from either perspective, but the motives and consequences differ. It is the perspective of rhetoric, rather than the figures and tropes themselves, that has uncertainty as its status and straddles borderlines, contact zones, and muddles. All language, from the screen of rhetoric, is enthymematic, and this is an assertion of a metaphor, not a truth, but a valuable one. In Burke's rhetoric, logic and grammar don't have a "natural affinity" and logic does not share "universality" with science" (de Man 14). In rhetoric, logic is not prior but enthymematic, in that it is persuasive when people agree to its being so and participate in creating the steps and the conclusions. Logical and enthymematic proof, within the realm of rhetoric, are differences in degree not in kind.

The radical extraction de Man performs is the removal of rhetoric's name from the *trivium* by first equating rhetoric and "literariness" and then inserting literariness and literature into the *trivium*. However, because of his commitment to logic, despite his argument that rhetoric redefined as literariness disrupts the trivium, de Man's "literariness," like current notions of rhetoricity and rhetoricality, becomes an object of study and stability rather than action and uncertainty. In sum, the resistance to theory is resistance to the uncertainties of rhetoric, particularly those of the enthymeme that require people to act together in uncertainty, about motives, judgments, actions, and consequences, to create temporary and partial sense of texts and life in order to stay alive. In other words, Burke emphasizes people acting; de Man deals in scholarship. He replaces people, interacting, entertaining and being entertained, and healing and being healed, with cognition. The resistance to reading is resistance to the non-verbal, to the non-human aspects of language, and to the human:

> Tropes used to be part of the study of grammar but were also considered to be the semantic agent of the specific function (or effect) that rhetoric performs as persuasion as well as meaning. Tropes, unlike

grammar, pertain primordially to language. They are text-producing functions that are not necessarily patterned on a non-verbal entity, whereas grammar is by definition capable of extra-linguistic generalization. The latent tension between rhetoric and grammar precipitates out in the problem of reading, the process that necessarily partakes of both. It turns out that the resistance to theory is in fact a resistance to reading, a resistance that is perhaps at its most effective, in contemporary studies, in the methodologies that call themselves theories of reading but nevertheless avoid the function they claim as their object. (de Man 14–15)

People are not actors in his historical analysis, certainly not as conscious agents who resist and collaborate. History, including the history of language, is determinate, and the messiness of life that includes people, their health and entertainment, does not interfere.

He does acknowledge that "it would appear that this concentration on reading would lead to the rediscovery of the theoretical difficulties associated with rhetoric" and that this is happening to an extent" (de Man 17). Burke helps us recognize that an exclusive emphasis on reading (or on writing) prevents attention to rhetoric, understood as the action of identification between and among readers and writers. There cannot be one without the other, and reading is human interaction. He also teaches us that the difficulties of rhetoric are the motives and grounds for action. Resistance to getting along with others *and* the desire for connection with others constitute the dance of life on earth for *animal symbolicum*.

In contrast, de Man suggests that

> [p]erhaps the most instructive aspect of contemporary theory is the refinement of the techniques by which the threat inherent in rhetorical analysis is being avoided at the very moment when the efficacy of these techniques has progressed so far that the rhetorical obstacles to understanding can no longer be mistranslated in thematic and phenomenal commonplaces. (17).

As he continues to discuss Ohmann and Fish, he distinguishes between "proof" and "seduction" or what, in chapter 2 and 3, I discussed as a distinction between qualitative and syllogistic progression, between logical and enthymematic proof, between persuasion in science and in rhetoric, and between sisterly persuasion and assertive logic:

> What awakens one's suspicion about this conclusion [Fish's] is that it relegates persuasion, which is indeed inseparable from rhetoric, to a purely affective and intentional realm and makes no allowance

> for modes of persuasion which are no less rhetorical and no less at work in literary texts, but which are of the order of persuasion by *proof* rather than persuasion by seduction. Thus, to empty rhetoric of its epistemological impact is possible only because its tropological, figural functions are bypassed. It is as if, to return for a moment to the model of the *trivium*, rhetoric could be isolated from the generality that grammar and logic have in common and considered as a mere correlative of an illocutionary power. (18–19)

Here, he seems to equate proof with logical proof only and relegates "seduction" to ethical and pathetic appeals. Although de Man doesn't refer to enthymematic or rhetorical proof, it seems likely that he would associate it with the affective and intentional in the way that many have linked the enthymeme with emotions and failed to recognize, that form the screen of rhetoric, a logical appeal is enthymematic. In chapter 3, using Burke, I argue that Fish persuasively uses logical appeals in his writing and ignores the enthymematic appeals of Anna, the Wolf Man's sister who seduced him. I argue for the value of sisterly persuasion that seduces through collaboration.

In sum, de Man equates instability with rhetoric and associates instability with figures and tropes, or what he calls "literariness." He turns from reading figures and tropes from the perspective of poetics, in terms of parts, kinds, and species, and reads them from the screen of rhetoric which he defines only in terms of uncertainty and instability, but for him these characteristics are inherent in figures and tropes themselves rather than in people's motives, actions, and situations. Consequently, he separates appeals to ethos and pathos from appeals to logos and uses only logical proof; yet, as he formalizes or theorizes instability, he performs his argument about resistance, and this performance requires audience participation in collaborative meaning-making. de Man says as much, but not about himself and not about the rhetoric of logical and enthymematic proof:

> In some cases, a link is reintroduced between performance, grammar, logic, and stable referential meaning, and the resulting theories (as in the case of Ohmann) are not in essence distinct from those of avowed grammarians or semioticians. But the most astute practitioners of speech act theory of reading avoid this relapse and rightly insist on the necessity to keep the actual performance of speech acts, which is conventional rather than cognitive, separate from its perlocutionary function. Rhetoric, understood as persuasion, is forcefully banished (like Coriolanus) from the performative moment and exiled in the affective area of perlocution. Stanley Fish, in a masterful essay, convincingly makes this point. What

awakens one's suspicions about this conclusion is that it relegates persuasion, which is indeed inseparable from rhetoric, to a purely affective and intentional realm and makes no allowance for modes of persuasion which are no less rhetorical and no less at work in literary texts, but which are of the order of persuasion by *proof* rather than persuasion by seduction. Thus, to empty rhetoric of its epistemological impact is possible only because its tropological, figural functions are being bypassed. It is as if, to return for a moment to the model of the trivium, rhetoric could be isolated from the generality that grammar and logic have in common and considered as a mere correlative of an illocutionary power. The equation of rhetoric with psychology rather than with epistemology opens up dreary prospects of pragmatic banality, all the drearier if compared to the brilliance of the performative analysis. (18–19)

The lines de Man draws cut across and reflect biases, as do all terms and distinctions. His distinction between epistemological and psychological, as if they are mutually exclusive, illustrates how his theory includes and excludes; and the "brilliance of performative analysis" as compared to "pragmatic banality" privilege forms of persuasion and power over others. He formalizes or theorizes instability and his performance, requiring an audience, persuades us to participate. In doing so, he, like Fish, incorporates persuasion by proof and persuasion by seduction.

As we have seen, Godzich states in the foreword to *The Resistance to Theory* that de Man "wanted very much to write for quite some time" an essay on Kenneth Burke "which he considered the 'social' counterpart to the more 'formalist' essay on Riffaterre included here, though equally meant to arrive at a notion of inscription that would wreak havoc with the attempt to deal with history and the social only through its representational forms" (xi).

Burke, as I have argued, develops the active, social, and enthymematic dimensions of forms as collaborative actions by writers and readers that prepare us for further collective actions. He deals with history as rhetorical and retrospective constructions, not as strictly "representational forms"; and through his rhetoric of identification he aims at affecting future history by teaching us to see around the corners of our terministic screens through revising our terms, identifying with others, and exploiting the comic correctives and thereby learning and practicing how to get along and avoid war.

Lessons from A Pedagogy of "Contractual Relation" and Its "Use Value" for Students

The final chapter of *The Resistance to Theory* includes Stefano Rosso's 1983 interview with de Man in its original form. Two points seem particularly relevant here, de Man's view of education and his explanation of Derrida's success in America, because they further distinguish between Burke's rhetoric of identification from de Man's "literariness" and between their understandings of the critic's role as educator.

de Man responds to Rosso's first question about his understanding of pedagogy based on his education in Europe and his teaching in Europe and in the US: "I have been teaching in the United States for the last thirty years and it's an experience which I take so much for granted that I don't reflect on it very much anymore" (115). The social responsibility of the critic seems to include theories of reading but not lessons in teaching reading. The difficulty of teaching in Europe, he explains, resulted from the fact that the material, scholarship, "was so separated from the actual professional use that students, who were mostly destined to teach in secondary school, would make of it" which resulted in "a real discrepancy between what one talked about and what the use value of this could be for students" (de Man 115–16).

He could "carry out" his "contractual relation" with students in the US, but in Europe there was a bizarre separation on two completely different levels:

> It's concretely visible in the fact that you stand up there, on that chair, with an abyss between you and the students, while here you sit at a table. I found bad faith in that ideological situation in Europe, worse than here. It is slightly more honest here, though certainly the political problem then gets transposed to the relationship between the "academic" and society at large. I found it easier to cope with that than with what one faces in Europe. (de Man 116)

When asked about Derrida's and deconstruction's success in the US, de Man explains that Derrida "works very close with texts, he *reads* very attentively" and this makes him "more accessible to an American audience" trained in New Criticism. Derrida's "ways of reading" are "exemplary," he says, in that he is aware of "the rhetorical complexities in a text which are applicable to the didactics, to the pedagogy of literary teaching, and as such there is an impact of Derrida which is, in a sense, purely pedagogical" (de Man 117). He explains that his own starting point is "not philosophical but basically philological and for that reason didactical, text-oriented"; therefore, he has a "tendency to put upon texts an inherent authority, which is stronger... than Derrida is willing to put on them" (de Man 118).

de Man grants authority to texts but little to readers. The abyss between himself and his European students is bad faith rather than an opportunity to identify and connect. Teaching at best is the carrying out of a "contractual relation" through a "very direct professional relationship" with students who will be "future colleagues" (116). His teaching, therefore, will have "use value" for them as academics. His disciplinary and professional conception of his identity and role as educator contrasts with Burke's commitment to human interaction and rhetoric "undisciplined."

What, then, would constitute de Man's desired yet unwritten essay on Burke, and how would he "wreak havoc with the attempt to deal with history and the social only through its representational form" (Godzich xi)? Godzich writes that de Man was "aware that the task he had embarked upon would always remain incomplete," and he states: "The texts he has left behind invite us to pursue his reflexion, challenging us to read them in the radical way he had begun to formulate" (xi). He acknowledges that his own "account" is "not meant to be canonical nor does it represent more than a punctual attempt to rationalize the publication in book form of essays written for a bewildering array of occasions that mobilize present-day scholarship" (xi).

Godzich leaves us with an attitude of inconclusiveness, an incomplete text, and an essay unwritten about Burke.

THE LIMITATIONS OF *ANIMAL SYMBOLICUM* AND LANGUAGE: NOT BLINDNESS AND INSIGHT BUT WHAT WE ARE BLINDED TO, INSIGHTFUL ABOUT, AND WHAT WE CAN DO TO CHANGE

It is the incomplete, essayistic, and "bewildering array of occasions," as well as Godzich's statements about Burke, that encouraged me to include this discussion of de Man's final work in this concluding chapter on living. But it is the juxtaposition of blindness and insight, in Burke's terms the dialectical relationship between a focus on being a focus off, that helps me round out my overall arguments and my understanding of Burke's rhetoric of identification as his "Epilogue on Earth." For Burke, our terministic screens, cultures, and bodies constrain and free us or blind us and give us insight. We cannot escape the limitations of *animal symbolicum* nor of our bodily selves, language, and situations, but we can learn to see around the corners of them by identifying with others, revising our terms, and adopting the comic corrective. Identification requires revisions in identities, terms, attitudes, and situations, so that we can come to terms with terms and with others, not to war: ad bellum purificandum.

In the conclusion to his introduction, Godzich summarizes his understanding of de Man's work:

> In a first movement, he restores the ancient relation between *aesthetics* and *theoria* and problematizes their relation, and most of us have followed with considerable interest what he has done there. But we ought not lose sight of the fact that de Man's remapping has liberated praxis from the hold that theory has had over it. It is incumbent upon us now to deal with praxis, though it becomes rapidly clear that our old ways of dealing with it, beholden as they were to the supremacy of theory and the autonomy of *aesthesis*, will not do. Praxis thus stands as a rather mysterious entity presently, the figure of the agency (*Handlung*) that we thought we had lost when we secularized but that now returns without the godhead that adorned, as the figure of history. (xviii)

Despite de Man's work, even his rhetoric as instability then literariness (independent of people and agency but a force in the *trivium* and *quadrivium*) has become praxis. But praxis has become "a rather mysterious entity" rather than action by people. The resistance to theory seems to be a resistance to life, as well as reading, as uncertain. The resistance seems also to be a resistance to people and our need to collaborate with each other. In contrast, Burke's is a rhetoric of people identifying with each other to get along in life and for various reasons.

Godzich, however, concludes the foreword with another brief reference to Burke: "The death of Paul de Man is thus a great loss as he was beginning to move into this phase of his, which was going to become apparent in the essays on Burke, Kierkegaard, and Marx. But there is enough for us to *read* here, and for quite a while" (xviii).

In conclusion, I want to summarize his lessons in reading, writing, and living that teach us to seek the good life defined by "vital social relationships" and to avoid war.

"The Experimental Method at Its Best": "Listening Rather Than Asserting" Because "Certainty Is Cheap"

Burke's rhetoric of identification requires an attitude of uncertainty and inconclusiveness as the grounds and motives for collaborating with others: Without acknowledging our limitations, we might think we can act alone.

By definition and practice, rhetoric deals with the uncertain and experimental because we can never be sure about the consequences of our actions: the word "tree" is not the tree (Burke, *RR* 283), and people, purposes, and places change. What we write will be translated and revised by readers; what we read is not exactly what the writer intended. Nevertheless, understanding both reading and writing as acts of identification—revisions of identities and situations and mutual meaning-making—is the heart and body of proof in Burke's rhetoric. For him, it is "in the areas of ambiguity that transformations take place; in fact, without such areas, identification and transformation would be impossible (Burke, *GM* xix).

He develops the attitude of uncertainty and inconclusiveness in himself and in readers using different terms throughout his rhetoric. He concludes "The Status of Art" in *Counter-Statement* with a discussion of effective and ineffective art that I extend beyond this issue: "We advocate nothing, then, but a return to inconclusiveness" (Burke, *CS* 91). In the realm of rhetoric, matters cannot be settled finally. We may reach a satisfactory conclusion in a context, but the people and situation will change. We therefore need flexibility of attitude and action. To return to inconclusiveness means we try to accept our limitations and our need to collaborate with others in order to get along. To return to inconclusiveness prepares us for further actions by allowing time and space for consideration of alternatives and preventing a rush to judgment. Later, in "Program," Burke defends the aesthetic because "it could never triumph" (*CS* 113): Certainties will always arise, impelling men to new intolerances. (Certainty is cheap, it is the easiest thing of which man is capable. Deprive him of a meal, or bind his arms, or jockey him out of his job—and convictions spring up like Jacks-in-the-box.) (*CS* 113) Aesthetic issues are rhetorical; aesthetics, like rhetoric, can never reach conclusiveness. The aesthetic is rhetoricized into action, and all forms are enthymematic actions that affect writer's and reader's thought processes and motivate both to collaborate.

Burke continues to advocate and practice inconclusiveness and uncertainty to encourage writers to accept their limitations and collaborate with readers and to encourage readers to accept theirs and participate. For another example, in *The Philosophy of Literary Form*, he explains the attitude in a more dramatic way of stooping to conquer and in more scientific language: "Such is the experimental method at its best. In so far as it is humanly possible, it begins by listening rather than by asserting. It is the postponed assertion, somewhat as investment is said to be postponed consumption" (*PLF* 407). In *Attitudes Toward History*, he asks his readers "merely to consider it [his writing] as being on the track of something. We are trying to bring up an issue—rather than to persuade anyone that we can make it crystal clear"

(*ATH* "Introduction" n.p.). He states in *A Grammar of Motives* that "[I]t is not part of our contract here to make final decisions on these many matters (Burke, *GM* 117). Perfection, thoroughness, conclusiveness, and certainty are the hierarchical and absolutist aims of *animal symbolicum* and our language: they are the motive for our doing and our undoing, between which we must find balance.

The "self-defeating emphases ('inner contradictions')" and limitations of Burke's rhetoric result from his focus on a rhetoric of identification and off other rhetorics. The "self-defeating emphases" and contradictions, however, give room for readers to identify with him and help him out. They are the rhetorical space for enthymematic proof.[47]

REVISION AS A WAY OF LIFE: CONFLICTS THAT ARISE BECAUSE WE DO NOT "TRAVEL LIGHT"

It is difficult to change: Insofar as we do not "travel light," we thus assemble much intellectual baggage, and the attempt to reshape this to new exigencies may require a considerable enterprise. Otherwise, a man either leaves himself in pieces or 'freezes' at a simpler state of development" (*ATH* 184n). In *The Rhetoric of Religion,* Burke associates this capacity to revise with the "linguistic marvel," the negative, and with notions of recycling, loss, death, and rebirth.

In the Epilogue to *The Rhetoric of Religion*, which is a "Dialogue in Heaven," he dramatizes TL. (The Lord) and S. (Satan) as they explain and demonstrate how knowing results from "no-ing," from recalcitrance, discounting, questioning, and recognizing that we don't know. His dramatic dialogue is interactive and collaborative; the main characters define each other, and we can't know one without the other. The "Impresario," who opens the drama and arouses our appetites, invites readers to imagine all definitions and all history coming together in a single flash and "a discourse that is not expressed in words at all, but rather is like the sheer aware-

---

47. As mentioned earlier, Jeffrey Walker in *Rhetorics and Poetics in Antiquity* states that the major advantage of Aristotle's enthymeme is the "recognition that the enthymeme, as an elliptical form of argumentation depending on shared assumptions, involves a dialogic, co-creative relationship between the audience and rhetor, in which the audience engages in a kind of 'self-persuasion' by completing or constructing for itself the tacit elided aspects of the enthymeme (170). Walker cites Bitzer's "Aristotle's Enthymeme Revisited" in the *Quarterly Journal of Speech* and John T. Gage's "An Adequate Epistemology for Composition" in *Classical Rhetoric and Modern Discourse.* See also Don M. Burks's 1970 "Persuasion, Self-Persuasion, and Rhetorical Discourse" in *Philosophy and Rhetoric.*

ness that goes with the speaking or the hearing of words" (*RR* 273). She/he concludes by alerting us to the "dialectical relationship among characters": "And, finally, imagine such intuitive expression as a dialogue between two persons that are somehow fused with each other in a communicative bond whereby each question is its own answer, or is answered even without being asked" (273). The "communicative bond" that fuses TL. and S., like the absolute communication possible only among angels, is an ideal unrealizable on earth. The "formal paradox underlying this discourse between The Lord and Satan" is that ends meet, in the beginning is the end, opposites define each other, each part is a whole of other parts and each whole is a part of other wholes, things are part of and apart from, logical and temporal priorities are one, and we are our others.

The Impresario speaks "preparatory observations" for "the author of the heavenly dialogue" who has asked him "to point out that his account is *purely dialogue*" and "involves a theory of purpose based on the definition of man as 'symbol-using animal'" (Burke, *RR* 274). Stage directions bring "the author" more directly though still symbolically onto the stage: "(Takes out a paper and reads.)" As the Impresario reads the author's words, we hear (or rather read) the author Burke whose language we recognize from earlier occasions. He is the multiple Burke: the Impresario, TL., and S. are part of and apart from Burke. They are his imaginings for his prologue in heaven that serves as an epilogue for his rhetoric designed for us here on earth. The dramatist creates characters with the help of actors and audiences, and we "believe" in and identify with characters who are also actors and constructions of the playwright and of other characters.

We can read *The Rhetoric of Religion* as a prologue of his "Prologue in Heaven," as it prepares us for understanding how we cooperate with others in creating god-terms that in turn recreate us and with which we are persuaded to identify because they are what we have in part created. The work also prepares us for the "Prologue in Heaven" by teaching us the possibilities and limitations in us and in language.

According to Burke, we "derive purposes from [our] physical nature," but with language, "a whole new realm of purpose arises, endless in scope, as contrasted with the few rudimentary purposes we derive from our bodies, the needs of food, drink, shelter and sex in their physical simplicity" (274). The differences between bodily and language purposes are "appetites differing not just in degree but in kind" (275), and the language purposes "amount even to a kind of built-in *frustration*" (275). He extends this point:

> In any case, obviously, the talking animals' way of life in a civilization *invents* purposes. Rationalized by money (which is a language,

a kind of purpose-in-the-absolute, a universal wishing well) empires arise. Such networks of production and distribution, made *possible* by language, become *necessary*. So, they raise problems—and many purposes are but attempts to solve those problems, plus the vexing fact that each "solution" raises further problems. (Confidentially, that's "the dialectic.") (*RR* 275)

Here the author speaks to readers in a parenthetical aside about how money and "networks of production and distribution" are "made possible by language" and "become necessary." He presents the "Prologue in Heaven" as a "Parable of Purpose" with the reminder that "language makes questioning easy" and "you can never be sure where quest ends and question begins" (*RR* 275). Both lead to the "search for some Grand Over-All Purpose, as with philosophers, metaphysicians, and theologians" (*RR* 275).

What follows is an imagined paradox, parable, oxymoron, or drama that serves as an epilogue/prologue set in heaven but created on earth. The fusion between The Lord and Satan is an enactment of the dialectic. Burke's identification, partial, temporary, and changing, cannot, however, be confused with this perfection, nor separated from the desire for it. To understand Burke's rhetoric as idealistic and romantic is to miss the limitations of his rhetoric and the limitations in *animal symbolicum* and in language, as he defines them.[48]

TL. summarizes the ambiguities that constitute life on earth for the "Word-People," the "talking animals":

> But, to the quick summation, and the perfect symmetry: In their societies, they will seek to keep order. If order, then a need to repress the tendencies to disorder. If repression, then responsibility for imposing, accepting, or resisting the repression. If responsibility, then guilt. If guilt, then the need for redemption, which involves sacrifice, which in turn allows for substitution. At this point the

---

48. See Arthur Quinn's "Teaching Burke: Kenneth Burke and the Rhetoric of Ascent" for a convincing argument for reading and teaching Burke as a romantic. He maintains that the "chief work for him is to overcome the sense of opposition between the one and the many" and that "the key to Burkean rhetoric is the 'identification' of the audience with the speaker, the sense that the speaker is not imposing his will from without but rather drawing up listeners' own common essence from within" (234). In Burke's rhetoric "consubstantiality" is implicit in identification, with the speaker and audience "united by the mediating logos" (234). We use language to come together and for further collective action. Identification may be described as a *kairotic* moment, a sense of harmony and wholeness in an otherwise chaotic world, but this is rhetoric, not reality.

logic of perfection enters. Man can be viewed as perfectly depraved by a formative "first" offense against the foremost authority, an offense in which one man sinned for all. The cycle of life and death intrinsic to the nature of time can now be seen in terms that treat natural death as the result of this "original" sin. And the principle of perfection can be matched on the hopeful side by the idea of a perfect victim. The symmetry can be logologically rounded out by the idea of this victim as also the creative Word by which time was caused to be, the intermediary Word binding time with eternity, and the end towards which all words of the true doctrine are directed. As one of their saints will put it: "The way to heaven must be heaven, for He said: I am the way." (*RR* 314–15)

This is the way of the world, and the way *is* the world, according to Burke.

The Power of the Negative: No-ing as a Way of Knowing

In *Permanence and Change*, Burke discusses our capacity to use language to reflect, critique, and revise our words, ourselves, and our world, despite bodily and language constraints:

> Though all organisms are critics in the sense that they interpret signs about them, the experimental, speculative technique made available by speech would seem to single out the human species as the only one possessing an equipment for going beyond the criticism of experience to the criticism of criticism. (*PC* 6)

Our terministic screens and orientations help us see by limiting what we see; we can learn to see around the corners of them through revising our terms and attitudes. Perspective by incongruity, joycing, dissociating, changes in identity, and the comic corrective are some ways of both recognizing our limitations and extending them. Seeing around the corner and making changes in moods, motives, orientations, frames, identities, and language are difficult, but they must occur if people and cultures are to live and grow:

> In a shift from one mood to another, there is no "conflict," there is simply "change." But if a mood has broadened into an *attitude*, and if that attitude has attained full rationalization, the shift to another attitude, requiring a different rationalization, does involve "conflict." Insofar as we do not "travel light," we thus assemble much intellectual baggage, and the attempt to reshape this to new exigencies may require a considerable enterprise. Otherwise, a man

either leaves himself in pieces or "freezes" at a simpler state of development. (*ATH* 184n*)

Identification with others in reading, writing, and living can also help us see beyond our own perspectives. Through acts of identification we learn to develop attitudes of uncertainty and ways of reading motives and contexts in order to collaborate with others. We revise ourselves, terms and situations, but we can put disparate aspects together in new ways and experience rebirth. If we don't risk change, we will "freeze" or "rot."

In *The Rhetoric of Religion*, this capacity for self-reflection, criticism of criticism, transformation, and revision is associated with the "linguistic marvel," the negative. Burke is able to round out the arguments he has been making and demonstrating with his rhetoric of identification from *Counter-Statement* on. For example, in *The Rhetoric of Religion*, he develops further his discussions of "Identity, Identification" in his "Dictionary of Pivotal Terms":

> To sum up: Identification is not in itself abnormal; nor can it be "scientifically" eradicated. One's participation in a collective, social role cannot be obtained in any other way. In fact, "identification" is hardly other than a name for the *function of sociality*. (*ATH* 266–67)

> Identity "involves 'change of identity' insofar as any given structure of society calls forth conflicts among our 'corporate we's,'" and from "this necessity you get, in art, the various ritualizations of rebirth." (*ATH* 268–69)

He again associates identification and identity with other means of change: "Change of identity is a way of 'seeing around the corner'" (*ATH* 269)." Burke continues: "In a sense, all perspectives are 'perspectives by incongruity.'" For they are obtained by 'seeing from two angles at once.'" (*ATH* 269).

In his discussion in *Attitudes* of how imagery works, he repeats and extends the idea of identification as rebirth ritual: "We believe that the coordinates of individual psychology invariably place a wrong emphasis upon symbolic acts. Individualistic co-ordinates are too non-social, whereas the basis of cure is socialization" (*ATH* 289). Still not content, he explains the relationship between the individual and the social as dialectical and as a set of bridges people must build. He generalizes his earlier idea of the artist dying and being reborn to include all acts of identification between the individual and social, since they all require a change in self and other, a dying and being reborn:

To be sure, there *is* the individual. Each man is a unique combination of experiences, a unique set of situations, a unique aggregate of mutually re-enforcing and conflicting "corporate we." But he must build his symbolic bridges between his own unique combination and the social pattern with relation to the social pattern, instead of treating his uniqueness as the realm of the uncrowned king. He forms and implements his individual role by utilizing the bureaucratic body of his society. In doing so, he must "die" and be "reborn" in quite the same way that a pure Utopian war plan could be said to die and be reborn, as it encounters the recalcitrance of objective factors. (*ATH* 289)

The individual and the communal are formed and reformed through the dialectical interaction and bridges people construct to connect them.

All these ideas from *Attitudes* are extended in *The Rhetoric of Religion*, as are his discussions in *A Rhetoric of Motives*. As we saw in chapter 2, Burke names the dialectical interaction between individuals, between individuals and the bureaucratic body, "identification," and he associates this term with Aristotle's notion of the enthymeme. According to Burke, we do not identify without "no-ing," without recognizing that we are not one with another, that we cannot be, but that we can do all we can to connect. Linguistic and bodily purposes motivate connections. We learn in interactions with others, in acts of identification and collaborative meaning-making, because we are not one with another. It is this idea of reading, writing, and living as identification, as revision and rebirth, that Burke discusses and demonstrates in his writing of *The Rhetoric of Religion*.

In "The Prologue in Heaven, Burke dramatizes the TL. and S. as they explain and demonstrate how knowing results from "no-ing" in the form of questions. In addition, language itself tends toward hierarchy, absolutes, and perfection, but language, being a social product, cannot reach this ideal or heavenly state: "The range of language being what it is, the very propounding and treasuring of such sanctions will lead in turn to the equally persuasive *questioning* of them" (*RR* 287). Satan reiterates this point: "Their task in ranging linguistically, then, will be to round out their sheer attitudinizing as thoroughly as possible" (*RR* 289). Burke himself ranges linguistically—he proposes "to go the full circuit" (*RR* 10)—in order to question his own assertions. He takes the roundabout rather than the direct route because he seeks to question and to engage readers in "no-ing" along with him. The reader learns through Burke's writing and revising to question what is said and to bring the negative to bear. The reader does not simply find knowledge but, rather, participates in a process of knowing through "no-ing."

Indirection to Find Direction and Identification: The Roundabout as Qualitative Rather Than Syllogistic Progression

Reflection allows Burke to transform "roundabout" to the "Grand Rounding Out" (*RR* 191), so that reflecting back becomes simultaneously reflecting forward. He reinforces the key-term "roundabout" by "telltale words" (*RR* 43) that cluster around it. He says that Augustine "introduces glancingly his theory of grace" (*RR* 100); later he says that by "glancing back" he can find what he is looking for (*RR* 161). Similarly, he writes of understanding "in retrospect" (*RR* 173), by borrowing back (*RR* 37). Two other members of a "terministic clan" (*RR* 70) having to do with roundaboutness are "unfold" (*RR* 298) and "foretold" (*RR* 49, 54). "Foresight" and "hindsight" provide clearer knowledge than does direct sight, for "totality is too immense for any partial view to encompass" (*RR* 313).

He affirms this indirect method on another level as well. His initial approach in *The Rhetoric of Religion* is to "analogize" by the "logological transforming of terms"; he then turns around to say that the process would be a kind of "de-analogizing." He refers to Augustine's approach which "readily leads to *allegorical* interpretations for natural phenomena," a "mode of thought to which logology is always, though somewhat coyly, prone" (*RR* 159). Throughout *The Rhetoric of Religion*, Burke juxtaposes the narrative and reflexive modes (*RR* 28, 124, 158) and the cyclical and rectilinear styles (*RR* 222), approaching them at times as differences in degree and at times as differences in kind. "Time" and "space" are terms that juxtaposed or set in opposition define each other and allow for transcendence. Dialogue is a process by which one partner defines the other and transcendence results from the reciprocity between opposites: "the dialogue form so readily permits one to say things with which one might personally disagree. (*RR* 5)

In addition to working with the roundabout and differences as ways for people to know by "no-ing," Burke incorporates the oxymoron, for it is an "intermediate term" which unites in one term what are understood as opposites or mutually exclusive terms (304; see, for examples, 46, 47, 52, and 304). The overall progression of the text is a verbal, temporary, and strategic transcending of opposites, time/space, narrative/reflexive, sound/sense, (*RR* 43, 53, 59, 67, 201) and part/whole. Throughout, he discusses the indirect approach of playing off polar terms (*RR* 18, 23, 32), counterparts, opposites of all kinds. As Burke demonstrates verbal transcendency, the reader (in a roundabout way) is instructed in how to transcend his text, to create meaning from the disparate parts. At the same time, he teaches us the necessity of being tentative in formulations of meaning because interpretations are situated, partial, tenuous, and revisable.

Burke continually turns back on himself, reflecting on his own "conversions" through writing. He justifies his failure to revise by saying that "in this study of conversion, the reader is given an opportunity to see how "the author's own thesis 'becomes converted'" (*RR* 85). Later, he explains the need to revise his initial dialectical pattern (*RR* 198). Elsewhere, he refers to his earlier ideas in *Counter-Statement*, where he considered the "same paradoxical interchangeability" as now "but as approached the long way round, through the study of a linguistic labyrinth that the author at that time glimpsed but 'in principle'" (*RR* 229). He admits that in the "Prologue in Heaven" "the conceit tended to take over, by developing unexpected quirks of its own" (*RR* 5). For Burke writing is both an extension and revision of the writer and the reader.

His roundabout approach is not merely circular, relativistic, and solipsistic, because, for him as for Bergson, the many perspectives "through the convergence of their actions" lead to "critical moments" (*RR* 187, 191, 192, 193, 284), times "when of a sudden he will feel unified" (*RR* 173). Throughout the roundabout process of language, the "word-men" (*RR* 280) can intuit, can know by circling, and can see anew by creating perspective by incongruity—but only for a moment before the negative sets in. As Burke reads Augustine and *Genesis*, he experiences "critical moments" when he transcends the division between himself as a reader and the text he is reading. Readers of Burke also experience "watershed moments," points at which they transcend to a higher unity, but these moments of insight lead to further questions and doubts. These "kairotic" moments of harmony and wholeness in an otherwise chaotic world are temporary, until the negative rears its head.

In *Rhetoric of Religion*, Burke summarizes his reading theory explicitly in the conjunction of knowing with "no-ing," while he demonstrates this way of knowing in the process of writing and rewriting his own text. To read *The Rhetoric of Religion*, we must remember that the subject of religion falls under the head of rhetoric. The reader experiences Burke's mind at work and develops intuitively a feeling for the principle of the negative. His meaning is not only in what he says but also in what he does: the roundabout approach, like a reversal or doubling of plot, requires readers to relate what happens to what happened to what might happen, stitching together a texture with threads readers rather than the writer supply. As readers learn to cope by making sense, they create a "way in," a positive intuitive identification with Burke, until the negative sets in and the cycling begins again. In this way, assent and dissent are complementary attitudes, each a necessary phase in the process of reading.

Burke's early explanations in *Counter-Statement*, of "formal identification" and how it works to engage writers and readers in creating meaning together, applies to individual figures, such as the oxymoron, when approached as actions. They also apply to broader structures of organization and development, such as indirection or juxtaposition of chapters. They function as proof in that readers are convinced by their own experiences in creating meaning collaboratively and persuaded by the meaning they have in part created. And they function enthymematically at all levels in affecting thought processes and generating action. What is certain in Burke's rhetoric is uncertainty and the recognition that what is missing, what cannot be realized for whatever reasons, is the motive and grounds for rhetoric.

Burke educates his readers to come to terms with each other and to avoid violence, war, and the kill, despite forces in language, in ourselves, and in others to do otherwise. Identification is the means and end of his rhetoric.

A quick tracking of the term *roundabout* in *A Rhetoric of Religion* documents Burke's methods of circling around his subject, defining by negation, and persuading by what's missing. He states his method directly at times, for example: "But such oversimplification of linguistic complexities can be avoided if we approach the subject roundabout, through a systematic concern with linguistic principles exemplified with thoroughness in the dialectics of theology" (Burke, *RR* 10). He continues throughout the book to demonstrate that indirection finds direction and avoids oversimplification. He allies himself with Augustine, who "indicates roundabout the strongly oral associations of words" (67), and then he turns with wit to Augustine's method on Augustine, saying, "we might find roundabout" the names of his mistresses "ambiguously lurking in odd places" (83).

Later, in discussing predestination, Burke adds a dimension to the roundabout approach: "If one is going to develop in a certain way, conceivably the logic of this ultimate development would manifest itself, however roundabout, at much earlier stages, in his peculiar way of assimilating experiences" (168). The "Prologue in Heaven," which is titled the epilogue, is Burke's indirect angle on earth. It's not as simple as that, but from his first work on, he develops the negative, the "linguistic marvel," that informs his notions of the ending in the beginning and vice versa; the relationship between temporal and logical priorities; and the qualitative or enthymematic dimension of linear, logical arguments. Terms define each other, and we know one in terms of the other; but we can still do things with words. The roundabout approach is not a-logical; its logic, perceived from within or in retrospect, is the logic of enthymematic or collaborative meaning-making that must stand pragmatic tests and the "'collective revelation' of testing and discussion" (*PLF* 4).

What's Negative about Identification?

In *The Rhetoric of Religion*, after Burke has named "identification" in *A Rhetoric of Motives*, he explores relationships of identity and identification further and argues that writing and rewriting are rebirth rituals, individual in that aspects of a person die in order for new aspects to emerge, and communal in that all writers undergo rebirth and revision. Early on, his attitude towards revision and his acts of on-going revision are complex although consistent: he revises constantly throughout a text, by qualifying, modifying, and contradicting whatever he says by "no-ing." He revises less after having written, by reversing "temporal priority" into "logical priority," except for the many notes, prefaces, prologues, forewords, epilogues, and appendices, all of which modify, qualify, extend, or undercut the text.[49] For the most part, he seems more interested in showing readers how he thinks—how he gets from here to there—with our help, than he is in creating a coherent and seamless text that persuades by appeals to the author's authority. For Burke, any particular argument will need to be revised for new circumstances. Therefore, his own false starts, qualifications, hesitations, repetitions, confusions, questions, and mistakes are essential for identification and for educating his readers how to get along with each other and create life collectively.

The rhetorical risks Burke was willing to take—to gain authority by sharing it—are great, as are the advantages. His ways of reading and writing were counter to ideas and styles flourishing and being published and paid for. He wrote for a wide range of audiences and tried different approaches and different audiences. He often disagreed with interpretations of his work, and readers were not persuaded by his methods of proof and persuasion. Appeals to authority, power, and logic remain dominant in academic discourse. The risks he took are evident in this fact.

At the same time, the advantages of identification are great. It is based in experience and experiential knowledge of collaborative meaning-making. It is a social method of proof with social consequences: people learn to get along with each other, at least temporarily and to some extent; more people

---

49. See Jack Selzer's *Kenneth Burke in Greenwich Village* and Ann George's review of *The Rhetorical Imagination*.

learn to act collectively; we share power, again only partially and temporarily; we learn to read motives and situations, calculate probable consequences, and act in uncertainty; and, finally, in doing so, we hesitate and equip ourselves for living, not killing and being killed. Dying will come soon enough.

Works Cited

Abraham, Nicolas, and Maria Torok. *The Wolf Man's Magic Word: A Cryptonymy*. Translated by Nicholas Rand. U of Minnesota P, 1986.

Abrams, M. H. *The Mirror and the Lamp: Romantic Theories and the Critical Tradition*. Oxford UP, 1953.

Alcorn, Marshall W. "Changing the Subject of Postmodernist Theory: Discourse, Ideology, and Therapy in the Classroom." *Rhetoric Review*, vol. 13, no. 2 (Spring, 1995), pp. 331–49.

—. *Narcissism and the Literary Libido: Rhetoric, Text, and Subjectivity*. NYUP, 1994.

Aristotle. *Art of Rhetoric*. Translated by J. H. Freese, Loeb, 2020.

Beach, Richard. *Reader-Response Theories: A Teacher's Introduction*. National Council of Teachers, 1993.

Bender, John and David E. Wellbery conclude their article "Rhetoricality: On the Modernist Return of Rhetoric" *Ends of Enlightenment*. Stanford UP, 2012.pp. 203–36

Berlin, James A. "Contemporary Composition: The Major Pedagogical Theories." *College English*, vol. 44, no. 8, 1982, pp. 765–77.

—. "Poststructuralism, Cultural Studies, and the Composition Classroom: Postmodern Theory in Practice." *Rhetoric Review*, vol. 11, no. 1, 1992, pp. 16–33.

—. *Rhetoric and Reality: Writing Instruction in American Colleges, 1900–1985*. Conference on College Composition and Communication, 1987.

—. *Rhetorics, Poetics, and Cultures: Refiguring College English Studies*. National Council of Teachers of English, 1996.

—. "Rhetoric and Poetics in the English Department: Our Nineteenth-Century Inheritance." *College English*, vol. 47, no. 5, 1985, pp. 521–33.

Biesecker's, Barbara A. *Addressing Postmodernity: Kenneth Burke, Rhetoric, and a Theory of Social Change*. U of Alabama P, 2000.

Bitzer, Lloyd F. "Aristotle's Enthymeme Revisited." *Quarterly Journal of Speech*, vol. 45, no. 4, 1959, pp. 399–408.

Bizzell, Patricia, and Bruce Herzberg. *The Rhetorical Tradition: Readings from Classical Times to the Present*. St. Martins Press, 1990.

Blakesley, David. "Defining Film Rhetoric: The Case of Hitchcock's *Vertigo*." *Defining Visual Rhetorics*, edited by Charles A. Hill and Marguerite Helmers, Erlbaum, 2004, pp. 111–33.

—. *The Elements of Dramatism*. Pearson, 2001.

Booth, Wayne. *Critical Understanding: The Powers and Limits of Pluralism.* U of Chicago P, 1979.

Britton, James, et al. *The Development of Writing Abilities (11–18).* NCTE, 1975.

Brooks, Peter. *Reading for the Plot: Design and Intention in Narrative.* Harvard UP, 1992.

Brueggemann, Brenda Jo. "The Coming Out of Deaf Culture and American Sign Language: An Exploration into Visual Rhetoric and Literacy." *Rhetoric Review*, vol. 13, no. 2 (Spring, 1995), pp. 409–20.

Burke, Kenneth. "Dancing with Tears in My Eyes." *Critical Inquiry*, vol. 1, no. 1, 1974, pp. 23–31.

—. "Methodological Repression And/or Strategies of Containment." *Critical Inquiry*, vol. 5, no. 2, 1978, pp. 401–16, doi.org/10.1086/447996.

—. "Rhetoric—Old and New." *The Journal of General Education*, vol. 5, no. 3, April 1951, pp. 202–209.

—. *Attitudes Toward History.* 1937. 3rd rev. ed., U of California P, 1984.

—. *Counter-Statement.* 1931. U of California P, 1968

Language as Symbolic Action: Essays on Life, Literature, and Method. U of California P, 1966.

—. *A Grammar of Motives.* 1945. U of California P, 1969.

—. *Permanence and Change: An Anatomy of Purpose.* 1935. U of California P, 1984.

—. *A Rhetoric of Motives.* 1950. U of California P, 1969.

—. *The Rhetoric of Religion: Studies in Logology.* 1961. U of California P, 1970.

Burks, Don M. "Dramatic Irony, Collaboration, and Kenneth Burke's Theory of Form." *Pre/Text: A Journal of Rhetorical Theory*, vol. 3, no. 4, 1985.

—. "Persuasion, Self-Persuasion and Rhetorical Discourse." *Philosophy & Rhetoric* 1970, pp. 109–19.

—. "Kenneth Burke: The Agro-Bohemian 'Marxoid.'" *Communication Studies*, vol. 42, Fall 1991, pp. 219–33.

—. *Rhetoric, Poetics, and Philosophy.* Purdue UP, 1978.

Butler, Judith. "Contingent Foundations: Feminism and the Question of Postmodernism." *Feminists Theorize the Political.* Edited by Judith Butler and Joan W. Scott, Rutledge, 1992, pp. 3–21.

—. *Gender Trouble: Feminism and the Subversion of Identity.* Routledge, 2006.

Bygrave, Stephen. *Kenneth Burke: Rhetoric and Ideology.* Routledge, 1993.

Carter, C. Allen. *Kenneth Burke and the Scapegoat Process.* U of Oklahoma P, 1996.

Clifford, John. "Burke and the Tradition of Democratic Schooling: Festschrift in Honor of Ann E. Berthoff." *Audits of Meaning*, edited by Louise Z. Smith, pp. 29–40, Boynton/ Cook, 1988.
Coe, Richard M. *Form and Substance: An Advanced Rhetoric*. John Wiley and Sons, 1981.
Conley, Thomas M. "The Enthymeme in Perspective." *Quarterly Journal of Speech*, vol. 70, no. 2, 1984, pp. 168–87.
—. "*Pathe* and *Pisteis*: Aristotle, Rhet. II.2–11." *Hermes*, vol. 110, pp. 300–15.
Corbett, Edward P. J., editor. *Rhetorical Analyses of Literary Works*. Oxford UP, 1969.
Crowley, Sharon. *Composition in the University: Historical and Polemical Essays*. U of Pittsburgh P, 1998.
Crucius, Timothy W. *Kenneth Burke and the Conversation After Philosophy*. Southern Illinois UP, 1999.
de Man, Paul. *The Resistance to Theory*. U of Minnesota P, 1986.
Derrida, Jacques. Foreword. *The Wolf Man's Magic Word: A Cryptonymy*. Translated by Nicholas Rand. U of Minnesota P, 1986.
—. "Some Questions and Responses." *The Linguistics of Writing: Arguments between Language and Literature*, edited by Colin MacCabe, Nigel Fabb, Derek Attridge, and Alan Durant, pp. 252–64, Manchester UP, 1987.
—. "Structure, Sign, and Play in the Discourse of the Human Sciences." *Writing and Difference*, trans. Alan Bass, pp. 278–94, Routledge, 1980.
Dowd, Maureen. "Film's 'Mad Prophet' Eerily Prescient." *Arizona Daily Star*, B5, September 11, 2001.
Duncan, Hugh Dalziel. Introduction. *Permanence and Change: An Anatomy of Purpose*, by Kenneth Burke, 1935, 3rd ed., U of California P, 1984, pp. xiii–xliv.
Eagleton, Terry. *Ideology: An Introduction*. Verso, 1991.
—. *Literary Criticism: An Introduction*. U of Minnesota P, 1983.
—. *Marxism and Literary Criticism*. U of California P, 1976.
Elbow, Peter, editor. *What Is English?* Modern Language Association, 1990.
Farmer, Frank. "Voice Reprised: Three Etudes for a Dialogic Understanding." *Rhetoric Review*, vol. 13, no. 2 (Spring, 1995), pp. 303–20
Felman, Shoshanna. *Jacques Lacan and the Adventure of Insight: Psychoanalysis in Contemporary Culture*. Harvard UP, 1987.
Fish, Stanley. "Why We Can't All Just Get Along." *First Things: A Monthly Journal of Religion and Public Life*, Feb., 1996, pp. 18–26.
—. "Withholding the Missing Portion: Power, Meaning, and Persuasion in Freud's *The Wolf-Man*." *The Linguistics of Writing: Arguments between Language and Literature*, edited by Colin MacCabe, et al., pp. 155–72, Manchester UP, 1987.

—. "Withholding the Missing Portion: Psychoanalysis and Rhetoric." *Doing What Comes Naturally: Change, Rhetoric, and the Practice of Theory in Literary and Legal Studies* 1989.

Foster, Dennis A. "Interpretation and Betrayal: Talking with Authority" *Reclaiming Pedagogy: The Rhetoric of the Classroom*, edited by Patricia Donahue and Ellen Quandahl, Southern Illinois UP, 1989, pp. 35–48.

Frank, Armin Paul. *Kenneth Burke*. Twayne Publishers, 1969.

Freud, Sigmund. *From the History of an Infantile Neurosis*. The Complete Psychological Works of Sigmund Freud, vol 17, Vintage, 2001.

Fulkerson, Richard. "Four Philosophies of Composition." *College Composition and Communication*, vol. 30, no. 4, 1979, pp. 343–48.

Gage, John. "An Adequate Epistemology for Composition: Classical and Modern Perspectives." *Essays on Classical Rhetoric and Modern Discourse*. Edited by Robert J. Connors, Lisa S. Ede, and Andrea A. Lunsford. Southern Illinois UP, 1984, pp. 152–69.

—. "Teaching the Enthymeme: Invention and Arrangement" *Rhetoric Review*, vol. 2, no. 1, Sep. 1983, pp. 38–50.

Gallop, Jane. *Reading Lacan*. Cornell UP, 1985

Gardiner, Ellen. "Peter Elbow's Rhetoric of Reading." *Rhetoric Review*, vol. 13, no. 2 (Spring, 1995), pp. 321–30.

Gardner, Muriel, trans., ed. *The Wolf-Man by the Wolf-Man: The Double Story of Freud's Most Famous Case*. Basic Books, 1971.

George, Ann. Review of *The Rhetorical Imagination* by Ross Wollin. *Rhetoric Review*, vol. 21, 2002, pp. 190–93.

Girard, Rene. *Violence and the Sacred*, translated by Patrick Gregory, Johns Hopkins UP, 1979.

Glenn, Cheryl. "Remapping Rhetorical Territory" *Rhetoric Review*, vol. 13, no. 2 (Spring, 1995), pp. 287–303.

Godzich, Wlad. Foreward. *The Resistance to Theory. The Resistance to Theory*. U of Minnesota P, 1986.

Graff, Gerald. *Professing English Literature: An Institutional History*. U of Chicago P, 1989.

Green, Lawrence D. "Aristotle's Enthymeme and the Imperfect Syllogism." *Rhetoric and Pedagogy*, edited by Winifred Bryan Horner and Michael Leff, Erlbaum, 1995, pp. 19–41.

—. "Rhetoric, Dialectic, and the Traditions of Antistrophos." *Rhetorica: A Journal of the History of Rhetoric* vol. 8, 1990, pp. 5-27.

—. "Enthymemic Invention and Structural Prediction." *College English*. vol. 41, no. 6, pp. 623–34, 1980.

Greenblatt, Stephen, and Giles Gunn, editors. *Redrawing the Boundaries: The Transformation of English and American Literacy Studies.* Modern Language Association, 1992.

Grimaldi, William M. A. *Aristotle, Rhetoric I: A Commentary.* Fordham UP, 1980.

Hassett, Michael. "Sophisticated Burke: Kenneth Burke as a Neosophistic Rhetorician." *Rhetoric Review*, vol. 13, no. 2 (Spring, 1995), pp. 371–390.

Henderson, Greig E. *Kenneth Burke : Literature and Language as Symbolic Action.* U of Georgia P, 1988.

Hunter, Susan. "The Case for Reviewing as Collaboration and Response." *Rhetoric Review*, vol. 13, no. 2 (Spring, 1995), pp. 265–72.

Hyman, Stanley Edgar. *The Armed Vision: A Study of the Methods of Modern Literary Criticism.* Vintage Books, 1955.

Iser, Wolfgang. *The Act of Reading: A Theory of Aesthetic Response.* John Hopkins UP, 1980

Jameson, Fredric R. "Ideology and Symbolic Action." *Critical Inquiry*, vol. 5, no. 2, 1978, pp. 417–22, https://doi.org/10.1086/447997.

—. "The Symbolic Inference; Or, Kenneth Burke and Ideological Analysis." *Critical Inquiry*, vol. 4, no. 3, 1978, pp. 507–23. *JSTOR*, www.jstor.org/stable/1343072. Accessed 5 Aug. 2023.

Jay, Paul. *The Selected Correspondence of Kenneth Burke and Malcolm Cowley 1915–1981.* U of California P, 1989.

Kastely, James L. *Rethinking the Rhetorical Tradition.* Yale UP, 1997.

Kennedy, George A., translator. *On Rhetoric: A Theory of Civic Discourse.* Oxford UP, 1991.

Knox, George. *Critical Moments: Kenneth Burke's Categories and Critiques.* U of Washington P, 1957.

Lauer, Janice M. "The Feminization of Rhetoric and Composition Studies?" *Rhetoric Review*, vol. 13, no. 2 (Spring, 1995), pp. 276–86.

Lentricchia, Frank. *After the New Criticism.* U of Chicago P, 1980.

—. *Criticism and Social Change.* U of Chicago P, 1984.

Lewis, Claudia. "N-Word Still Stings Civil-Rights Fighters." *Arizona Daily Star*, B5, September 11, 2001.

Lloyd-Jones, Richard, and Andrea A. Lunsford, eds. *The English Coalition Conference: Democracy Through Language.* Modern Language Association, 1989.

Lunsford, Andrea A., and Lisa S. Ede. "On Distinctions Between Classical and Modern Rhetoric." *Essays on Classical Rhetoric and Modern Discourse*, edited by Robert J. Connors, et. al., Southern Illinois UP, 1984, pp. 37–49.

Lynch. Dennis A. "Teaching Rhetorical Values and the Question of Student Autonomy." *Rhetoric Review*, vol. 13, no. 2 (Spring, 1995), pp. 350–70.

Mailloux, Steven. *Reception Histories: Rhetoric, Pragmatism, and American Cultural Politics*. Cornell UP, 1998.

Miller, Arthur B., and John D. Bee. "Enthymeme: Body and Soul." *Philosophy & Rhetoric*, vol. 5, no. 4, pp. 201–214.

Miller, Thomas P. *The Formation of College English: Rhetoric and Belles Lettres in the British Cultural Provinces*. U of Pittsburgh P, 1997.

Nelson, Cary. "Writing as the Accomplice of Language: Kenneth Burke and Poststructuralism." *The Legacy of Kenneth Burke*, edited by Herbert W. Simons and Trevor Melia, U of Wisconsin P, 1989, pp. 156-73.

Nienkamp, Jean. *Internal Rhetorics: Toward a History and Theory of Self-Persuasion*. Southern Illinois UP, 2001.

Nussbaum, Martha C. *The Fragility of Goodness: Luck and Ethics in Greek Tragedy and Philosophy*. Cambridge, UP, 1986.

Olson, Gary A. *Justifying Belief: Stanley Fish and the Work of Rhetoric*. State U of New York P, 2002.

Perelman, Chaïm, et al. *The New Rhetoric: A Treatise on Argumentation*. U of Notre Dame P, 1969. *JSTOR*, doi.org/10.2307/j.ctvpj74xx. Accessed 7 Sept. 2023.

Quandahl, Ellen. "'More Than Lessons in How to Read': Burke, Freud, and the Resources of Symbolic Transformation." *College English*, vol. 63, no. 5, pp. 633–54 May 2001

Quinn, Arthur. "Teaching Burke: Kenneth Burke and the Rhetoric of Ascent." *Rhetoric Society Quarterly*, vol. 25, 1995, pp. 231–36.

Raymond, James C. "Enthymemes, Examples, and Rhetorical Method." *Essays on Classical Rhetoric and Modern Discourse*, edited by Robert J. Connors, et. al., Southern Illinois UP, 1984, pp. 141–51.

—, ed. *English as a Discipline; or, Is There a Plot in This Play?*

Rodriguez, Richard. "Migrants, the New Rebels." *Arizona Daily Star*, B5, September 11, 2001.

Rueckert, William H. *Kenneth Burke and the Drama of Human Relations*. U of Minnesota P, 1963.

Scholes, Robert E. *Textual Power : Literary Theory and the Teaching of English*. Yale UP, 1985.

Selzer, Jack. *Kenneth Burke in Greenwich Village: Conversing with the Moderns 1915–1931*. U of Wisconsin P. 1996.

Southwell, Samuel B. *Kenneth Burke and Martin Heidegger: With a Note Against Deconstruction*. UP of Florida, 1988.

Stafford, William. *Writing the Australian Crawl*. U of Michigan P, 1978.

Tompkins, Jane P, editor. *Reader-Response Criticism: From Formalism to Post-Structuralism.* John Hopkins UP, 1980.
Toulmin, Stephen. Introduction. *The Quest for Certainty. The Later Works of John Dewey, Volume 4, 1925–1953: 1929: The Quest for Certainty*, vol. 4, edited by Jo Ann Boydston, Southern Illinois UP, 1984.
Vitanza, Victor. *Negation, Subjectivity, and the History of Rhetoric.* State U of New York P, 1996
—. "'The Wasteland Grows'; Or, What Is 'Cultural Studies for Composition' and Why Must We Always Speak Good of It?: ParaResponse to Julie Drew." *JAC : a Journal of Composition Theory*, vol. 19, no. 4, 1999, pp. 699–703.
—. "The Wasteland Grows," Research Network Forum., College Composition and Communication Conference, Chicago, April, 1998. Rpt. in *James A. Berlin and Social-Epistemic Rhetorics: A Seminar* by Victor J. Vitanza. Parlor, 2021.
Walker, Jeffrey. "The Body of Persuasion: A Theory of the Enthymeme"
—. *Rhetoric and Poetics in Antiquity.* Oxford UP, 2000.
Warnock, John. "The Relation of Critical Perspectives to Teaching Methods in Composition." *College English*, vol. 34, no. 5, 1973, pp. 69–70.
Warnock, Tilly. "Making Do, Making Believe, and Making Sense: Burkean Magic and the Essence of English Departments." *Redrawing the Boundaries: The Transformation of English and American Literacy Studies*, edited by Stephen Greenblatt and Giles Gunn, Modern Language Association, 1992, pp. 143–59
—. "Reading Kenneth Burke: Ways in, Ways out, Ways Roundabout." *College English*, vol. 48, no. 1, 1986, pp. 62–75.
Wess, Robert. *Kenneth Burke: Rhetoric, Subjectivity, Postmodernism.* Cambridge UP, 1996.
West, Cornel. *The Cornel West Reader.* Civitas, 2000.
White, Hayden. *Tropics of Discourse.* John Hopkins UP, 1986.
Winterowd, W. Ross. *The Contemporary Writer.* Harcourt, 1981.
—. *The English Department: A Personal and Institutional History.* Southern Illinois UP, 1998.
Wolin, Ross. *The Rhetorical Imagination of Kenneth Burke.* U of South Carolina P, 2001.
Zaner, Richard. *Philosophy, Rhetoric, and Argumentation*, edited by Maurice Natanson and Henry W. Johnstone, Pennsylvania UP, 1965.

Index

1935 American Writer's Congress, 218

9/11, 152, 156, 167, 179, 183, 184, 189–190, 195, 205, 208, 212

Abraham, Nicholas, 136–141, 143
Abrams, M. H., 169, 206
absence, 45, 64, 100, 140, 154
academic essay, 151
Act, 19, 23, 49, 150
ad bellum purificandum, 12, 23, 86, 186, 234, 250
Adorno, Theodore, 35
Agency, 19, 23, 25
Agent, 19, 23
Alcorn Jr., Marshall W., 118, 198
alienation, 3, 31, 32, 170
all living things are critics, 157
Althusser, Louis, 33, 34, 222
ambiguity, 13, 24, 145, 146, 168, 251
American criticism, 20, 22
animal symbolicum, 3–5, 23, 29, 65, 88, 99, 117, 150, 152, 157, 160, 187, 200, 220, 236, 238, 245, 249, 252, 254
antithesis, 149, 210
appetite, 59, 62
Aristotelian rhetoric, 211
Aristotle, 14, 43–50, 53–54, 74–78, 83, 86–89, 91, 92–93, 95–97, 101, 103, 111, 118, 161, 211, 212, 215, 221, 238, 244, 252, 257
art, 18, 27, 44, 46, 47, 50–54, 56, 57–59, 62–74, 77–82, 87, 89, 90, 112, 141, 160, 171, 178, 206, 232–234, 251, 256
Art for Art's Sake, 59, 69

assessment, 11, 151, 169, 173, 218, 221
attitudes, 5, 9, 15, 24, 54, 60–61, 66, 69, 74, 76, 80, 82, 85–86, 94, 96, 104, 130, 141, 145, 149–151, 156, 161, 170–172, 177, 181, 188, 203, 221, 236–237, 239, –, 255–256, 260
Atwill, Janet M., 103
Augustine, St., 86, 88–89, 258–260
Austin, J. L., 33
authority, 7–8, 13, 32, 64, 71, 81, 90, 100, 107, 118, 120, 125–126, 128, 130, 132, 150, 161, 163–169, 178, 180, 182–183, 185, 191–192, 196, 204, 206, 222, 227, 239, 249, 255, 261
available means of persuasion, 4, 67, 80, 92, 143, 221

Bakhtin, Mikhail, 232
Baldwin, Charles Sears, 208
Barnyard, The, 157
Barthes, Roland, 53, 202
Bartholomae, David, 203, 211
being driven into the corner, 170
Beisecker, Barbara A., 45
Benjamin, Walter, 176, 231, 232
Bergson, Henri, 259
Berlin, James A, 95, 153, 169, 182, 190–198, 200–203, 206, 208–211, 215, 216–220, 222–226
Bin Laden, Osama, 167, 227
Bishop, Wendy, 205
Bitzer, Lloyd, 46, 48, 83, 252
Bizzell, Patricia, 161, 200, 203
Blackmur, R. P., 176
Blakesley, David, 46
Bloom, Harold, 9, 143

271

bodies, 4, 21, 23, 66–67, 141, 145, 157, 187, 201, 219, 249, 253
body of proof, 8, 12, 29, 36, 44–45, 47, 77, 83, 87–88, 91, 96, 109, 161, 177, 212, 213, 251
Bohemian, 44, 69, 70, 73
Booth, Wayne C., 52, 161, 207
Borges, Jorge Luis, 121
Bourdieu, Pierre, 35
bourgeois/Bohemian conflict, 70
bricoleur, 9, 112
bridging devices, 172–173, 180
Britton, James, 169
Brock, Bernard L., 45
Brokaw, Tom, 188
Brooks, Peter, 118–123, 126–127, 130, 132–133, 143, 241
Brueggemann, Brenda Jo, 201
bureaucratization of the imaginative, 172
Burke, Kenneth: *Attitudes Toward History*, 3, 14, 30, 43, 49, 55, 77, 91, 116, 149, 150, 152, 155, 157, 161, 169, 170–180, 182, 209, 232–237, 239, 251–252, 256, 257; *Counter-Statement*, 12–14, 44, 49,–51, 53, 55–64, 66–82, 85–86, 92, 94–96, 111, 161, 173, 179, 182, 209, 213–215, 233, 239, 251, 256, 259–260; *Grammar of Motives, A*, 21, 25, 146, 150, 161, 238, 251–252; *Language as Symbolic Action*, 4, 6, 16, 40, 117, 207, 209, 234, 238, 239; *Permanence and Change*, 3, 6, 77, 98, 150, 155, 157–161, 173, 179, 182–183, 214, 227, 239, 255; *Rhetoric of Motives, A*, 3–5, 14, 21–22, 44–45, 49, 58, 74, 83, 85–96, 161, 192, 214, 221, 257, 261; *Rhetoric of Religion*, 4, 16, 92, 161, 231, 234, 239, 251–261; *Symbolic, The*, 150; *White Oxen, The*, 51
Burks, Don M., 44, 83–84, 252
Bygrave, Stephen, 6–7, 35–40

Caesar, Julius, 75, 77
casuistic stretching, 43, 46, 49, 62, 90, 170, 172, 174, 180
casuistry, 43
catharsis, 244
certainty, 13, 73, 100, 131, 135, 152, 164, 167–168, 180, 186, 203, 238, 252
Chesebro, James W., 45
Cicero, 86, 89
classrooms, 155, 200, 212, 217
Clifford, John, 215
coercion, 13, 115
collective selves, 191, 236
college writing, 151
comedy, 176, 178, 180, 234
comic corrective, 103, 105, 130, 145, 150, 155–156, 158, 169, 174–175, 180, 187, 218, 227, 235, 247, 249, 255
composition courses, 151
Conference on College Composition and Communication (CCCC), 103
contradictions, 35, 56, 59–60, 88, 133, 149, 152, 160, 168, 171, 186, 197–198, 216, 219, 220, 222, 236, 252
conventional form, 74, 80
Corbett, Edward P. J., 192, 205, 206, 207
Corder, Jim, 204, 205
Covino, William, 103
Cowley, Malcolm, 49, 58, 75, 78, 213, 214
Critical Inquiry, 7, 8, 11, 27, 52
Crucius, Timothy W., 58, 154
cultural studies, 37, 190, 192, 196, 203, 216, 218
current-traditional rhetorics, 151, 193, 212
Cushman, Ellen, 205

Davis, D. Diane, 205
De Gourmont, Remy, 50, 52, 56, 59–61, 72, 111

de Man, Paul, 9, 114, 222, 232, 237, 239–250
deconstruction, 9, 109, 110–113, 139, 141, 248
deductive logic, 167, 168, 169
definitions, 22, 45, 74, 79, 96, 151, 170, 174, 180, 237, 238, 252
Derrida, Jacques, 108–114, 122, 132, 138–143, 145, 248–249
desire, 3, 31, 48, 56–57, 59, 62, 64–65, 67, 82, 100–101, 104, 116, 121, 129, 138, 140, 150–151, 154, 163–164, 166, 187, 190–191, 199, 218, 223–234, 236, 238–239, 245, 254
Dewey, John, 30, 154–155, 215; *The Quest for Certainty*, 154
dialectic, 48, 84, 88–90, 144, 179, 254
disidentification, 215, 221, 223
dissociation, 59–60, 110, 111
division, 69, 146, 194, 259
Dowd, Maureen, 184
Dowst, Kenneth, 202
dramatism, 24, 40, 46, 161
dreams, 124

Eagleton, Terry, 6, 32, 202
ecology, 235, 236
economics, 4, 155, 161, 191, 192, 217, 220
Ede, Lisa, 103
education, 28, 30, 70, 115, 150, 151, 154–156, 158–160, 163, 191–194, 215, 222, 236, 239, 248
Elbow, Peter, 198, 202, 203, 226
Eliot, T.S., 51, 64, 75, 77, 121
eloquence, 63, 66, 111, 214
English departments, 190–191, 193, 196, 203
Enos, Theresa, 224
enthymeme, 6, 8, 34, 36, 44–49, 53–54, 74, 77, 83–85, 87–88, 91–93, 96, 97, 101–103, 109, 139, 161, 168–169, 211–213, 215, 221, 243–244, 246, 252, 257
epideictic, 9, 46–47, 109
epistemic rhetoric, 190–192, 193–196, 201, 202, 208, 210–211, 224
epistemology, 154, 210–211, 247
equipment for living, 13, 35, 39, 81, 103, 151, 162, 178, 187, 233
Euclid, 74, 76
expressive criticism, 206
expressivism, 151, 193, 195, 205

Farmer, Frank, 198
Felman, Shoshana, 164
figures, 45, 49, 52, 66, 79, 83, 95, 102, 135, 141, 161, 163–164, 173, 202, 234, 238, 244, 246, 260
Fish, Stanley, 98–118, 121–138, 141, 143–145, 161, 168, 245–247
Flaubert, Gustave, 52, 56–58
Flower, Linda, 197
folklore, 192
formal logic, 167
formalists, 9
forms: incidental, 75, 79
Foster, Dennis A., 163–168
Foucault, Michel, 27, 200, 202–203, 209, 211, 220
Frank, Armin Paul, 5, 27, 49, 51, 52, 99, 154, 198, 202
Frankfurt School, 241
Freud, Sigmund, 35, 98–108, 114–138, 141, 143–145, 168, 221–222
Frye, Northrop, 9, 241
Fulkerson, Richard, 206

Gage, John T., 46, 48, 211, 252
Gallop, Jane, 165
Gardiner, Ellen, 135, 198
Genesis, 259
Gide, André, 72, 121
Gilyard, Keith, 205
Glenn, Cheryl, 103, 197
God-terms, 239

Godzich, Wlad, 232, 237, 239, 247, 249, 250
Good Life, The, 170, 232, 233
gradatio, 66, 95
Graff, Gerald, 203
Gramsci, Antonio, 28, 222
Greenblatt, Stephen, 203
Grimaldi. William M. A., 44, 46, 48, 54, 211–212
Gunn, Giles, 203

Halloran, S. Michael, 211
Hamlet, 61, 62, 64
Hassett, Michael, 200, 201
Hayden White, 9, 52, 202, 209
Hayes, John, 197
Heidegger, Martin, 154
Henderson, Greig, 6, 205, 207
hermeneutics, 25, 139
Herzberg, Bruce, 161
hierarchy, 3–4, 13, 23, 29, 88, 107, 117, 163, 192–193, 197, 215, 227, 236–238, 257
Hindman, Jane E., 205
hip-hop, 184
Hirsch, E. D., 9
history, 9, 15, 17–19, 21–22, 28, 37, 39, 46–47, 52, 68, 71, 73, 85, 87, 100, 115–117, 119, 121–122, 134, 138, 154, 160–161, 165, 191–192, 194, 196, 201, 203, 205–206, 216, 232, 241–242, 245, 247, 249–250, 252
Hitler, Adolph, 26, 105, 106
humanism, 178, 199, 200
Hunter, Susan M., 197
Hussein, Saddam, 227
Hyman, Stanley Edgar, 50

identification, rhetorics of, 5, 39, 51, 56, 151–152, 170, 180, 186, 192, 194, 198, 221, 226–227, 247–250, 252, 256
identity, 14, 18, 20– 22, 59, 64, 79, 91, 99, 151, 157, 163, 167, 169, 175, 185, 190–191, 198, 216, 218, 222–226, 236, 249, 255–256, 261
ideological analysis, 7, 15, 17–20, 23–24, 26, 154
ideology, 4–8, 10–15, 18–22, 27–29, 33–39, 48, 49, 59, 90, 163, 185, 192, 195, 197–200, 205, 210, 212, 216, 218–222, 224–226; of form, 7–8, 10
imagery, 48, 124, 149, 173, 175, 256
images, 34, 44, 62, 63, 69, 78–79, 91, 94, 111, 153, 173, 183–185
inconclusiveness, 24, 72, 179, 249–251
incongruity, 6, 43, 49, 58, 60, 77, 174, 176–177, 214, 255–256
inductive experience, 168
intellectuals, 31, 154, 193, 208
intuition, 168, 237, 238, 242
invention is the mother of necessity, 157

Jakobson, Roman, 169
James, William, 154
Jameson, Fredric, 5–27, 30, 35–40, 49, 156, 166, 201–202, 233
Jarratt, Susan, 103, 200
Jay, Paul, 49, 58, 205, 213, 214
John Reed Clubs, 28
joycings, 62, 160
Jung, Julie, 205

Kastely, James, 103, 107, 213
Keats, John, 26, 27
Kenner, Hugh, 53
Kinneavy, James, 211
Knox, George, 50
Krieger, Murray, 9
Kuhn, Thomas, 202

Lacan, Jacques, 16, 132, 163–168, 219, 222, 223, 224
Langer, Susanne K., 202
Lauer, Janice M., 194, 197
Leff, Michael, 210

Lentricchia, Frank, 5–6, 9, 27–32, 35, 36, 38–40, 49, 52, 99, 154, 202, 222
Levi-Strauss, Claude, 9
Lewis, Claudia, 184
literature, 4, 8–9, 26, 30, 32–35, 49, 56, 57, 70, 74, 77–88, 99, 106, 109, 160–162, 190, 192–194, 203–204, 206, 208, 213–215, 233, 238– 244
Lloyd-Jones, Richard, 203
logic, 18, 25, 37, 48, 68, 76–77, 78, 80, 87–88, 93, 97, 102, 106, 110, 115, 121, 124–126, 128, 145, 149, 167–168, 177, 221, 237, 238, 240, 242–247, 255, 260–261
logology, 234, 236, 258
Lunsford, Andrea A., 46, 103, 203, 211
Lynch, Dennis A., 198–201

Macbeth, 64, 75, 77, 111
MacCabe, Colin, 108–112, 122
Macdonell, Diane, 220, 221
Macherey, Pierre, 34–35
Macrorie, Ken, 202, 204, 205
Mailloux, Steven, 154
Malinowski, Bronisław, 176
Mann, Thomas, 50, 72, 119, 121, 123
margin of overlap, 44, 63, 71, 76, 81– 82, 112, 244
Marinara, Martha, 205
Mark Bracher, 223
Marx, Karl, 28–29, 31, 176, 210, 221, 250; *German Ideology, The*, 22, 28
Marxism, 14, 28, 31–32, 34, 52, 107, 159, 161–162, 201–202, 209, 217, 222
maxims, 93
McCain, John, 189
McKeon, Richard, 176

means of persuasion, 8, 13, 18, 38, 57, 68, 77, 87, 114, 175, 192–193, 205, 212, 233, 243
metaphors, 6, 37, 52, 79, 83, 93, 129, 138, 154, 168, 172, 214, 244
Miller, Richard, 205
Miller, Thomas P., 203
mimetic criticism, 206
miso-philanthropic, 3
Modern Language Association (MLA), 239
moralized by the negative, 4–5, 238
Murray, Donald, 9, 202, 204, 205
music, 48, 63, 79, 160, 242
Mussolini, Benito, 28
myth, 29, 120–121, 199–200

naïve verbal realism, 4
Nelson, Cary, 16
New Criticism, 9, 241
New Historicism, 9
Nietzsche, Friedrich, 6, 16
novels, 57
Nussbaum, Martha C., 171

objective criticism, 206
occupational psychoses, 155
Ohmann, Richard, 210, 245, 246
Olbrechts-Tyteca, Lucie, 46, 199–200; *The New Rhetoric*, 198–200
Ong, Walter J., 161
opinions, 46, 49, 81, 83, 87–93, 96–97, 240
Osgood, C. E., 105, 122

paradox, 79, 163, 168, 235, 253–254
Pater, Walter, 56, 58–59
Pearl Harbor, 189
Peirce, Charles Sanders, 154
peitho, 88
Perelman, Chaïm, 46, 199–200; *The New Rhetoric*, 198–200
perfection, 3–4, 75, 78, 81, 95, 145, 186–187, 236, 238–239, 254–255, 257
Perl, Sondra, 205

perspective by incongruity, 6, 22, 58, 60, 62, 72, 77, 82, 100, 144, 152–153, 172, 174–175, 180, 214, 236, 259
persuasion, 4, 6–8, 13–14, 19, 32, 45–47, 49, 54, 81–96, 99, 101–105, 108–109, 111–113, 121–125, 128–132, 135–139, 143, 151–152, 161, 163, 169, 185–186, 194, 207, 210, 216, 221, 237, 244–247, 252, 261
philologists, 9
philosophy, 4, 46, 60, 68, 83, 121, 154, 161, 190, 210, 242
Plato, 50, 110, 144, 176
poetic process, 64, 67, 71
poetics, 44, 46–47, 64, 67, 71, 86, 91, 95, 136–137, 149, 169, 182–183, 194, 206, 208–209, 227, 238
Polanyi, Michael, 202
polemic, 178
politics, 4, 46, 83, 87, 93, 95, 155, 190–192, 195–196, 198, 205, 208, 210–211, 220, 225, 227
post-ideological, 184–185, 186, 217
postmodernism, 152, 198, 219, 223
postmodernist pedagogy, 198
pragmatic criticism, 206
pragmatism, 154
presence, 34, 45, 75, 77, 111, 222
propaganda, 178
Proust, Marcel, 119
proverbs, 93
psychoanalysis, 9, 40, 104, 115, 119, 137, 142, 164, 191, 198, 216, 223
psychology, 20, 53, 62–63, 72, 87, 105, 160–161, 190, 192, 197, 206, 216, 218, 220–222, 225–226, 247, 256
purification, 50, 186, 224
Purpose, 19, 24–25, 26, 161, 254

qualitative progression, 19, 44, 51, 54, 62, 64, 66, 68–69, 71, 74–78,
80, 82, 92, 100–111, 130, 141, 173, 214
Quinn, Arthur, 254
Quintilian, 89, 95

rationalization, 160, 255
Raymond, James C., 46, 203
reader response criticism, 9, 53, 191
rebirth, 151, 161, 180, 252, 256–257, 261
religion, 4, 160–161, 192, 239, 259
reorientation, 150
repetitive form, 74–75, 79, 80
representative anecdotes, 159, 215, 176
rhetorical analysis, 19, 23, 29, 192, 206–207, 245
rhetorical criticism, 206
rhyme, 75, 79–80
Richards, I. A., 104–106, 113, 122
ritual, 91, 149, 256
ritualistic naming, 169, 175
Rodriguez, Richard, 184, 187
Rorty, Richard, 154, 200, 202, 209
Rose, Mike, 205
Rosso, Stefano, 239, 248
rotten with perfection, 4, 16, 59, 117, 157, 238
Rowell, Edward, 84
Royster, Jacqueline Jones, 205
Rueckert, William H., 51

Safire, William, 184
Said, Edward, 202–203, 211
Sand, George, 56
scapegoat mechanism, 160
Scene, 19, 23
Scholes, Robert, 169
science, 26, 68, 70, 73, 89, 93, 99, 106, 115, 118, 137, 160, 168, 190, 197, 203–214, 243–245
Scott, Robert L., 210
Selzer, Jack, 49, 58, 208, 213, 261
Shakespeare, 43, 61–62, 64, 77, 175–176

Shaughnessey, Mina, 205
simile, 93, 180
situations, 4, 13, 17, 21, 23, 25–26, 33, 39, 43, 45–46, 53, 59–62, 76, 83, 93, 98–100, 102, 104, 112, 133, 145, 150–152, 155–156, 159, 161, 163, 167, 171–174, 185, 190–191, 197, 205, 212, 218–222, 233, 236, 238, 246, 249–251, 256–257, 262
Sloan, Thomas O., 207
Sloterdijk, Peter, 217
Smith, Paul, 222
social epistemic rhetoric, 190–192, 194–195, 197, 205
society, 3, 13, 18, 30, 34, 51, 69, 71, 119, 142, 154, 176, 199, 215, 222, 248, 256–257
sociology, 160
Sommers, Nancy, 205
Southwell, Samuel B., 154
Stafford, William, 204
Stalin, Josef, 169
stealing back and forth of symbols, 172
strategies of containment, 12, 26
stylistic identifications, 85
substance, 29, 223
suffering, 150, 226
syllogisms, 45, 47–49, 54, 76–77, 87, 93, 96–97, 101, 168–169
syllogistic progression, 44, 54, 74–75–78, 100, 111, 138, 173, 178, 245
symbol-making, 4, 238
symbol-misusing, 4, 238
symbols of authority, 161, 178
synthesis, 89, 149, 198

teaching, 18, 53, 117, 126, 135, 143, 150–151, 155–156, 163, 168, 189–190, 192, 194–198, 200, 204, –, 208, 215–216, 226–227, 239–241, 247–249, 253–254; writing, 150–151, 163, 189, 192, 194, 196, 204–205, 216, 227
technology, 69, 73, 155, 189
terministic screens, 5, 15, 19, 24, 30, 37, 100, 130, 145, 156, 173, 209, 247, 249, 255
terrorism, 187, 227
theory despair, 145
theory fear, 112, 145
theory hope, 113, 145
theory of reading, 75, 140, 164, 246
theory of verbal praxis, 7
Thomism, 149
thymos, 48, 101
Todorov, Tzvetan, 208–209
Torok, Maria, 136–141, 143
Toulmin, Stephen, 154
trained incapacity, 98, 150, 155, 160
transcendence, 9, 20, 84, 170, 172, 232, 258
transference, 43, 122, 164–165, 168
transformation, 7, 15, 27, 84, 146, 194, 219, 223, 251, 256
trivium, 240, 242–244, 246–247, 250
tropes, 9–10, 18, 36, 45, 49, 52, 66, 79, 83, 93, 95, 102, 141, 161, 173, 237–238, 244, 246
trout (educated), 98, 157–158, 160
truth, 25, 31–34, 38, 49, 54, 55, 76, 81, 83, 87, 89–91, 93, 96–97, 106, 116–118, 121, 124, 130, 132, 145, 164, 167–169, 184, 186, 206, 223, 244

uncertainty, 4, 13, 22, 24, 33, 39, 50–51, 55, 73, 83, 86–87, 91, 97, 112, 121, 125, 130, 140, 145–146, 150–152, 154, 168–169, 175, 177, 180–181, 190, 218, 220, 226, 233, 238, 243–244, 246, 250–251, 256, 260, 262
unintended by-products, 171, 236
Upward Way, The, 187

Veblen, Thorstein, 98, 155, 157
verbal sparring, 3
Vietnam, 196
Villanueva, Victor, 205
violence, 4, 13, 45, 112, 139, 143, 152–153, 160, 162–163, 180, 186, 260
Vitanza, Victor J., 16, 103, 196, 198, 215–219, 225

Walker, Jeffrey, 46–48, 101, 103, 252
war: rhetorics of, 30
Warnock, John, 52–53, 206
Wess, Robert, 16, 21, 213
West, Cornel, 171
White, Hayden, 9, 52, 184, 209
Whitehead, Alfred North, 202
Williams, Raymond, 202
Williams, William Carlos, 175
Wimsatt, W. K., 105–106, 122, 206
Winterowd, W. Ross, 151, 203, 210

Winters, Yvor, 15
Wittgenstein, Ludwig, 154
Wolf-Man, The, 98–107, 114–115, 118–119, 123–124, 128, 134–136, 142–144
Wolin, Ross, 49, 58, 173, 205, 208, 212–215
World Trade Center (WTC), 184
writer-reader relationship, 82, 166, 192
writing as identification, 150–151, 153, 168, 211, 216, 239
writing for public audiences, 151
writing to identify, 152, 182
WW I, 155
Wyoming Conference, The, 204

Yancey, Kathleen Blake, 205

Zaner, Richard, 83
Žižek, Slavoj, 217

About the Author

Born in Columbus, Georgia, Tilly Warnock is Professor Emerita at the University of Arizona, where she taught in the graduate program in Rhetoric, Composition, and the Teaching of English and directed the first-year writing program. She received her BA from Tulane University, MAT from Emory University, and PhD from the University of Southern California (Rhetoric, Linguistics, and Literature). In the 1960s, she taught in schools in North Carolina. At the University of Wyoming in the 1970s and 1980s—the early days of the emergence of the academic field of rhetoric and composition—she published articles on James Joyce and directed the writing center and the Wyoming Conference on English. She hosted Kenneth Burke at the Wyoming Conference in 1985. Her textbook, *Writing Is Critical Action* (Scott, Forseman & Co.) was published in 1989. She lives with John in Tucson.

www.ingramcontent.com/pod-product-compliance
Lightning Source LLC
Chambersburg PA
CBHW030530230426
43665CB00010B/830